3   363.2 WRI

LEARNING. services

01209 616259

Cornwall College Camborne
Learning Centre - Second Floor

This resource is to be returned on or before the last date stamped below. To renew items please contact the Centre

Three Week Loan

Policing

An introduction to concepts and practice

Alan Wright

WILLAN
PUBLISHING

Published by

Willan Publishing
Culmcott House
Mill Street, Uffculme
Cullompton, Devon
EX15 3AT, UK
Tel: +44(0)1884 840337
Fax: +44(0)1884 840251
e-mail: info@willanpublishing.co.uk
website: www.willanpublishing.co.uk

Published simultaneously in the USA and Canada by

Willan Publishing
c/o ISBS, 5824 N.E. Hassalo St,
Portland, Oregon 97213-3644, USA
Tel: +001(0)503 287 3093
Fax: +001(0)503 280 8832
e-mail: info@isbs.com
website: www.isbs.com

First published 2002

ISBN 1-903240-17-4 Paperback
ISBN 1-903240-18-2 Hardback

British Library Cataloguing-in-Publication Data

A catalogue record for this book is available from the British Library

Printed and bound by T J International Ltd., Trecerus Industrial Estate, Padstow, Cornwall, PL28 8RW

Contents

List of figures

Preface

Understanding the nature and meaning of policing is just as important for members of the police and other criminal justice agencies is it is for academics. The complexities of the subject mean that practitioners need to reflect on their work. In doing so, they need to draw upon theory, empirical evidence and practical experience. Like criminology itself, 'police studies' is a hybrid discipline. In reflecting on the practice of policing, it draws upon sociological, psychological and historical insights. However, as Michael Oakeshott argued in *Experience and Its Modes* (1933), no single mode of experience (practice, history or science) is complete in itself. Although it might sometimes seem to cut against the grain of contemporary criminology, I hope that this narrative is a balanced account across these modes of experience. That I have injected some (admittedly lightweight) philosophical discussion into the arguments of this book should perhaps be not too surprising, given that my long-term interest is in political theory. In my view, it is crucial to clarify the origins and meaning of policing in order to make sense of empirical claims about its character. The latter do not 'speak for themselves' in any significant way that is prior to an understanding of the origins and meaning of the practice. In this sense, although this book contains no radical research findings or profound claims for changes to policing, I hope it provides a reasoned overview of a complex subject. Inevitably, there will be faults and omissions. The narrative has not travelled far but I hope it is in the right direction.

My thanks are due to a number of people who have commented on drafts of the manuscript. In particular, Marc Jacobs (Institute of Criminal Justice Studies, University of Portsmouth), Amanda Matravers (Institute of Criminology, University of Cambridge) and Rob Mawby (Staffordshire University) deserve special thanks for their constructive comments. Thanks are also due to Les Johnston and Frank Leishman (series editors) for their help and advice. The publisher, Brian Willan, deserves an accolade for his patience and for encouraging me to finish the manuscript. Finally, my sincere thanks are due to the many people who have provided me with a great deal of inspiration over the years. The encouragement of John Alderson, Mike Chatterton, Frank Gregory, Barry Loveday, Ian McKenzie, Ken Pease, Steve Savage and Jerry Skolnick are greatly valued. I am particularly indebted to Dr Rob Mawby of Staffordshire University for his kindness, patience and ability in more than one project. If there is anything worthwhile in this book, it will be to the credit of their influence. Readers will rightly lay its failings at my door.

Alan Wright
University of Portsmouth
August 2001

Introduction

This book is an introduction to the study of policing. Often surrounded by controversy, policing is a subject that arouses considerable interest from the public and professionals alike. Indeed, the subject is intrinsically interesting. In fact and in fiction, policing has been awash with human drama. As a consequence, it has been the frequent subject of media and literary attention since the 19th Century. Since the 1960s, however, it has also come under intense critical scrutiny from criminologists and sociologists. There has been a rapid expansion of the academic literature on the subject, aimed at producing a more rigorous account of the phenomenon and its effects.

Of course, there are already many excellent books on policing. Reiner's *The Politics of the Police* is a seminal text (Reiner, 1992a; 3rd edition, 2000a). Bayley's *Police for the Future* (1994) is a blueprint for a new approach to policing and crime prevention. Waddington's *Policing Citizens* (1999) puts forward a theory of the exercise of power and authority by the modern police. Johnston's *Policing Britain: Risk, Security and Governance* (2000) analyses the changing forms and functions of the police and their implications for society. *Core Issues in Policing* sets out a wide-ranging analysis of policing from a number of contributors (Leishman, Loveday and Savage, 2000). All of these works are notable for their scholarship and depth of analysis. Despite the evident value of these volumes, there remains some space for an introductory but critical text, providing a study of policing practice in the context of historical and contemporary paradigms of social and political thought.

The main aims of this book are:

- to explore the concept, context and practice of policing;
- to provide an accessible text for those who are comparatively new to academic debate on the subject;
- to provide an analysis of sufficient depth to reflect the complexity of the issues.

It does not seek to justify any particular type of policing or to convince the reader of the effectiveness of any single form of policing. On the contrary, its central thesis is that policing in a democracy takes many forms. Focusing primarily on British policing, the book discusses the ways in which the meaning and practice of policing are changing in the light of the challenges faced by the public police and other criminal justice agencies.

In addition to the critical content, the text asks readers to explore questions of meaning that criminology sometimes ignores. From the outset, it raises questions about the variety of ways in which the terms 'police' and 'policing' are used: about their conceptual contestability and ambiguity. It suggests that we will not find answers to the question, 'What is policing?' in the empirical analysis of functions of the police. We will find them in the conflicting paradigms of thought within which policing is located. In this sense, as we shall see in Chapter 2, policing can no longer simply be understood solely as the activity of the public police institution. Accordingly, where the term 'policing' appears in the text, we need to take care not to assume that it refers only to the activities of the public police. We use it in this sense in Chapter 1, because the public police have in the past been the primary agency for carrying out policing activities. However, from Chapter 3 onwards, we extend the meaning of the term to include the activities of other agencies. For these reasons, it has been necessary to pose a few questions about the way in which the meaning of the terms 'police' and 'policing' have developed. I hope that readers who have an aversion even to a little philosophy will persevere with the sections that deal with these questions. They are important because they provide some of the answers to why it is now necessary to think differently. Why we now need to think not just of the public police which has existed in institutional form since the early nineteenth century, but of policing in its wider sense.

The arguments of each chapter show how policing practice is developing to reflect a 'new logic' of diversity and change. The outline of the arguments is as follows. Chapter 1 opens with a basic discussion of police work. Building upon these ideas, it goes on to discuss how police work has come to take the form that it does and how modern policing was the response of the state to particular problems of social order. It discusses the importance of the prevention and detection of crime in this respect. In particular, it examines the role of police in promoting and sustaining local social order. In reflecting upon these developments, it argues that there has been an increasing crisis in the modern police in recent years. By the 1990s this seemed to have reached almost epidemic proportions. In parallel to this crisis, criminology has developed an extensive critique of the subject, heralding a radical challenge to the meaning of policing itself.

Chapter 2 examines the extent to which it is still valid to regard the functions of the public police as definitive of policing. It raises questions about the meaning and conceptual contestability of policing. It argues that we can now define policing as an activity which a number of agencies, groups or individuals (including the public police) may deliver. In this sense, it is better to understand policing in terms of the modes of its practice, each one of which is policing seen from a distinct perspective. This chapter argues that the modes of policing practice include policing as:

- peacekeeping;
- crime investigation;
- risk-management; and
- the promotion of community justice.

This chapter also emphasises the reciprocity between agencies and citizens who are involved in the practice. Policing in this sense is not simply a list of functions or the effective completion of a number of tasks by a single institution. It is the name of a complex set of activities that are necessary in a democratic society. Chapters 3–6 elaborate these arguments, setting out detailed discussions of each of the modes of policing.

Chapter 3 discusses peacekeeping as a mode of policing practice. It examines the tension between liberty and order and how different types of state adopt different approaches to this problem. It discusses four different models of policing in this respect. This chapter also discusses the use of paramilitary methods by the police in most jurisdictions. Even democratic states make extensive use of such methods. Many police forces, however, also increasingly make use of conflict management instead of coercion for the purpose of peacekeeping. Here, the use of paramilitary methods seems to be at odds with the idea of conflict management. This chapter discusses the as yet unresolved tensions between them.

Chapter 4 discusses the investigation of crime as a mode of policing practice. It examines the investigative culture of the police in the context of the development of crime investigation work. It sets out a typology of investigation, from the investigation of high-volume crime to serious and organised crime. It also criticises the role of investigators as crime-fighters and the beliefs about the efficacy of crime-control that this approach implies. It concludes that science, due process and the recognition of the rights of victims and offenders should guide this mode of policing practice.

Chapter 5 sets out arguments for the management of risk as a mode of policing practice. This includes the implications for policing of the so-called 'risk society'. It also discusses the role of the police in crime prevention and the trend towards a more holistic concept of community safety. Finally, it examines aspects of policing the risk society. This includes a review of claims as to 'what works' and trends towards multi-agency partnerships and citizen participation.

Chapter 6 builds upon this debate by evaluating the promotion and delivery of community justice as a mode of policing practice. It does this in several ways. It discusses different approaches to justice and distinguishes the concept of community justice from that of law enforcement. It raises questions about whether it is possible to 'save' professional policing or whether community policing is the best means for delivering community justice. It relates these arguments to the idea of the policing of diverse cultures. In a pluralist society, specific forms of policing may be necessary to meet differences in demands and community needs. This has to be reconciled with other demands for the impartial application of the law.

Finally, Chapter 7 discusses the politics of policing in terms of the tensions present in late modernity. Here, contemporary influences may suggest that policing is moving into an era that we might describe as post-modern. Evidence for this includes:

- pressures of new public management;
- changes to the original conception of the public police;
- redistribution of responsibility for investigation, crime reduction and community safety;
- changes in the political, economic, social and technological contexts of policing;
- continued uncertainty about the role and the very meaning of policing.

More positively, however, this chapter discusses reflexive modernisation as a possible way in which progress might still be achieved. By reflecting on its problems, it may be possible to learn new lessons. Here, communication may provide a way through which policing can be developed. However, the dangers of relying on image management rather than seeking real changes of substance need to be recognised. The trajectory of these influences confirms that a modal logic of practice of the kind identified in Chapter 2 and elaborated in Chapters 3–6 best describes policing in late modernity. This, it concludes, provides a more cohesive account of the nature of policing in its wider sense than one based on a functional account of the police as an institution.

Chapter 1

The rise and fall of modern policing

This opening chapter sets out a critical account of the police as a modern institution. Beginning with everyday ideas about police work, it examines the factors that influence our understanding of the subject. It discusses the contemporary debate on the police, focusing particularly on the crisis in policing over the decades since the 1960s. As a preliminary to the more positive account of policing later in this book, this chapter summarises the influences that have led to this state of affairs. It argues that the paradigms of thought that underpin modernity have served to influence both the rise and fall of the modern police. The time is now right for a reappraisal of policing in the light of new conditions.

The arguments of this chapter are set out in five parts. The first examines some basic ideas about the nature of police work, drawn from everyday knowledge and from criminological studies. This section begins to indicate why we need to get beneath the surface to develop a deeper understanding of the concept of policing. The second part of this chapter explores the origins of the police and the way it has developed within the modern state. This includes a review of the founding of the professional police in the nineteenth century as a rational move by the state to deal with specific problems. The third part examines how the modern police developed as a mechanism for the promotion of social order and discusses the implications of that role for liberty in Victorian Britain. The fourth part explores the contemporary police in more detail. It raises the question of whether the police are now experiencing a form of crisis that is beginning radically to alter its character. It questions the extent to which the police institution can survive the pressures that now challenge its very legitimacy. The concluding part of the chapter addresses the central question, 'What is policing?' from the perspective of a number of influential criminological studies. It suggests that the catalogue of failure that these studies represents diverts attention away from a more positive account of policing which can be constructed from the changing social and political conditions of the present.

Police work

What is police work and how do we acquire our knowledge about it? Initially, it may appear relatively easy to describe police work simply by listing the kinds of tasks and activities carried out by the police. We may see police officers going about their work and we can gain insight into what they are doing in a variety of ways: through direct contact or indirectly from people who have such contact. More often, because for most people direct contact with the police is a comparative rarity, it comes from the media. Both documentary and fictional accounts of police work provide important sources of our perceptions. In Britain, television programmes such as *Crimewatch UK*, *The Bill* and *The Thin Blue Line*, however, each provide very different perspectives on police work. For readers who are unfamiliar with these programmes, *Crimewatch UK* provides factual accounts of unsolved serious crime and its investigation and encourages the public to come forward with information. *The Bill* is a series that dramatises the work of police in a city police division, highlighting the professional and private lives of those involved. (The name of the series is drawn from the Victorian nickname for the London police, namely, the 'Old Bill'.) *The Thin Blue Line* is a comedy series lampooning police work in a local police station.

Depending on what we prefer to watch, these programmes produce very different perceptions of the nature of police work. We can make a similar point about the diversity of representation of the police in the US in programmes such as *NYPD Blue*, *Hill Street Blues* or on *CNN* news. Fly-on-the-wall documentaries and public appeal programmes such as *Crimewatch UK* provide information that may seem closer to reality, although even they do not give an objective overview of the whole field. In fact, although television programmes make up a very large proportion of public knowledge about police work, it is knowledge that is often partial, fragmentary and incomplete. In contrast, the task of this book is to analyse and assess the realities behind these perceptions: to establish a more cohesive account of policing than that available from everyday experience.

At the simplest level of analysis, the tasks carried out by the police reflect the reality of police work. For example, we can gain a very basic insight into what the police do by looking at the career of a police officer in Britain, which may span many years and encompass a number of roles. For the first two years in the service, officers work in a local police unit as uniformed probationary constables. During this time, they receive a considerable amount of training in law and policing skills, from basic training to training on the job. This includes tutoring by more experienced officers before constables are ready for independent patrol. Thereafter, their work includes such things as foot and motor patrols, dealing with reports of crime, traffic accidents, motoring offences, public disorder, emergencies and other incidents. They also respond to a variety of calls for service from the public. Increasing demands upon the police in recent years mean that police work is often concerned with reacting to such calls. However, they are also encouraged to engage with community-based activities, such as crime prevention and local problem-solving.

After two or three years, officers may continue in local uniformed policing or may apply to carry out more specialised work. This could include roles such as crime investigation, traffic patrol work, public order or community policing. Some specialist roles have even more specialised pathways within them. These include accident investigation, criminal intelligence, surveillance and community liaison work. Although some specialist work is local, in many cases special units or squads carry out the work. Murder squads, drugs squads and other units are often part of the central structure of police forces, although they may be part of local commands in some places. Other units, such as the National Crime Squad (NCS) and National Criminal Intelligence Service (NCIS), carry out investigations and provide intelligence on organised and cross-border crime. They are not part of local police forces but are autonomous policing agencies. Even if they go into such specialist police work, many officers return to ordinary duty later in their careers. After two years as a probationary constable, an officer can start to think about taking the first steps on the ladder to supervisory rank. A variety of management tasks, including such things as the supervision of the arrest, detention and questioning of suspects, are included in the work of those who take this route.

The purpose of this very basic account is simply to indicate the kinds of roles that police work entails. Of course, not every police officer will carry out every role. An elementary catalogue, however, starts to emerge. Even in the comparatively brief assessment offered above we can already identify the following:

- foot patrols;
- motor patrols;
- responding to incidents and emergencies;
- dealing with public disorder;
- crime investigation;
- criminal intelligence;
- surveillance;
- crime prevention;
- local problem-solving;
- community policing;
- dealing with motoring offences;
- dealing with traffic accidents;
- specialised traffic patrols;
- traffic accident investigation;
- supervising arrest, questioning and detention.

This list is not exhaustive. Many readers, especially police officers and those who have made a study of policing, will be able to add to it. What it shows, however, is that police work involves an evident diversity of tasks and activities. As Manning (1977) argues, however, police work is not what it may seem on the surface. It is often full of ambiguity, especially where there is controversy about its functions, effectiveness or legitimacy. For this reason, at every level, whether in ordinary duty or specialist roles, police officers need to reflect on the nature of policing in order to make sense of its complexities. From their very earliest days in the service, a police officer may meet difficult circumstances. However, the public does not lower its expectations because an officer has only limited experience.

Criminological studies of police work have sought to show the relative proportions of the types of work carried out by the police. For example, Shapland and Vagg (1988) suggest that dealing with 'potential crime' amounts to 53 per cent of police work; social disorder 20 per cent; information and service 18 per cent; and traffic 8 per cent. Bayley (1996: 39) in contrast, in a study aggregated across a number of countries, suggests that patrol work amounts to 59 per cent; criminal investigation 15 per cent; operational support 11 per cent; traffic 8 per cent; administration 8 per cent; and crime prevention 3 per cent. Although there are apparent similarities in category in these studies, the differences in quantification show the need for extreme care in identifying what is counted in particular cases. Other criminologists postulate models that cluster the different categories of police work. Fielding (1996: 42–59), for example, argues that three models characterise policing, namely the enforcement, service and community models. The enforcement model concentrates on the control of crime and enforcement of the law. The service model sets policing priorities for dealing with crime control, order maintenance and service delivery in consultation with the public. The community model gives priority to maintaining public tranquillity over crime control. Police and public share responsibility for dealing with crime and disorder. There is, he says, 'no perfect model of policing and it is probably necessary to borrow elements from each model to arrive at a police service that meets all the demands of the public' (Fielding, 1996: 42–3). In many ways, this is a more useful approach for our purposes. As will be evident from Chapter 2 onwards, this is the method we will adopt in this book, clustering and comparing in order to interpret, rather than quantifying different categories to put forward a scientific theory of policing.

The criminological literature also provides us with other kinds of information about police work, including criticism of the way the police operate. Many scholarly and research-based texts follow this critical approach. We will discuss this critical trend later in this chapter. However, it is noticeable that such texts usually refer to the work of 'the police' rather than to the concept of 'policing' *per se*. The problem is that if we specify our study as that of 'the police' we are already starting to make assumptions about the concept that interests us. Reiner's (1992a, 2000a) *The Politics of the Police* specifically focuses on the development of the police in modern society. This enables him to interpret the nature of the police organisation, its history, culture and social construction. Similarly, Bayley's (1994) *Police for the Future* focuses on the way in which the police (in the US and elsewhere) should adopt a more community-based approach to crime prevention. Again, it is worth emphasising how concepts delimit and qualify the ways in which we might think of the police institution. It is important to remember, however, that studies of the police are not necessarily theories of policing. As we shall see in Chapter 2, there are good reasons for expanding our understanding of policing beyond this focus on the police. As Fielding (1996) suggests, it is as much the role of criminologists to make the logic of policing clear as to provide an empirical critique of the work of the police. Indeed in recent years, writers such as Johnston (1992; 2000) have extended the debate on policing far beyond discussion of the public police alone.

Although sociologists may have a different view, historical accounts are as relevant to our understanding of policing as are those based upon scientific research. Historical accounts of the work of the police are a primary means through which we can assess its relation to the state and its record in ensuring or denying the liberty of citizens. This applies particularly to the form of police introduced in early nineteenth-century Britain. It is also interesting to consider even earlier forms of policing and to assess the historical trajectory of which both they and the modern police are part. Although this book focuses on British policing, comparative studies also are helpful. There are certainly similarities in police work across the world. However, as Mawby (1990) shows, it is dangerous to assume too much from the superficial similarities in policing in different jurisdictions. There are also differences in constitutions, history and operating styles. The British and US models of policing, for example, have aspects that remain, to some extent, local. The fact that police accountability in both Britain and the US often includes a degree of local public involvement makes a difference to police work on the streets. It is in this sense that we can safely talk about 'the British policing tradition'. In contrast, policing in some European states has so far shown a higher degree of centralisation and state control than that in Britain or the US. As we discuss in Chapter 3, this affects the policing of public disorder. In former totalitarian regimes, it also affects the viability of involving local people in anything resembling community policing. The implication of these points is that it is well worth looking at the context within which policing has developed. For this reason, throughout this book we will draw upon historical sources in addition to conceptual and empirical studies.

The rise of the modern police

The modern police developed in the nineteenth century as the specific response of the state to problems of crime and security. For those who accepted the civil authority of the state, this represented a rational development. As such, it was considered appropriate to develop legitimate institutions to protect the life, liberty and property of citizens within the rule of law. However, whether the police promote order and provide protection or simply provide a means of state oppression geared to class interests is an important question for those studying the rise of policing. To answer it, we must seek evidence in the historical development of the police institution. The study of policing before the police helps us to understand the changes in conditions that led to the foundation of the 'new police'. This new departure in keeping order was to some extent based upon perceptions of the failure of older methods. The following can only be a sketch of the terrain. Detailed discussions are to be found in specialised accounts of police history such as that of Emsley (1996a, 1996b) and Rawlings (2002).

In most of medieval Europe, the system of feudal land tenure provided private jurisdictions for keeping order. Military commitment of the vassal to the lord in exchange for grants of land was the main feature of the system. Ultimately, the king held all land as feudal superior. In Britain, the *soke* or district, in which the lord had private jurisdiction over free-men, came from Danelaw and existed well into the second millennium. The use of mercenary armies, however, gradually led to the decline of the feudal system and the rise of the system of royal justice. In Britain, royal power was absolute, especially after the Norman Conquest. However, it often had little direct effect. On the contrary, pre-modern law and order in England was largely localised and community based. As such, policing before the police continued to follow the earlier model of the Anglo-Saxon tithing-man, responsible for keeping the peace and enforcing the law within his group. The local focus of order had a longer-term impact. In the eleventh century, the Normans developed the system of constables from these earlier Anglo-Saxon structures (Reith, 1943: 14). The de-scendents of the Norman constable existed in some parts of England well into the nineteenth century (Emsley, 1996a: 11–23).

In 1285, the Statute of Winchester gave a more formal sense of legitimacy to these local measures for keeping order. It also gave militia-style roles to armed freemen under the so-called Assize of Arms. Importantly for policing, it provided for watch and ward guards for local communities. Later, the Justice of the Peace Act 1361 also provided conservators of the peace to ensure order in counties and boroughs. However, as Choong (1997: 2–3) suggests, until the mid-seventeenth century, the theory of governance under which these measures were enacted was that in which absolute power lay with the Crown. Parliamentary rule came only after the demise of the divine right of the monarchy in the English Civil War (Bill of Rights 1689). The rule of Parliament, however, did not imply universal franchise, even after the Reform Act of 1832. Nevertheless, these changes signalled the develop-ment of a state based more upon law and reason. The rise of a modern police was only possible after such a transition.

Economic change in the late seventeenth century also led to social and political change. The Industrial Revolution led to the rise of a property-owning middle class but also to an impoverished working class. As Hill (1969) remarks, summarising the changes to be observed in Britain in the late seventeenth and eighteenth centuries:

> … we have moved from a backward economy to one on the threshold of industrial revolution: from an agricultural to an industrial economy … We have moved from a society in which it

was taken for granted that a fully human existence was possible only for the narrow landed ruling class to a society in which an ideology of self help had permeated into the middle ranks.

(Hill, 1969: 287)

These changes also led to the growth of a large urban working class who provided labour for the new industries (Evans, 1996: 107). Concern for equality or moral restraint did not drive these developments. This was especially the case where commercial exploitation of workers or the proceeds of the slave trade were the basis for new wealth. As a result, the economic ground was far from level. There was widespread poverty. Social conditions were poor. Social and political unrest in the cities during this time provided problems of order that were categorically different to those of pre-modern Britain (Evans, 1996: 147–75). This called for a form of policing different from that which was appropriate to largely agricultural communities.

Emsley sets out details of the events leading to the setting up of the Metropolitan Police in 1829. According to Emsley:

Developments in the last decade of the eighteenth and first quarter of the nineteenth centuries took place against a background of increasing debate about the state of the police in the metropolis, with the word 'police' increasingly being used to describe the system for maintaining public order, for preventing theft and for detecting offenders.

(Emsley, 1996a: 21–2)

Rising crime and disorder provided the impetus for a new police for London. Although a Tory, Peel was committed both to reform and to social order. He supported the Reform Act of 1832 and other measures. He also provided the basis for the longer-term Tory acceptance of the principle of reform in the so-called 'Tamworth Manifesto' of 1834. It is not surprising, therefore, that ideas of reform and social control should come together so forcibly in his proposals for a new police. In this sense, Peel was simply following modern thinking. He also overcame the objection to using a word associated with napoleonic measures for political control instituted by Joseph Fouché. Eventually the new police emerged to encapsulate these reforming ideas. The development of police in the rest of Britain soon followed.

Modernity generated many problems that were difficult to resolve, despite its goal of social progress. However, it did provide the basis for the development of the new police in the nineteenth century. As Johnston

(2000) suggests, the new professional police were characterised by bureaucracy and functional rationality. In this sense, they were distinctively modern. According to Johnston:

> The new police forces established under Peel's reforms were specialized public bureaucracies with responsibility for internal security. These organisations were staffed by salaried personnel, possessing full constabulary powers, and personifying, at street level, the state's monopoly of legitimate coercion. These three features of police organisation – differentiation of function, rationalization of structure and location within the state – defined the police solution as a characteristically modern one.
>
> (Johnston, 2000: 12)

Reith (1938; 1943), Critchley (1978), Reiner (1992a) and Emsley (1996a) describe the problems of the years after the founding of the new police. A detailed review of these issues is beyond the scope of this present work. However, the real reasons for their founding still exercise the minds of critics. Disputes as to its real role are to found in the difference between 'orthodox' (conservative) and 'revisionist' (radical) accounts of the history of the police (Reiner, 1992a: 12–56). For Critchley (1978) and Ascoli (1979), the setting up of a body for preventing crime and maintaining order was essential to deal with the social problems which resulted from the rapid growth of cities. They are criticised, however, for ignoring the rationality of working-class opposition to the new police. In contrast, revisionist accounts such as that of Storch (1975) suggest that the growth of police is better explained by the clamour of the propertied middle classes for a body to protect their assets. The true role of the police, in this sense, was the control of a supposedly delinquent (but actually deprived) working class.

What is the truth of this debate? The Metropolitan Police Act 1829 certainly indicated (on the surface at least) that the new police were primarily intended to deal with property offences. The preamble to the Act says:

> Whereas offences against property have of late increased in and near the Metropolis; and the local establishments of nightly watch and nightly police have been found inadequate to the prevention and detection of crime … It is expedient to substitute a new and more efficient system of police in lieu of such establishments of nightly watch and nightly police within the limits hereinafter mentioned …
>
> (Metropolitan Police Act 1829 – 10 Geo. 4, c. 44)

This seems largely in line with the orthodox construction. However, it does not take into account the extensive mob disorder preceding the formation of the new police. What is reasonably clear from most accounts of the new police is that those who founded it conceived the role of police as modern. In this sense, the degree of control it provided would contribute towards social progress rather than to political oppression. For Henry Fielding and Patrick Colquhoun, the 'science of the new police' certainly implied social progress. The control of robbery in London and crime on the Thames were valuable social outcomes. Some limitation of liberty was a price well worth paying (Fielding, 1757 and Colquhoun, 1796, in Emsley, 1996a: 18–22; Reith, 1943: 20–1). Peel also emphasised the urgent need for social control in parliamentary debates on the new police. He saw this as important because of the failure of the military to deal with disorder and of the existing runners and constables to control crime (Reith, 1943: 26–32).

It is difficult to make a judgement between the orthodox and re-visionist versions of police history. Both have a degree of truth, although attitudes to this probably depend as much upon modes of explanation as upon the historical facts. In comparing these positions, Reiner suggests that neither the orthodox nor the revisionist versions fully take account of the facts. He says:

> All historians of the emergence of professional policing in Britain have shown that it was surrounded by acute political conflict. The orthodox historians are clearly wrong in their lack of appreciation of the rational basis of opposition to the police, rooted in different social interests and political philosophies. On the other hand, the revisionists overemphasise the extent of continued working-class opposition, and the overt role of the police in class and political control.
>
> (Reiner, 1992a: 55–6)

Reiner argues instead for a synthesis of the opposing positions. This recognises the need for new measures of social control in the context of the time. It also recognises that policing was (and still is to a great extent) embedded in a social order which is 'riven … by conflict, not fundamental integration'. It also gives credit, however, to the success of police reformers and to the tradition they created (Reiner, 1992a: 56).

Although we should not claim too much for the relationship between modernity and policing, there are clear linkages between them. The modern state has long provided the principal means through which institutions such as the police can be conceptualised. This is as relevant to states based upon theories of 'possessive individualism' (Macpherson, 1962), as it is to those based upon collectivism (such as those argued by Rousseau and Hegel). As we shall see in Chapter 3, the latter have fostered quite different policing systems. In democracies, however, legitimate authority is underpinned by the rule of law (at least in theory). For those who agree with John Locke, legitimate government does not rely on state violence but upon legislation that has the consent of the people (Locke, 1690: 80–1). Of course, claims about the state's monopoly of coercive force may affect this principle. Again, we will discuss this further in Chapter 3. The argument that consent is little but a mask through which a state promotes hegemony and hides its intentions may also affect our attitudes (Hall *et al.*, 1978: 227–39; Brogden, 1982). Neither of these counter-claims, however, denies the role of the modern police in the promotion of social order. As we shall see later, other ideas are now emerging about the role of the police and policing more generally. But without the idea that its initial role was to promote social order, the very idea of a modern police simply could not have arisen.

The police and social order

Descriptions of the police role in contemporary documents provide an important clue to the nature of policing. From such documents we know that preventing and detecting crime and preserving public tranquillity defined the official role of the new police. Pronouncements by Colonel Sir Charles Rowan and Sir Richard Mayne, the first Commissioners, clearly set out the importance of these functions. This was also emphasised in the books of instruction issued to every London police officer – a practice that has continued up to the present in many police organisations. Victorian accounts of policing, however, show that crime prevention and detection were not the only roles of the police. Their work included a wide range of other activities. They would often intervene in ways not concerned with infringements of specific liberties. For much of their time they focused upon more mundane aspects of local social control. This included dealing with emergencies, minor public disorder and matters affecting the local environment.

Most of the instructions and orders issued to police officers were not about policing functions on the grand scale. They were about the detailed day-to-day implementation of rules and procedures and minor measures to ensure social order. The pocket books of regulations and orders issued in the nineteenth century contained a wide range of such material. There were regulations for preventing and dealing with drunkenness (including their own). People were to be discouraged from putting oyster shells down gratings in the streets, thereby blocking the drains. Boys should not fly kites dangerously in the streets. Constables should inspect cellar-flaps, as much for reasons of safety as for crime prevention (Metropolitan Police 1851: 92, 94, 96). From the early days after the formation of the new police, therefore, social order and the 'use and condition of the streets' were major and crucial roles for the police. Although the prevention of crime was strategically predominant, and there was much policing of demonstrations during the period 1829–1856, the day-to-day routine of social control was a characteristic of police work from the very first. To a great extent, it has continued to be so.

The social control role of the police was not merely a matter of following the procedures set out in regulations and police orders. Legislation increasingly underpinned this aspect of police work. However, there were deeper purposes to this work. The goal was social improvement rather than mere enforcement of the law. According to Emsley:

> The police constable was the 'domestic missionary' charged with bringing civilisation and decorum: he was armed with a battery of legislation to achieve this end.
>
> (Emsley, 1996a: 74)

A good example of their missionary zeal was the vigorous enforcement of new liquor licensing laws. Such enforcement led to serious and continuing friction between the police and the poorer sections of the working class, notably in the industrial towns of the north (Emsley, 1996a: 75). This new licensing legislation was the product of sustained pressure from the temperance movement and the churches.

This agenda for social improvement had its basis in the work of social theorists such as T.H. Green, who argued for state intervention as a means of dealing with social deprivation and moral danger (Vincent and Plant, 1984: 70–1). For Green, liberty was meaningless outside the context of a system of justice that promoted human development in a positive way. The gin-shops that were widespread in Victorian London were no more than machines of slavery for the working-class people who frequented them. Liberty, therefore, meant restricting some freedoms. According to Green:

> ...when we ... speak of freedom, we should consider carefully what we mean by it. We do not mean merely freedom from restraint or compulsion. We do not mean freedom to do as we like irrespective

of what it is that we like. We do not mean a freedom that can be enjoyed by one man or one set of men at the cost of a loss of freedom to others. When we speak of freedom as something to be so highly prized, we mean a positive power or capacity of doing or enjoying something worth doing or enjoying, and that too, something that we do or enjoy in common with others.

(Green, 1880, in Nettleship, 1885–8: 371)

This placed the onus on the state to improve the conditions under which rights and obligations could have real meaning (Milne, 1962: 125–44; Berlin, 1969: 131–4). Although it was not easy to repair the effects of earlier laissez-faire attitudes, the principle of positive freedom did help to improve social conditions during the latter part of the nineteenth century. Examples include such things as urban planning, hospitals and social welfare. It also influenced some aspects of the police role. It was an influence on senior politicians such as H.H. Asquith, R.B. Haldane and Alfred Milner. Like utilitarianism, it was the product of the reforming middle class. In practice, however, its application was often at the expense of working-class freedoms. As popular resistance shows, the claim that it was for the good of the recipients certainly did not have universal approval. More recent examples include the enforcement of laws on drinking and driving, seat belts and crash helmets, and measures for dealing with the misuse of drugs.

Other aspects of the theory of liberty are relevant to other forms of police work. For example, the police in some circumstances can intervene in the liberty of a citizen who infringes the rights and freedoms of others. Arrests for theft and assault are examples of the police intervening to redress the negative liberty of citizens. Negative liberty, in this sense, means that a citizen has the right to act freely, unless it affects the rights and freedoms of others. In such cases, the citizen whose rights and freedoms are affected is entitled to redress. In cases where police themselves infringe a citizen's rights the principle is no different. Instead of redress against another citizen in such cases, the citizen seeks redress against the police. In democracies police are not in a privileged position. There is no theoretical problem in applying the principle of negative liberty to them. This is unlike the position in totalitarian states where police are not subject to prosecution. This has been a major issue in the transition of some states to democracy, for example in Eastern and Central Europe (Benke *et al.*, 1997).

Some studies of the police argue that police work is not concerned with preserving liberty at all, in either the positive or the negative sense. They suggest it has a more political purpose in promoting order, namely to maintain the social and political *status quo*. This may be an unspoken adherence to the predominant ideas of its day. Alternatively, it may reveal itself in certain kinds of police action. For Waddington (1999), this is clear in police attitudes to social order. He says:

> ... the police do not maintain order *per se*, but impose a particular order. The distinction is crucial, since many deviant subcultures could be considered to exhibit their own order; conforming to their own values and norms and not at all behaving in a disorderly manner. Their behaviour is not unordered, but ordered in ways that do not conform to prevailing notions of respectability.
>
> (Waddington, 1999: 42)

There are certainly cases where the imposition of a particular order by the police is evident. Choong (1997: 3–11), for example, points to the consistency of action of the police in coercing suspects from the earliest times. In such cases, there is no instrumental justification for such coercion, outside the application of due process. However, the long-term evidence of such coercion seems to imply something more, namely that the very act of offending provides a challenge to authority and, by implication, to the *status quo*. As such, it demands the reassertion of police control. There is also a suggestion that the control of dissent sometimes appears at a strategic level, for example in the case of police action against the so-called 'flying pickets' in the miners' strike of 1984 (Waddington, 1999: 82). Here, the police response was coordinated by the National Reporting Centre (NRC) and the Association of Chief Police Officers (ACPO). In this case, police action may have gone beyond the management of disorder to the political control of dissent, raising the question of whether it was in direct support of the policies of the (then) Conservative administration.

What conclusions can we draw from this debate? First, the role of the police in promoting liberty in comparison with promoting social order is certainly ambiguous. On the one hand, police work is '... the exercise of the authority of the state over the civil population' (Waddington, 1999: 30). On the other hand, concern for the state does not appear to drive the vast majority of social order police work at all. More often, it is a response to local pressure to keep the peace, to promote safety or simply to avoid trouble. In this sense, policing has often been concerned with the exercise of low-level discretion. Some commentators point to the tendency in this respect to avoid on-the-job trouble or trouble with the public (Chatterton, 1983; Norris, 1989). This applies both to routine street policing and serious disturbances. Although senior police officers may have a more strategic view, it is difficult to reconcile the idea of policing as the exercise of authority on behalf of the state with some of the realities of routine police work. Indeed, since the mid-1980s, containment has been the main principle in the policing of potential public disorder. In most circumstances, even if there are moral or political considerations, police now appear more likely than ever to follow due process or simply to contain the situation.

The demonstrations against the export of live animals to Europe in 1995 are a good example. In these cases, the moral high ground was clearly with the protesters because of the appalling treatment of the animals. Legally, however, the police had to act against the protesters to enable the exports to continue and did so. Waddington (2000: 156–9) rightly points to this as an example of the moral ambiguity the police constantly face. In some cases, maintaining order may simply be a matter of inaction by the police unless enforcement is subject to legal or political direction. For example, during the September 2000 blockades of fuel depots by the road haulage industry across Britain, police did little more than prevent breaches of the peace. More recent events, however, such as the disturbances in the summer of 2001 in Oldham and Bradford, where Asian and white youths were in violent confrontation, indicate that conflict resolution is not simply a matter of ensuring an appropriate degree of policing. We will discuss this further in the context of policing as peacekeeping in Chapter 3.

In general, social control without the widespread use of oppression has been the major success of the modern British police. This was so despite the ambiguities of police work and the problem of balancing the positive and negative aspects of liberty. The focus of police work in local communities was an important factor in bringing this about. Whether it involved law enforcement or not, its careful application led to consent to policing in most cases. At least, this was so until the late 1950s, when other factors began to predominate. Reiner confirms the consolidation of policing into a respected and generally depoliticised force between 1856 and 1959. He says:

> By the 1950s 'policing by consent' *was* achieved in Britain to the maximal degree it is ever attainable – the wholehearted approval of the majority of the population who do not experience the coercive exercise of police powers to any significant extent and the *de facto* acceptance of the legitimacy of the institution by those who do.
>
> (Reiner, 1992a: 60)

This era marks a high point in the development of the modern police. It indicates its contribution to social cohesion, evidence for which is provided by approval across the class structure. Things were never the same thereafter. For this reason, we now need to examine the decaying legitimacy of the institution since the late 1950s and to explore the factors that may have led to this decline.

The crisis in policing

There is strong evidence for the existence of a crisis in modern policing. On the one hand, extensive malpractice has begun to undermine the status and effectiveness of the professional public police. On the other hand, a more community-based police seems as yet unable to meet the needs of a diversity of cultures or to be able to control extremes of deviance. New models for ensuring public safety are challenging the primacy of the public police in this role. A wide variety of agencies (public, commercial and voluntary) are now involved in the delivery of a number of policing services. The proper role of the public police has become even more ambiguous. It becomes more necessary than ever to establish the underlying reasons for this relentless challenge to the role of the public police. In this section, we will identify and discuss specific aspects of the crisis in British policing. 'Crisis', in the sense in which the term is used here, conveys the idea of an institution that is finding it increasingly difficult to cope conceptually and practically with the extreme demands upon it. In this section, therefore, we will focus upon the factors that have led to the crisis. These include the effects of increased police malpractice, management problems and the difficulties of police reform. We will conclude that because of the intractability of these problems, it is now necessary to reassess the nature of policing itself, as it tries to cope with contemporary pressures and re-establish its legitimacy.

Although we will focus mainly on British policing, there are many examples of similar problems in other jurisdictions. The video recording of the beating of Rodney King by police in Los Angeles in the 1990s led to the prosecution of several officers. This case produced severe public reaction and rioting in some places. Acquittal of the police officers who were involved did not reduce the resentment. Long-term difficulties of dealing with crime in some American cities have undermined public support for the police. Corruption in the police has reduced public trust in their work in some parts of Australia. Commissions with wide powers are now tackling this problem. In the Netherlands, there has been criticism of government ministers and senior police officers for failing to deal with organised crime effectively and a working group was set up to analyse the problem (Punch, 1997; Fijnaut *et al.*, 1998: ix–xii). The widespread nature of these problems indicates an endemic flaw in public policing in late modernity. This is not simply a matter of the failure of individual police officers or institutions.

The evidence for the crisis in British policing is substantial. The catalogue of concerns has increased rapidly in the past forty years. Indeed, the 1962 Royal Commission on the Police (chaired by Sir Henry Willink) was set up in the wake of disturbing trends in the previous decade. Cases included impropriety by some provincial chief constables. There was an increasing number of cases of brutality against suspects and the 'planting' of evidence (Ascoli, 1979; 274–6; Rose, 1996). Whether this merely brought to the surface types of cases that had existed clandestinely in earlier years is difficult now to determine. However, the Royal Commission was under no illusions about its task. They wished to halt the slide in the integrity of the police that these scandals represented and their potential impact on the ability of the police to tackle crime. They said:

> We do not think that anyone acquainted with the facts can be satisfied with the state of law and order in Britain in 1960. Society has in our opinion, a duty not to leave untried any measure which may lead not only to detection, but above all to the prevention of crime.
> (Royal Commission on the Police 1962, quoted in Ascoli, 1979: 276)

In the event, despite their reiteration of the doctrines that were supposed to underpin modern policing from its outset, the Commission was not able to halt the slide. The Commission introduced measures to improve accountability and the handling of complaints against the police. They were not effective as long-term safeguards. Neither did the increase in police pay and numbers following the Commission's recommendations have the sought-after effect. A large number of subsequent events showed that this was the case. These include the corruption scandals of the 1960s, the failed 'Yorkshire Ripper' investigation of the 1970s and the flawed investigation into the murder in 1993 of Stephen Lawrence. All are indicators of the long-term decline in the police as an important public institution. As never before, this catalogue of problems now raises the fundamental question of whether the British police has run its course in the form originally intended by its founders.

To understand the implications of this, we need to look more closely at some of the detail. The 1960s provide the starting point. Initially, there was no suggestion that the scandals of the 1960s represented a trend. In

1962, Detective Sergeant Harry Challenor took control of a team of aides-to-CID at West End Central police station in London. In the following months, this squad made a large number of arrests, including those for offences of demanding money with menaces and possessing offensive weapons. The crime-fighting work of the squad was energetic but not especially controversial (except for the members of the Soho underworld who were their targets). A number of convictions resulted from their operations. However, in July 1963 the squad made an arrest at a demonstration in London against a State visit by Queen Frederika of Greece. One of the demonstrators, who had been carrying a banner, subsequently had an offensive weapon (a piece of house brick) 'planted' on him. In this case, problems over the credibility of the evidence led to acquittal. A mounting number of complaints against Challenor and his squad included allegations of corruption in the 'planting' case. Challenor and other officers appeared at the Central Criminal Court in June 1964 on this and other charges. Three officers received sentences of up to four years imprisonment. Challenor, however, was committed to a mental hospital as unfit to plead. The subsequent official enquiry criticised the Metropolitan police but this malpractice was generally regarded as an isolated case (Morton, 1993: 114–22). This was also the stance taken by the Force. The 'frailties of the few', it was argued, should not be used to discredit the force as a whole (Ascoli, 1979: 287).

The decade of the 1960s, however, produced yet more evidence of serious malpractice. This included corruption in the South East Regional Crime Squad (the 'Times Enquiry'), the Metropolitan Police Drugs Squad and the Obscene Publications Squad (Cox *et al.*, 1977). In the 1970s, the so-called 'Yorkshire Ripper' killed thirteen women in the north of England. A prolonged investigation failed to find the killer, despite a heavy commitment of police resources. This failure also led to a further undermining of public confidence. (For discussion of the implications of this case for crime investigation, see Chapter 4.) As Roger Graef shows in *Talking Blues* (1990), the 1980s was a 'decade of trouble' for the police. The inner city riots and the miners' strike showed the need for radical change in policing. The Scarman Report (Home Office 1981) temporarily eased concerns about the way that the police were dealing with visible ethnic minority groups. However, reviews of police attitudes did not promote confidence in the future of inner-city police work (Smith *et al.*, 1983). What little optimism there was around at the time has proved short-lived.

Attempts to sustain the due-process model of criminal justice by means of legislation have secured some improvements. The Royal Commission on Criminal Procedure 1981 tried to secure a better balance between the need for justice and the rights of suspects. The Police and

Criminal Evidence Act 1984 (PACE) was the result. PACE tightened the rules under which the police investigate crime, make arrests and detain suspects. However, despite new controls to ensure that the prescribed procedures are followed, miscarriage of justice cases continue to appear. The Guildford Four, Birmingham Six and Carl Bridgewater murder cases have now been joined by post-PACE examples, such as the Cardiff Three (Rose, 1996; Ashworth, 1998: 11–15; Walker and Starmer, 1999). The inquiry into the Steven Lawrence murder investigation added more fuel to the fire. Consequently, the police stand accused both of incompetence and institutionalised racism (Macpherson, 1999). Claims against the police for assault and other torts have risen, both in terms of their operational work and their internal failures to deal with issues such as sexual harassment and discrimination in the workplace.

Despite the undoubted impact of these problems, attempts to reform the police have met only with limited success. The 1993 White Paper on Police Reform identified a lack of clear objectives and defects in the police framework as major problems. It set out a new strategy to meet the aims of policing (Home Office 1993a). There were also reports from three other inquiries during this time. First, an inquiry chaired by Sir Patrick Sheehy recommended a number of changes to the police management structure (Home Office 1993b). Secondly, an inquiry chaired by Ingrid Posen of the Home Office reviewed the delivery of police core and ancillary services (Home Office 1995). Thirdly, the Police Foundation and Policy Studies Institute (PSI) set up an independent inquiry into the roles and responsibilities of the police (Police Foundation/PSI 1994, 1996). The output from these inquiries did not produce lasting results, although the work of the Audit Commission and HM Inspectors of Constabulary has been more influential.

These pressures have placed exceptional demands upon the police at every level, from chief officers down to newly appointed constables. According to some police officers with whom the author discussed these matters during 2000, the problems are as great as ever. As a result, police morale continues to ebb away. As yet, there is nothing to indicate the turning of the tide. Scrutiny of the police and new systems of performance management have not increased effectiveness or reassured the public. Work by ACPO, the Home Office or by what Young (1988) has called 'administrative' criminologists has not yet been able to steer the police into calmer waters. Indeed, disclosure of major difficulties may have had precisely the opposite effect. The most disturbing effect of this stream of problems and criticism is that it has not merely been a challenge to accountability. It has begun to call into question the very rationale of the public police as an institution. Consequently, the police now appear to be in the midst of a revolution that draws its fuel from an ever-growing catalogue of malpractice and organisational uncertainty.

The criminological critique of police work

Over the past 40 years, criminologists have carried out extensive research into the work of the police. The first study of the police by a British sociologist was that by Banton (1964). Other research followed with a number of influential studies both in the UK and the US. Skolnick (1966) studied the 'working personality' of the police and the dilemmas they face when they try to reconcile the needs of law enforcement with those of peacekeeping. Bittner examined the functions of the police and the way in which they exercise their discretion in routine police work (Bittner, 1967a, 1967b, 1970, 1974). Black and Reiss (1967) and Wilson (1968) carried out research on transactions between the police and the public and on policing styles. Cain and Manning carried out sociological studies of police work in the UK and US (Cain, 1973, 1979; Manning, 1977).

The researchers that followed this first generation built upon these foundations. Research by Reiner (1992a) focused upon the politics of the police, including factors that influence the police culture. Holdaway (1979, 1983) studied the way in which the exercise of control by lower rank officers conceals and protects a range of dubious policing practices. Research by Punch (1979a, 1979b, 1985) examined the service role of the police and the propensity for endemic corruption in some kinds of policing. Research by Chatterton (1979, 1983) and Chatterton and Rogers (1989) examined the complex social processes of police work and the ways in which the police try to meet their objectives. Bayley (1985, 1994) reviewed different styles of policing, arguing for a shift in focus from crime-fighting to a more community-based from of policing. Left-wing criminology has provided critiques of the control of the police, the relationship between police, society and the state and crime-control methods (see, for example, Jefferson and Grimshaw, 1984; Lea and Young, 1984; Scraton, 1985; Kinsey *et al.*, 1986). The above listing is not exhaustive. It does not do justice to the richness and variety of the research. For a more comprehensive review of the development of police research, see Reiner (1994, 2000b).

There is a clear connection between the research interest in policing and the problems of the modern police discussed above. That the rise of research into the police happened at the very time when the practice of policing was in crisis is not merely coincidental. Of course, it may be that criminology itself has affected the comfortable certainties of earlier forms of policing. Whether or not this is the case, by the 1990s the crisis in the modern police seemed to have reached almost epidemic proportions. The continued prevalence of malpractice and stress in the police organisation showed that this was the case. In the *Oxford English Dictionary*, the meaning of the term 'epidemic' is a malaise prevalent among a people or a community. We use the term here in much the same way, indicating a widespread upheaval in the practice and purpose of the police institution. In many of the examples set out above, the main role of criminologists (or of sociologists of the police) has been to identify and explain the failure of policing methods. Consequently, a negative critical consensus about police work has built up over the past four decades.

Reiner (2000: 213) argues that this research has five distinct phases. The first of these, that of *consensus*, relates to the work carried out, for example, by Banton (1964), when the work of the police organisation was considered worth celebrating. This research sought to learn from the police as a successful form of social organisation. The second category, that of *controversy*, reflects the growth of malpractice and the abuse of power by the police. The research carried out by Reiner (1992a), Holdaway (1983) and Chatterton (1983) suggests that it is the use of police discretion and the power that this entails which shapes deviance of this kind. By the 1980s, however, due to the increased politicisation of the police, the research had changed to focus on the idea of *conflict*. The role of the police in conflicts such as the urban riots and the miners' strike of the 1980s led Jefferson and Grimshaw (1984) and others to question who should control the police.

By the late 1980s, a new more *contradictory* phase of police research began to emerge. According to Reiner, a number of tendencies were in competition. The left-realist approach put forward by Lea and Young (1984) challenged the earlier left-idealist conceptions that had opposed the role of the criminal justice system in the control of crime. Left-realism also rejected the more disciplinary version of realism that could be found in the work of writers such as Wilson (1975) and Wilson and Kelling (1982). Left-realism, however, did agree with the right-realists that a degree of crime control was necessary. The victims of crime were often as socially disadvantaged as were its perpetrators. This justified intervention by the criminal justice agencies for the purpose of crime control, but with a greater degree of community control over their work. For discussion of the distinctions between radical criminologies, left-idealism and left-realism, readers should refer to White and Haines (1996: 135–71) or to Coleman and Norris (2000: 73–82).

According to Reiner, *crime control* is now the predominant mode of police research. Reflecting upon its contemporary political implications, he says:

> Research is integral to Labour's crime reduction agenda in general and to the role of the police in particular. The driving paradigm for police research now is clearly *crime control*… There has been explicit rejection of the earlier 'nothing works' pessimism …
>
> (Reiner, 2000b: 216).

For Reiner, it is unfortunate that the trajectory of research is away from fundamental questions about the social role of policing towards questions about crime control and the police reforms that might make this more effective. Fundamental research is still necessary, covering such things as the social characteristics of those who call upon the police for help. Research of this kind would be a constructive way of gaining a better understanding of the social role of the police (Reiner, 2000b: 226).

Waddington (1999) makes use of the lessons of the research in a way that is quite different to that of Reiner, namely in support of a definitive theory of policing. There is, he suggests, agreement about the failure of policing across a wide range of research. Reflecting upon his own experience of the realities of police work, he points to a striking similarity in a large number of research studies. He says:

> My experience is far from exceptional, indeed it is the norm. Many writers on the police describe essentially similar events … In various American police departments things seem to be much the same as in Chicago (Bittner, 1967a, 1967b; Wilson, 1969; Rubenstein, 1973; Muir, 1977; Sykes and Brent, 1983); Ericson (1982) found that policing was essentially similar in a municipal police force in Ontario during the 1970's; Cain (1973), Manning (1977), Chatterton (1983), Holdaway (1983), McClure (1980), Young (1991), Smith and Gray (1983) and Kemp *et al.* (1992) depict similar scenes in various English police forces over a thirty year period: and Punch (1979a) revealed that policing in Amsterdam conformed to this general picture.
>
> (Waddington, 1999: 1–3)

There is certainly a high level of agreement in the research that the police are not effective as crime-fighters. This is so, despite the fact that police and politicians often claim that this is their key role (Hough, 1996: 60–71; Waddington, 1999: 6–7). This is confirmed by studies of motorised and foot patrols in Kansas City and Newark, New Jersey, which have shown that police are ineffective in this respect (Kelling *et al.*, 1974; Police

Foundation, 1981). The research also shows that the police are ineffective in the detection of crime, peacekeeping and the more service-oriented aspects of police work. Rarely, do they produce the results claimed for them by politicians and practitioners. Also, in law enforcement and crime prevention, police are now simply one agency among many. According to Waddington:

> ... the police cannot lay claim to be society's 'thin blue line' against disorder and lawlessness, for they are supplemented by a host of social controls which, if absent, would leave the police virtually powerless.
>
> (Waddington, 1999: 11)

In all of these functions, however, it is not just that the police are ineffective. Examples drawn both from Waddington's own field research and from other published work show that the supposed functions of the police simply do not represent their true role.

For Waddington, the lessons of the research leave only one viable answer to the question 'what is policing?' It is '... the exercise of the authority of the state over the civil population' (Waddington, 1999: 30). By 'authority', Waddington means command of an area or a situation. For example, illegal street traders cease trading when the police pass by. Motorists invariably conform to traffic laws when the police are about. The public obeys police cordons. As the exercise of authority, police work is a 'demand for deference'. He agrees with Walker (1996) that the only real function of patrolling is symbolic. It is an affirmation of the authority of the police. Such authority is not subordinate to their coercive power because they exercise it in many other ways, for example when informing someone of the sudden death of a relative. Authority also serves to keep citizens and dissenters in their place. It does not do this by law enforcement and due process but by the use of discretion that is inherently discriminatory. This is the sense in which the police use their authority to impose a particular social order. He says, authority 'imbues *everything* they do' (Waddington, 1999: 19–20).

The list of writers and works cited above are certainly not exhaustive. However, they do emphasise the extent to which the critical consensus now provides the central rationale for the criminological study of policing. It is evident that the implications of this research are different for Waddington and Reiner. For Waddington (1999), the research paves the way for a strong theoretical claim. His conclusion that policing is the exercise of the authority of the state over the civil population could be entitled 'Waddington's Law'! Despite the fact that there is evidence that the authority of the police has declined in recent years, this is a compelling argument. However, it is also reductionist in the sense that it reduces the role of the police to a single function under the modern state.

For Reiner, in contrast, critical research on the police does not represent a single well-defined theory of policing. Unlike the paradigms that characterise most natural sciences or human sciences such as psychology, it does not provide overarching law-like explanations. Both Reiner's classic *Politics of the Police* (1992a, 2000a) and his review of research on the police (2000b) contain more interpretative narratives. Also for Reiner, moral and political standpoint is very important. The *Politics of the Police*, the first edition of which appeared in 1985, reflects this approach. An earlier series of articles ranging widely over the work of the police was the basis for this book. Starting from a standpoint on the political left, Reiner says that he intended the book '... to contribute to the enormously impassioned debates then raging round the police and ... to intervene in this polarized argument in support of a middle way' (Reiner, 1998: 87). It is in this sense that his work is interpretative. There is no single overarching theory of the police or policing. On the contrary, for Reiner the purpose of criminological research is to interpret the world of policing in order to change it.

How can we assess the merits of these different approaches? Both Waddington's theory of policing and Reiner's interpretative approach contribute greatly to our knowledge and understanding of police work and the police institution. The critical consensus they both represent calls into question the rationale of a wide range of policing practice. In this sense, there is a considerable amount of intellectual agreement between them. However, their findings are a far cry from the reforming ideas which were common to those who founded the modern police, namely that it had a broadly defined range of roles, intended to make a positive contribution to social progress. For this reason, before we can start to consolidate our conclusions on policing practice, we need to ask some further questions about the nature of that practice. In particular we need to examine the whole idea of police functions. This entails a conceptual critique of policing practice, an enquiry that questions the assumptions about meaning that are implied by modernity and their continued relevance to policing. For these reasons, it is to the debate about the functions of the police and the use of the terms 'police' and 'policing' in a variety of practices that we must now turn.

Chapter 2

Policing as a rational function: back to basics?

In Chapter 1 we saw that the rise of the modern police resulted from a particular way of thinking about controlling crime and promoting social order. As such, the police fulfilled an important rational function in the modern state. We saw that the crisis of the modern police, and the important questions which criminology has raised, poses serious challenges to this idea. Given the endemic nature of these problems we argued that it is now necessary to find new ways of conceptualising policing. We suggested that new understandings are also are necessary to provide a more cohesive account of the relationship between state, police and citizens.

This chapter extends the debate by criticising the way in which policing is understood in terms of its functions. It reviews a number of studies of the functions of the police and reveals the inadequacy of a functional explanation of police work. In contrast to claims about functionality, this chapter suggests that we should pay more attention to the diversity of meaning of 'police' and 'policing'. It explores the contested nature of the terms and shows that their meaning is not un-ambiguous and unequivocal. It questions why, despite the evident puzzles that surround them, social science and practitioners alike tend to regard their meaning as transparent. It suggests that clarification of the different meanings of 'police' and 'policing' can help dispel some of the puzzles that still dog attempts to provide robust accounts of their character. Finally, it argues that because policing has a variety of meanings, it is now more appropriate to understand it in terms of its various modes of practice. This is a central contention of the book. The placing of this conceptual analysis at this stage of the book is important because it forms the basis of the more detailed discussion of the modes of policing practice in the chapters that follow. As the introduction indicates, it will discuss a number of philosophical points. Although these may make some demands upon readers who have no specialist knowledge or interest in the philosophical literature, they are important to the chain of argument of the book as a whole.

Policing functions: reality or myth?

A function is a special purpose or activity that is part of a greater social system (Merton, 1957). To make use of a mechanical analogy, it resembles a part of a machine. Functionalism is the tendency to think of social organisation in terms of the patterning of its functions. For social anthropologists such as Malinowski (1944), in every type of civilisation, every custom, material object, idea and belief fulfils some vital function, has some task to accomplish, and represents an indispensable part within a working whole. Functionalism, therefore, sees the modern police in terms of its place within the system of the state or society generally. To use another example, as the heart has the function of conveying oxygen around the body, so the police have the function of preventing and detecting crime and preserving social order within the modern state. This functional way of thinking has dictated the character of the modern police from its inception until the present. It has underpinned the rationale and aims of the institution. It has dictated the formal structure within which the police were supposed to operate. It has defined the means of judging its effectiveness. It has set the parameters within which subsequent criticism has developed. The police *are* what the police *do* in respect of their internal functionality and their wider role in society and the body politic. In the most pessimistic analysis, the police are simply agents for the functional imperatives of the state.

The analysis of functions is crucial to many sociological accounts of police work. This is not surprising, given the high level of interest in functionalism during the years in which many sociologists of the police were developing their careers. Accounts of this kind have provided important insights into the nature of police work. They show how police work involves a range of moral dilemmas. They show how police adopt pragmatic solutions to control crime and take action aimed at keeping the peace rather than following legal process. However, it is the comparison between the formal functions of police and empirical evidence of the range of informal behaviours that actually opens the deepest questions about the way in which the police really operate.

This is certainly the case in Bittner's influential study *The Functions of the Police in Modern Society* (1970). Here, Bittner provides a compelling analysis of police functions and the factors that make the police what they are. The pattern of their relationships with the courts, with communities and with politicians enables them to play a controlling role. Bittner's study also challenges the official claim that the police mandate is that of a law enforcement agency guided by due process. For Bittner, police work has three characteristic traits. First, it is a 'tainted occupation'. Inevitably, it involves getting 'dirty hands' in carrying out work that society will not (or cannot) do for itself. Secondly, police work tends to provide peremptory solutions to complex human problems. In this sense, the need to 'be right' and 'do something' means that the police have to compromise even before they act. Thirdly, the police inevitably discriminate against citizens. This is because of their class and educational background and because of the type of work they do. According to Bittner:

> Because the preponderant majority of police interventions are based upon mere suspicion or on merely tentative indications of risk, policemen would have to be expected to judge matters prejudicially even if they personally were entirely free from prejudice.
>
> (Bittner, 1970: 11)

For Bittner, however, there is one core function that serves to distinguish police from other functions of the state, namely the capacity to use force. He says:

> Because only a small part of the activity of the police is dedicated to law enforcement and because they deal with the majority of their problems without invoking the law, a broader definition of their role was proposed. After reviewing briefly what the public appears to expect of the police, the range of activities police actually engage in, and the theme that unifies all of these activities, it was suggested that the role of the police is best understood as a mechanism for the distribution of non-negotiable coercive force employed in accordance with the dictates of an intuitive grasp of situational exigencies.
>
> (Bittner, 1970: 46)

Thus, for Bittner, of all the functional aspects of the role of the police, the capacity to use force is *the* core function. This aspect of policing, which draws upon Max Weber's claims about the role of the state in maintaining a monopoly of coercive force, is further explored in Chapter 3 (Gerth and Wright Mills, 1970: 78).

In addition to its role in studies of police work, there is evidence that functionalism was prominent in areas of government policy on the police. In the 1990s, for example, a number of initiatives used the analysis of functions as the key to police reform. They drew upon the central idea that policing is made up of a number of functions, some of which might prove to be 'core' or definitive of the basic role of the institution. Police would give priority to these core functions. Other agencies would take over the less important ancillary functions. There would be gains in effectiveness and welcome savings in costs. These initiatives were part of a concerted review of policy.

In 1993, the government's White Paper on the subject identified a lack of clear objectives in policing and defects in the police framework. It set out a new strategy to meet the aims of policing (Home Office 1993a). The main aims (broad functions) of policing were said to be:

- to fight and prevent crime;
- to uphold the law;
- to bring to justice those who break the law;
- to protect, help and reassure the community;
- in meeting those aims, to provide good value for money.

The White Paper also proposed the strengthening of local police authorities. The aim of this was to help improve local police account-ability. It also proposed that there should be increased direction by central government who would set key policing objectives in accordance with the government's law and order policies (Home Office 1993a: 2–3). These proposals were incorporated in the Police and Magistrates Courts Act 1994.

Also in 1993, the Association of Chief Police Officers Quality of Service Committee (ACPO 1993) highlighted five similar functional areas for the delivery of police services, namely:

- crime prevention and detection;
- traffic control and related matters;
- community relations and dealing with community-related problems;
- public reassurance and public order maintenance;
- answering and responding to calls for assistance.

It is questionable whether their efforts to specify these functions succeeded in clarifying the role of the police. They are convenient for measuring performance but they do not reflect the ambiguities of police work. Overall, it is doubtful if these measures have improved the accountability or effectiveness of the police. However, more importantly for the arguments of this chapter, they show that the conception of policing as an array of functions was very much alive in official thinking.

In Chapter 1, we briefly mentioned the Sheehy, Posen and Cassels inquiries. (Home Office 1993b, Home Office 1995 and Police Foundation/Policy Studies Institute 1994, 1996). Each of these inquiries drew heavily on the functional analysis of police work. The Sheehy inquiry examined the range of functions associated with each rank. It proposed the following:

- 'delayering' of the structure by the removal of some senior ranks;
- changes to the reward structure;
- introduction of performance-related pay;
- local pay flexibility;
- fixed-term appointments.

The inquiry recommended that pay should depend upon the extent to which a particular job was difficult or dangerous. In this way, length of service and the promotion system alone would not be the only means of rewarding performance (Home Office 1993b). The police staff associations were strongly against these proposals. They successfully argued for retaining the *status quo*. As a result, the Home Office made only minor modifications to the rank structure and to senior officer contracts. Once again, the Sheehy Report relied heavily upon the analysis of functions. As was the case with the reform White Paper, policing functions were the underpinning concepts for reform.

Two other inquiries at this time also relied on the analysis of policing functions. Ingrid Posen of the Home Office chaired the first of these. Its terms of reference were to examine police work and to make recommendations about the most cost-effective way of delivering core services (Home Office 1995). The inquiry asked chief constables to examine 85 tasks and to say whether these were core or ancillary. The inquiry also made a distinction between the inner core and outer core tasks. However, task lists were mainly classified according to primary function, such as preventing crime, upholding the law and so on. This inquiry foundered because of two problems. First, there was controversy regarding the whether this was merely a cost-saving exercise. Secondly, the police considered that the ancillary tasks were an important influence on public consent for carrying out their core role. Eventually, the review team concluded that there was little scope for the police to withdraw completely from large areas of current police work.

The independent Cassels inquiry, which was set up in 1993, also examined the functions of the police (Police Foundation/Policy Studies Institute 1994, 1996). For this inquiry, the patrol function was of considerable importance. The most radical proposal to emerge was for a two-tier patrol system. The inquiry proposed that this should include a new local patrolling force or designated patrol officers who would remain part of the local constabulary. This is similar to the approach adopted in some parts of continental Europe. The rationale for this suggestion was analysis of the function which has long appeared to be central to police work, namely that of patrol. The Kansas City Preventive Patrol Experiment had shown that an increase in mobile patrols did not make a significant impact upon crime (Kelling *et al.*, 1974). A study of foot-patrols in Newark, New Jersey had similar results (Police Foundation 1981). However, targeted police activity in crime hot spots did meet with some success. The Audit Commission paper, *Streetwise: Effective Police Patrol*, also made similar claims (Audit Commission 1996). As the Cassels inquiry pointed out, however, it is the view of the public that patrolling is an important police function. This is a paradox for policing strategies. It places senior police managers in a dilemma if they make patrolling a priority. Cassels claimed that the adoption of alternatives to patrols by the regular police could solve this dilemma. According to their final report:

> Police strategies ... which increase confidence and trust in the police are likely to be important as part of a broader strategy to tackle local crime problems. Thus, although in strict crime control terms it is clear that there are limitations upon the effectiveness of patrol, its popularity, its potential impact on security and the likelihood that it may help sustain public confidence in the police all suggest that a visible uniformed presence must continue to play a significant part in modern policing.
>
> (Police Foundation/PSI 1996: 28)

The inquiry also noted that private security or special constables had carried out some very successful patrol work. However, the inquiry did not recommend the full implementation of two-tier policing, nor a system that would be outside the control of the local chief constable. They concluded that if local authorities wished to experiment with the use of private patrols, they should be free to do so. They have not adopted this on a national scale but some chief constables and local authorities have endorsed the idea.

Mawby (2000) has rightly characterised these core-function studies as a seductive myth. He claims that there are two ways in which they are flawed. The first is because they failed to consider public perceptions of the role of the police. In this sense, they did not relate the functions to wider social and community needs. The second is because they over-estimated the viability of dispersing policing tasks to other agencies to allow the police to concentrate upon the 'real' task of fighting crime. A deeper failure, however, is the fallacy of understanding policing in terms of its functionality at all. In this sense, the core functions studies promise something that they can never deliver. They can never pull apart the complex web of purposive activities and practices. The definition of functions can never overcome the moral or practical ambiguities of police work. In this sense, policing functions are not the loose and separate entities that these inquiries supposed.

These inquiries show that it is not possible to make an institution more effective by ignoring the ambiguity inherent in its practice. Indeed, they illustrate why the whole modern idea that institutions are rational structures defined by their functions is deeply flawed. Political, economic, social and technological change means that we can no longer associate policing with the police alone. In fact, reference to the functions of the police can no longer answer the question, 'What is policing?' at all. The only way to do this is to provide an account that interprets policing practice in terms of its social and political purposes. Such an account will point to the rich pattern of relations between policing, the state and other agencies, groups and individuals. It will recognise that policing can only exist in an 'informational society' of the kind discussed by Bell (1980) and Castells (1989). We will discuss this further in Chapter 7. In the light of the evidence, therefore, we should abandon any attempt to understand policing as a range of functions of the police. Instead we should develop an account which recognises the diversity of meanings which now characterise the terms 'police' and 'policing'.

Diversity of meanings

Functionalism has not led to a unified scientific account of police work. Nor has it produced practical measures for police reform. As we have argued above, the reason for this is that we can no longer simply under-stand policing in terms of the functions of the police. We need to look anew at the meaning of 'police' and 'policing' to establish new ways of approaching these questions. It is true that there is a rapidly expanding literature on the police. However, it seldom discusses the deeper meaning of the concept. Studies of police work regard policing as a transparent concept. Those who recognise the difficulties, however, are aware that there are problems associated with the meaning of the term 'policing'. Indeed, it is now unsafe to use the term as if it refers to the activities of a single institution.

The fact that the meanings of 'police' and 'policing' are ambiguous makes them difficult to define. The context in which they are used makes a difference to the meaning. For example, the use of the term 'police' by criminologists discussing police accountability may not be the same as its use by the police or those who make complaints against them. Its meaning for practitioners will not be the same as that in the minds of those who consider themselves 'policed against'. The concept of policing may have had very different meanings for protesting students who faced the *Compagnies Républicaines de Sécurité* (CRS) in Paris in 1968 than for the members of the CRS who were on public order duty at that time. This is so, despite the fact that both may have believed that they were influencing the future and very legitimacy of the French state. It is all the more problematic in such cases if theoretical accounts assume that the meanings of the terms 'police' and policing' are unequivocal. However, even where the meaning is elusive, 'police' and 'policing' cannot simply mean anything we want them to mean. For this reason, we need to clarify the way in which the various forms of discourse use the concepts, both in theory and in practice.

We should recognise that the terms 'police' and 'policing' have always borne a variety of meanings, both in the pre-modern and modern eras. Early understandings of the term 'police' locate its roots in the ancient world. A connection between policing and *polis* (the Greek city-state) seems intuitively correct. Of course, this is not to say that there are direct links between policing in fifth-century Greece and modern policing. However, *polis*, 'politics' and 'police' share the same root. In this sense, the term 'police' and the political world are connected. This is so from the Greeks onwards, where, according to Emsley, 'The Greek *politeia* meant all matters affecting the survival and well being of the state (*polis*).' (Emsley, 1996a: 3).

History shows that there is a clear connection between policing and politics. Up to the nineteenth century, the descendants of tithing-men and Norman constables carried out local policing in England. However, as elected representatives of the parish and as officers recognised by the Crown, they were not servants. In fact, they were deeply involved in local politics (Critchley, 1978: 5). From the sixteenth century onwards, however, the German states used the word 'police' more widely. Raeff (1983: 43–56) points to the use of police ordinances (*Polizeiordnungen*) as the means of expressing the government's philosophy, goals and methods. A strong connection between police and state was also the case in France, even before the Revolution and the demise of the *Ancien Régime* (Stead, 1957: 20–41). According to Emsley (1996a: 3), by the eighteenth century the words, *la police* or *die Politzei* were being widely used in continental Europe: to denote '… internal administration, welfare, protection, and surveillance of a territory'.

In Britain during the eighteenth century, the word 'police' was also used occasionally to denote measures for administrative oversight and audit. According to the *Oxford English Dictionary*, the first official use of the concept in this sense was in the reign of Queen Anne. She appointed Commissioners of Police (six noblemen and four gentlemen) for this purpose in Scotland for the general administration of the country. However, many people regarded this use of the term as a trend towards political absolutism. As we have shown, the use of the term 'police' by Henry Fielding and Patrick Colquhoun during the late eighteenth century (*The New Science of the Preventive Police*) marked a more limited approach. Although the connection between police and social control was retained, closer identification with local communities provide the ground upon which the British policing system was later established (Fielding, 1757; Colquhoun, 1796; Reith, 1943: 19–21). This was quite unlike the more centralised state-oriented policing systems and *gendarmarie* that existed in most parts of Europe at that time. What is noticeable here is the extent to which the terms 'police' and policing' took on different meanings in different contexts. In late modernity, similar factors influence our understanding of the terms, including developments in the theory of meaning itself.

This diversity of meanings leads to difficulties when we ask, what roles are essential to the definition of policing? Unfortunately, this is precisely the question that has led to the functionalist position criticised above. To develop a more satisfactory answer to the question 'what is policing?' it is necessary to further explore the use of the term in different circumstances. Here we need to jettison the pretence that meaning is *only* about the relationship between the word 'policing' and a limited set of real-world conditions. Of course, the link between the word and its object is certainly *one* of the things we can expect to consider when we ask 'what is policing?' Indeed, we have already tentatively explored some of the answers to this question in the section on police work in Chapter 1. Policing is certainly about many of the things listed there. However, we also need to identify in what different senses the term can properly be used.

Meaning relates to human interaction in the use of language. Meanings relate to each other in many different ways, like members of a family which have resemblance one to another but who may have no particular essence or 'thing in common'. It is not difficult to see that there may be many different senses in which we can properly use the word 'policing'. Different aspects of policing in different jurisdictions may have similarities without there being one essence with which they all comply. For example, as we will see in Chapter 3, the policing of public disorder in France in the eighteenth century may be different in many ways to the policing of public disorder in the Netherlands in the twentieth century. They may also differ in certain ways from the front-line combat role of the Israeli police on the West Bank in 2001. And these forms of policing are certainly very different from problem-oriented policing in Madison, Wisconsin, community policing in Brixton, London and mobile patrol policing in Helsinki. Although there may be family resemblance and similarity between them, there are also enough differences in types of policing to convince us that we should be very careful to establish the sense in which we are using the term. A simple analogy illustrates the point. In some ways, I look like my cousin Brian, who also shares some facial characteristics with his brother Martin. I do not, however, share any of cousin Martin's characteristics. This is common in human families – and so it is in family resemblance between different types of policing.

It is clear that we also need to recognise the importance of other types of meaning beyond those describing the relationship between the police and what they do by way of tasks and activities. From the very beginning of the police, emotive or evaluative meanings have also held an important place in understanding the concept. Such meanings neither denote a word–object relationship or a particular sense of the term. Rather, they express speakers' emotions or attitudes. For example, the early British reluctance to accept the term 'police' indicates that it had something of an emotive meaning in English. From the earliest times, it did not merely denote a particular institution but indicated a certain strained relationship between the police and the policed.

This concern remained even after the foundation of the new police in the early nineteenth century. However, according to Reith (1943: 135) the performance of the police themselves later placated public reluctance in this respect. Meanings have continued to change since the foundation of the new police. No doubt, ever-changing perceptions of the police role drove these changes in meaning. For example, hardly anyone ever refers to the 'bobby' now, except sentimentalists who mourn the passing of some supposed golden age of British policing. The reference by Storch (1975) to the police as a '... plague of blue locusts' points primarily to public attitudes to policing, not to their function. Similarly, the reference by Reiner to the transitions from 'crushers' to 'bobbies' and from 'plods' to 'pigs' says as much about emotive meaning as about the reality of policing styles (Reiner, 1992a: 73–104).

When considering the question of the emotive meaning of 'police' for the police themselves, attachment to the institution may have a meaning that is strongly embedded in loyalty expressed in discourse. Although political correctness now constrains them, much of what police officers actually say about their occupation still exhibits a high degree of emotive meaning. This often aims at producing solidarity, loyalty and shared moral commitment. It is not just a matter of using colloquialisms and slang. Frequent reference to 'the job' rather than to 'the police' is a commonly observed characteristic of practitioner discourse, among other more reprehensible terminology. However, it is a mistake to see emotive meaning simply as an unfortunate optional extra or by-product of a perverse police culture. Evaluative usage by non-practitioners also conveys the speakers' beliefs about the police. The emotive content of both ordinary and slang expressions is embedded in discourse because users of language are human agents with feelings. It is an ineradicable linguistic phenomenon implied by using language in the process of making a particular practice 'meaning-full'.

A further distinction is worth recognising in our efforts to get clear about discourse that uses the terms 'police' and 'policing'. Austin (1962) maintained a distinction between the meaning of an utterance (what the utterance says) and the speech act performed in making the utterance. He refers to the latter as an illocutionary act: in effect, an act that we perform in saying something. We can easily understand the role of such performatives in relation to police discourse, not least because of the action-orientation of many aspects of policing. Take, for example, a plain clothes police officer making an arrest. The police officer announces him or herself and says, 'I am a police officer. I arrest you for murder!' How are we to understand the linguistic role of this statement and how does it square with the ideas about meaning discussed above? First, it does not tell us much about the function of policing or about emotive meaning, although it may have some elements of these. It is a performative utterance of the Austinian kind. In such cases, the utterance itself actually constitutes the most important part (if not the whole on some occasions) of the act of arrest. In fact, using verbs is this way often names the very sort of act that we are performing. Similarly, the use of the term 'police' in this utterance is not simply about the meaning of the concept. It is about the performance of the act itself. One can easily see the difference if this was a citizen's arrest, where the arresting person was not able to use the word 'police' meaningfully as part of the speech act.

It is clear, therefore, throughout pre-modernity and into the current era, that the terms 'police' and 'policing' have borne a variety of meanings, reflecting the nuances of relations between police and people at different times and places. Their meaning has been subject to change throughout history, reflecting both structural (institutional) factors and the impact of interactions between state, police and people. For these reasons, we should take particular care in using the terms. We should not assume that they are self-evident and transparent. This diversity of meanings also emphasises the importance of understanding the contested way in which the discourse of our subject works.

Policing: a contested concept?

We can empirically describe aspects of the work of the police institution in terms of its tasks and activities but even this becomes more difficult at higher levels of abstraction and generalisation. As we have already seen, the idea of understanding the wider concept of policing in terms of its functions has a number of flaws in this respect. Although it seems deceptively simple, the concept of policing is very difficult to pin down. Indeed it will not have escaped the attention of many readers that this is precisely what criminology thrives on. Like policing itself, because it necessarily deals in conceptual controversy, there is little likelihood that it will go out of fashion!

Modern philosophers have shown that apparently simple action concepts such as policing often turn out to be highly complex. Ryle (1951), for example, has addressed the problem of action concepts in this respect. He argues, in relation to a paradigm pair of action concepts (namely working and thinking), that nothing answers to a general description of what 'working' and 'thinking' actually consist of. In the case of working, according to Ryle, '… there is nothing going on in one piece of work which need be going on in another.' Although each specific instance of work is capable of description, the polymorphous nature of the concept means that there is no necessary overlap between them. Here, 'polymorphous' means, literally, 'having many forms'. In addition to working and thinking, other concepts, such as trading, playing, housekeeping and farming, are also polymorphous, whereas the concept of apple picking is 'nearly enough non polymorphous' (Ryle, 1951: 258–71).

We can argue with some justification that the concept of 'policing' meets Ryle's criteria for polymorphism. As already suggested in relation to differences in meaning, there need be nothing going on in some kinds of policing that needs to be going on in others. For example, the action content of community policing need not be the same as the action content of law enforcement. There is no *necessary* overlap between them, although there may be overlap under some specific conditions. Technically speaking, our use of the term 'policing' does not rigidly designate the action content of policing practice other than the one we are specifically referring to at the time. It is an abstract general term but it does not label only one thing. This is not a complicated point. We often distinguish between forms of police work in terms of their action content, as we also often distinguish between them in terms of their context, both organisationally and historically. We can talk about paramilitary policing and not get it confused with the kind of policing which is concerned with putting identifiable marks on children's bicycles. However, we still want to make use of the word to denote some kind of association between these different kinds of practice. This indicates that we should be looking for an understanding of policing in terms of a modal logic of practice that recognises this variability. A provisional model for such a modal logic of policing practice is set out later in this chapter.

Whether we assume that there is one and only one thing called 'policing' or whether, as we have argued above, it covers a range of tasks and activities, it is all too easy to get into disputes about it. Following similar logical themes to those of Ryle, Gallie (1964: 157–91) shows that concepts of this kind are 'essentially contested'. In Gallie's contention, there is not and cannot be a final and conclusive agreement about meaning between the users of such concepts. It is not merely the case that there are factual disputes about them (saying in effect either function x is policing or it is not – this is the 'functional fallacy'). In the case of essentially contested concepts, there are endless disputes over their proper application (Gallie, 1964: 158). Gallie's arguments relate to any concept that satisfies the following criteria:

1. That the concept is appraisive in the sense that it signifies some kind of valued achievement. (Many concepts within the political universe of discourse including police and policing, get included under this rubric.)

2. That the achievement is of a complex character and entails a range of compound activities to achieve it. (As we have seen, the concept of policing falls into this category.)

3. That it is of an open character in that we cannot specify in advance with any accuracy what might fall within the concept. (This again, has been argued by commentators such as Waddington (1986a) to be a characteristic of policing.)

4. That each party recognises that other parties will contest its use. (A degree of friction between proponents of different policing styles often illustrates this point. We will discuss zero-tolerance policing in this respect in Chapter 6.)

For Gallie, in the field of politics, democracy is a typical essentially contested concept. Policing, which as we have seen has its roots in politics, is also an essentially contested concept. We have already alluded to its complexity, compound nature and open character. A wide range of controversies in criminological studies and in practice shows that this is the case.

In the senses intended by Ryle and Gallie, therefore, it is logically impossible to give a singular definitional account of the essence of policing. We cannot specify in advance all the kinds of intentions, actions and outcomes that the concept might entail. The conceptual clarity that would be necessary to underpin essentialist claims is always lacking. It is always necessary to resort to argumentation about the nature of the concept in the actual world in which we find ourselves. In this sense, we are right to regard the meanings of 'policing' as contested. It does not suffice to suggest that such concepts have a natural meaning and that contestedness is simply a mistake over their true nature. In the words of Douglas (1992: 9), 'Knowledge always lacks, ambiguity always lurks'. Also, as Gallie shows, to understand the nature of such concepts, we need not only ask for their use in practice but also for their history. Understanding such concepts, as this discussion has tried to show, is as much a matter of grasping their historical development in practice (in dispute and discussion) as it is for empirical criminological science.

Of course, if these claims about the problematic nature of meaning are correct, it should not be surprising that there are seemingly endless disputes among both criminologists and practitioners about policing. However, it is precisely the contested nature of policing that should alert us to the fact that no single function or set of functions can serve to define its essence. Indeed, it is the very diversity and contested nature of policing that now allows us to break free from the pretence that its meaning is defined by the functions of 'the police'. When we review the concept of policing, therefore, we should interpret the whole range of meaning implied by the use of the term in practice. In doing so, we find that the variety of usage leads us towards comparison of particular kinds of resemblance. For example, in using the term 'policing', we connote different types of activity that are alike in some ways but different in others. The danger is that we might persist in the essentialist claim that there is one and only one thing that is truly policing or that the essence of policing should be defined in some irreducible way. Even Bittner, who has provided us with perhaps the most illuminating accounts of certain kinds of policing, has been tempted to take this line (Bittner, 1970). Although he shows that local police often have the end of peacekeeping in mind more than that of law enforcement, his purview of policing across a wider range of its contemporary practice remains limited.

Many kinds of policing are possible within the variety of ways in which we can legitimately use the term. Indeed, it now becomes clear why some of the classical works on policing have not tried to create a unified theory of policing. They have not done so because their authors have long recognised the futility of the exercise, given the endemic ambiguity of the subject. In any discussion of police science, serious conceptual problems will always arise that will confound even the most determined determinist. Given the conceptual polymorphism and contestability that is endemic in the practice and study of policing, we should not be surprised at this. Nor should we be surprised at the recourse to historical narrative and interpretation in much recent criminology, including that in Reiner (1992a, 2000a). But we can certainly no longer resort to an analysis of the functions of the police to provide us with either a theoretical or practical understanding of the complexities of policing. To rely on this, given the difficulties outlined above, is no longer a viable option.

Deconstructing practice

How, then, should we proceed? In aligning the question of the meaning of policing so strongly to the idea of practice rather than function, it is necessary to say more about the notion of practice and to show why it is of crucial importance. Policing practice, in the sense in which we use the term here, is concerned with the sphere of conduct. Conduct configures actions carried out by individuals, agencies or by parts of the formal police organisation. Like the new police and its successors, contemporary policing is beginning to be characterised by new forms of conduct. Policing is now the output of a variety of agencies with multiple objectives and lines of accountability. We can no longer speak of policing as though it relates to the activities of a single organisation. According to Coleman and Norris:

> The police should not be equated with policing, an activity that can be performed by a number of agencies. The role of the police is better thought of as the reproduction of order by authoritative

intervention and symbolic justice, rather than in terms of crime control.

(Coleman and Norris, 2000: 145)

The correctness of the latter remains to be seen. Although it is clear that we should talk of policing in this wider sense, it is important not simply to replace single-agency functionalism with multi-agency functionalism. For this reason, we have to be more careful than ever about what we mean by the term 'policing'. The ambiguity and contested nature of the concept means that the very idea of policing and its practices need to be under continual review.

The alternative that characterises the remaining chapters of this book is to adopt an approach that both interprets and deconstructs policing practice. 'Interpretation' means that as a practice evolves we explain it in a way that gives it meaning. 'Deconstruction' reflects the need to interpret practice throughout its whole possible range. The sense in which we use the term here reflects the idea that a text (in this case a text that both configures and explains the role of the police institution and other kinds of policing practice) is subject to multiple meanings (Derrida, 1976).

For policing practice, however, it is not sufficient to identify the fact that multiple meanings of policing exist. We need to know how the discourse of and about policing actually uses them. Discussion of the primary functions of policing in the discourse of modernity and the state has provided a starting point. Here the focus was on law and order. The transition to law reflected the contrast with the application of raw power in pre-modernity. The transition to order reflected the contrast with a state of anarchy or with a 'war of each against all' of the kind feared by Hobbes (1651). These contrasts generated the policing functions of controlling crime and disorder. However, given the diversity of meaning of policing, it now needs to take account of the expanded range of concepts and contrasts. These will need to cover a plurality of contemporary policing.

Figure 2.1 provides a tentative outline of the modes that constitute contemporary policing practice. Columns 1 and 2 reflect the transition from pre-modern to modern policing. As shown in column 3, the modes of policing practice in late modernity include peacekeeping, crime investigation, the management of risk and the promotion of community justice.

Column 4 reflects the idea that modern policing practice has mainly been concerned with 'controlling' as its context of influence. Modern policing, therefore, was arguably concerned with controlling disorder,

| Pre-modern construct (1) | Modern policing construct (2) | Late-modern mode of policing practice (3) | *Trajectory of contexts of influence* / *Modernity to late modernity* | | |
			Controlling (modern) (4)	Managing (late-modern) (5)	Enabling (ideal type) (6)
Anarchy	Maintaining order	Peacekeeping	Disorder	Conflict	Liberty
Sin	Crime/detection	Crime investigation	Crime in the individual	Due process	Justice
Fate	Crime/prevention	Management of risk	Crime in the aggregate	Risk and contingency	Community safety
Power	Law enforcement	Community justice	Deviance (individual offenders)	Reduction of offending	Community security

Figure 2.1. Table of policing concepts

controlling crime committed by individuals, controlling crime in the aggregate and controlling deviance. In contrast, contemporary policing shows a range of other approaches to these domains. These provide ways of thinking about policing beyond the simple model of policing as control of crime and disorder.

Column 5 indicates that these modes of practice relate to more managerial notions. These include managing conflict, due process, risk and contingency and reduction of offending. The use of the term 'managing' in this context diverts the primary focus from the use of force as a sole defining characteristic as in modern policing to something which is no more than a reserve power. We discuss this in more detail in Chapter 3. Column 6 indicates that these modes of practice are enabling concepts aimed towards the achievement of the ideals of liberty, justice, safety and security.

Such a framework is not immutable. It does, however, set out a range of concepts showing the transition from pre-modern to late-modern thinking and the contexts of influence within which they operate. The deconstruction of contexts of influence is as important as the description of the modes of practice. This is because they help to show the new ways in which the plurality of policing practice is realised and articulated. Again, this emphasis on plurality moves the debate away from the idea of essential functions. In particular, it questions the primary category of control that was central to the idea of 'the police' as a modern institution.

As the framework in Figure 2.1 implies, the 'force versus service' distinction does not do justice to the diversity of policing practice. Both caring and controlling concepts may be appropriate at each level. Again, however, this also emphasises that policing practice is full of ambiguity and conflicts of value. For more detailed debates on this topic, see Stephens and Becker (1994: 227–9) and Wright and Irving (1996.) It does not mean that controlling concepts are no longer relevant. Nor does it mean that there is no necessity for this aspect of policing in dealing with some types of problem. But the belief that control is all, when viewed in the context of the contemporary socio-political environment, reflects an approach to policing whose time has passed.

In our analysis of policing practice we have identified its modes and its contexts of influence. However, we need to make a further important point, namely to distinguish between a practice and actual behaviour. Although analysis of behaviour can tell us much about what goes on within a practice, it does not serve to define the practice. Examples of actual behaviour exhibited in the relationship between a policing agency and citizens does not define the practice of policing. Policing is not simply about the satisfaction of wants in particular transactions. It is about the way in which distinctive forms of conduct configure the police–citizen relationship. For Oakeshott, it is the idea of conduct that is important in the consolidation of practice, not simply purposive action or behaviour. He says:

> Conduct is not to be understood (as it is often understood) as performing actions designed to achieve imagined and wished for situations.
>
> (Oakeshott, 1975: 38)

In purposive action, human agents bargain with each other and 'with the future'. Important though they are, such transactions are only possible because of more durable relations that are not themselves transactions but which are the 'conditional contexts' of all such transactions (1975: 54). For Oakeshott, therefore, practices are:

> ... a set of considerations, manners, uses, observances, customs, standards, maxims, principles, rules and offices specifying useful procedures or denoting obligations which relate to human actions and utterances.
>
> (Oakeshott, 1975: 55)

In the sense in which we use the term in this current work, actions and transactions between police and individual suspects, victims, colleagues or members of the public either singly or collectively are not policing practices. Forensic psychology and the sociology of the police deal more than adequately with these transactional aspects of policing. Practice, in contrast, is concerned with conduct, understood as a legal, moral, social and political category. It is the subject of social and political theory.

Policing practice, then, is the set of rules, procedures and values that configure police conduct. The practice of policing upon which we will concentrate, therefore, focuses upon the conditional contexts within which an indeterminate range of specific policing behaviour takes place. To make the logical relationship between them clear, a mode of practice is not a set of functions but the whole of policing viewed from a particular perspective. In the case of this current work, we consider policing practice from the perspectives of the modes of policing of peacekeeping, crime investigation, the management of risk and the promotion of community justice. Figure 2.2 shows the interlocking relationship between the four modes.

It is important to recognise that the rationality of these modes of practice is totally different from the functional rationality which is

Figure 2.2   The modes of policing practice

associated with the work of the 'modern' police. This departure reflects the diversity of policing and the fact that a number of agencies and groups now provide it.

Reciprocity and performativity

It is important to emphasise that because it is concerned with conduct rather than with behaviour, the idea of practice does not imply a contract, either tacit or express, between the police and citizens. This is not its means of justification. At the level of practice, reciprocity between policing and citizens provides the justification for policing. Citizens' rights are the basis for such reciprocity.

Although there are many reasons why these things do not always become reality, we can put the formal argument in the following way. First, the logical conditions for citizenship are a recognition of the necessity of a system of law, adjudication and security. It is only under such a system that citizens can have rights and obligations. Citizens' fundamental rights include the rights to liberty, security, safety and justice. As we have seen in Chapter 1, citizens have moral and legal obligations to respect the rights of others. The primary reason citizens have for meeting their obligations in addition to demanding their rights is that they believe that the rights and obligations of others will also be met. It should again be emphasised that this is not a matter of contract between the citizen and the state but a matter of rights. A contract that cannot be broken is meaningless. There are no circumstances, either on behalf of the state or the citizen, in which the relation of reciprocity based on rights can be broken.

It is clear that under some circumstances, individuals, groups or agencies of the state may deny these rights to citizens. The role of policing is to help prevent this happening or to deal with it when it does. Policing is therefore part of a complex system that enables citizens to make their rights and obligations a reality. It is about providing the legal and social context under which citizens may live in liberty, security, safety and justice. Policing is only possible because the law confirms and consolidates citizens' rights to these goods. This applies to each of the modes of practice. As citizens we are entitled to expect that peacekeeping will only operate under the law and will respect and defend the rights of citizens. Crime investigation should only operate under law in the investigation of dishonest or violent offences. Policing as the management of risk should provide the lawful means of minimising threats to personal security and property. Community justice should provide the legal basis through which citizens can live together in harmony.

The fact that policing depends upon reciprocity means that policing agencies are obliged to act in accordance with principles based on citizens' rights. Policing should only adopt means for defending rights that are legitimate and proportionate to the rights themselves. In this sense, policing agencies should work towards the achievement of citizens' rights without using means that contradict them. This applies equally to the rights of suspects. This means that policing should not try to secure liberty, security, safety and justice for citizens by using means that are illiberal, dishonest, unsafe or unjust. It is in this area of reciprocity, as we have shown in the debate about the crisis in policing, that the police have sometimes failed to deliver.

Of course, citizens know that policing practice will involve the exercise of discretion. However, they also expect the law to define and constrain the extent of the discretion. Policing may not do whatever it likes without sanction. Citizens also expect policing to be accountable. They expect effective democratic processes to be in place to monitor and regulate its activities. Of course, this means that policing (in its widest sense) will also be subject to policing. An independent agency with separate powers can do this more effectively. This, however, does not affect the principle of reciprocity.

Policing is not always successful. Policing failures, as shown in the crisis in the police since the 1960s, are largely failures of behaviour. They range from sheer malpractice to overstepping the limit in of the use of discretion. Persistent failures in behaviour which do not respect citizens' rights will lead to changes in practice because they attack the very roots of reciprocity. This is why the crisis in the police is of such crucial importance. For example, where the law itself is brought into disrepute, as was the case with section 4 of the Vagrancy Act 1824 (the 'sus' law), changes are made. Where patrolling systems have no impact upon crime, policing tries other methods.

In fact, the actual demise of a whole mode of practice (as the conditional context of a vast range of activities) is very rare. One that springs to mind is the virtual disappearance of police responsibility for traffic control since the 1970s. Of course, this does not mean that policing does not provide advice, take part in traffic planning or carry out law enforcement. But the day-to-day routine responsibility for directing moving traffic has gone. Technology has replaced this form of policing. In other cases, rather than discarding the mode of practice what are required are changes to behaviour and procedure. For example, the Macpherson inquiry did not say that the policing practice should no longer include crime investigation because of the failure of the Stephen Lawrence murder investigation. It said that there should be an improvement in behaviour: in investigative competence and fairness. However, in some future cases, changes to a mode of practice may be necessary. Political action or social evolution may drive whole modes of practice onto the scrap heap when they fall into decay or no longer have reciprocal meaning. New modes of practice will arise to replace them.

Policing practice, in the sense that we use the term here, is also performative. We have already made reference to the sense in which the discourse of much policing practice is performative, on the terms put forward by Austin (1962). In many cases, a speech act replaces the use of force, thereby rendering coercive action unnecessary. Lyotard has also drawn attention to a stronger sense of performativity, in particular to the way in which it serves to legitimise beliefs about the efficacy of practice itself. He claims that it is not the scientific testing of hypotheses that provides the strongest evidence for the viability of research and education. If it works, it has value (Lyotard, 1984: 62–3). We can apply the same principle to policing practice. What is both viable and legitimate in policing is what works in practice in its immediate context of influence.

As discussed in Chapter 1, a considerable amount of critical 'what does not work' research has been carried out by criminologists and is well documented. However, policing and crime-reduction practice also require 'what works' and 'why it works' judgements. Much of the 'what works' research has been carried out by so-called 'administrative criminology'. 'What works' methods provide good examples of the use of performativity in policing and criminal justice practice. We discuss these 'what works' claims in more detail in the context of policing as the management of risk in Chapter 5. They provide an antidote to arguments that suggest that because *some* forms of police work are ineffective, the key functions of policing must be the exercise of the authority of the state or the use or threat of coercion (Bittner, 1970; Waddington, 1999). The logical structure of policing practice that we have set out above shows that we should take other factors into account in addition to those that define the failures of the police.

This chapter has argued the need to take seriously the ambiguity and contestability of the concept of policing. These problems of meaning, it has suggested, provide serious difficulties for a theory of policing based on the functions of the police. A number of official inquiries into police functions have fared little better. The problems of meaning, however, have a more positive side. They mean that we can get a better understanding of policing from the perspective of the diversity of its practice. In looking at the transition to late modern conditions from the logic of this more diverse model of policing, we have proposed four modes of policing practice. These modes include policing as peacekeeping, as crime investigation, as the management of risk and as the promotion of community justice. We have also noted the change from the largely controlling style of policing up to the 1980s to a more managerialist approach thereafter. We have shown that the concept of reciprocity is central to an understanding of the logic of policing practice. Performativity, in terms of 'what works', provides an antidote to the pessimistic 'nothing works' epidemiography discussed in Chapter 1.

The following chapters discuss each of the four modes of practice that are set out in Figures 2.1 and 2.2 above. The order in which we shall discuss them implies no particular precedence. In Chapter 3, we review peacekeeping as a mode of policing practice. This includes the relationship between order and liberty and the various methods adopted by states for ensuring public order. In Chapter 4 we review crime investigation as a mode of policing practice. We explore policing as the management of risk in Chapter 5. Chapter 6 discusses policing as the promotion of community justice. In particular we raise the question of whether a professional police is sustainable or whether community justice requires other forms of policing. It is to the first of these constitutive modes of policing practice, namely that of peacekeeping, that we now turn.

Chapter 3

Peacekeeping: policing as social order

Adopting the framework for analysis introduced in Chapter 2, this chapter examines policing from the viewpoint of the mode of practice of peacekeeping. It maps the trajectory of this aspect of policing from pre-modern conditions through to late modernity. It discusses the development of policing for the control of public order and the way in which states of different kinds use the police to create the basis for a 'well-ordered state'. This trajectory provides the text of a long discourse about liberty and order between the state and citizens. Often, it has been characterised by extreme noise and violence. However, radical positions have not lacked able communicators, from Tom Paine's *Rights of Man* onwards (Paine, 1791). The dissent implied in direct public action has often been in a just cause. For example, there has been public resistance again oppressive regimes, such as that in the abortive Hungarian up-rising of 1956 and in other parts of Central and Eastern Europe in recent decades. Such resistance has been effective in promoting political and social change. The role of the police in these transitions has been crucial. In democracies, however, dissent does not of itself necessarily lead to the application of coercive force, although all states retain the means for countering potential threats. The police have an undeniable role in dealing with such confrontations. As physical protest increases, so the role of the police becomes more prominent. A degree of confrontation between protesters and the police in such cases is almost inevitable. In this sense, public disorder is the most visible sign of the clash between dissenting voices and the authority of the state.

To understand peacekeeping, however, we need to do more than simply analyse the behaviour involved in controlling disorder. The analysis of practice means that it is more important to examine the kinds of transactional contexts within which peacekeeping takes place. This debate, therefore, is not about the success or failure of specific interactions between police and those who demonstrate dissent. It is about the underlying contexts of state, liberty and order within which such transactions take place. The underlying transactional context is equally important where the dissent is against the police activity itself. This was the case in the riots in Britain in the early 1980s, which were initially a reaction to heavy-handed policing (Home Office 1981). For these reasons, we cannot understand peacekeeping as a mode of practice outside of its social and political contexts. This chapter will discuss the background to that debate. It will review the relationship in this respect between the police and the state. It will question assumptions about the nature of police authority and the means for asserting that authority. This includes not only the problems surrounding the application of coercive force but also the nature of the power that this mode of practice entails.

This chapter provides an overview of this mode of policing practice in four parts. First, drawing upon a number of examples from historical contexts, it reviews the development of the means for dealing with public disorder in different types of state. In particular, it explores the extent to which some states regard policing as a primary means through which they are able to exercise political will. Although recognising its importance, it is not the aim of this chapter to provide an in-depth review of the role of the police in terms of the justice or otherwise of particular causes. We will suggest, however, that some forms of public order policing are more appropriate to promoting freedom and liberty than are others. In particular, we suggest that a policing system that is not under the central political control of the state is best for democracies. Such a system will be subject to multiple accountabilities. It will be subject to the rule of law. Such police forces, in contrast to those that developed in jurisdictions with centralised and militarised systems, are more likely to promote liberty than to deny it, at least in the longer term.

Secondly, it explores the extent to which policing contributes either to the (somewhat negative) objective of ensuring order or the (more positive) objective of promoting liberty. Does the fact that the police sometimes make use of coercion simply confirm the monopoly of coercive power of the state or does it actually make it possible for conditions to be restored within which rights and liberties can be enjoyed? This question is at the centre of the debate about the meaning of policing as 'law enforcement' or as 'peacekeeping'. The monopoly of the legitimate means of coercion is crucial to this debate. It poses serious dilemmas for this mode of policing practice and leads to a considerable amount of moral ambiguity for the police (Waddington, 2000).

Thirdly, it focuses upon the relative roles of the police and the military in promoting a well-ordered state. This part of the chapter discusses the extent to which there should be clear lines of separation between their civil and military roles. This section compares policing of public order in the established democracies and the transitional states of Eastern and Central Europe. It sets out four models of policing, which contrast the means by which states organise the control of public disorder. Only two of these models are appropriate to the policing of democracies. Finally, this chapter discusses the extent to which a so-called paramilitary style of policing has become the norm in most states. It analyses the way in which police have sought to maintain their capacity for keeping order by such methods, while at the same time attempting to keep the peace by means of conflict management.

Policing, state and public order

The debate about the role of the state in promoting liberty while ensuring order is as old as politics itself and has provoked a wide range of responses. There are historical differences in the way different states have dealt with this problem. The history of policing reflects these different styles. In particular, we can draw important lessons from the differences between Greek and Roman conceptions of the role of the state and their relative attitudes to the means employed for ensuring order. It is worth taking a little time here to explore those differences before examining their impact upon contemporary policing.

For thinkers of the city-states of classical antiquity, it was not possible to achieve justice without first creating an ordered society. According to the fifth-century philosopher Plato, reason was the basis for the construction of the 'just city'. Because of their familiarity with use of reason, Plato argued that philosopher-rulers would be the best people for establishing social and political order (Hamilton and Cairns, 1961: 656). These measures alone, however, would not be enough to ensure the survival of the state. If the constitution were to be preserved, a permanent overseer would be required. This was to be found in a military caste of guardians. Plato conceived this as a specially trained fighting force, whose business it would be to control internal and external enemies. They would forgo private property so that they would not be in economic conflict with the population. His conception was perhaps the first systematic attempt to promote the idea of an organised body for social order and peacekeeping.

This model for a republic based on reason and on structured political responsibility is surprisingly modern in its claims. It was, however, no more than a blueprint. It had no democratic structure. Neither did it recognise the political realities of social and political organisation in fifth-century Greece. These were quite different from the ideal republic proposed by Plato. Indeed, Plato's only attempt at involvement with the realities of politics was doomed to failure. His attempt to help King Dionysius II of Syracuse to set up a state based on these principles came to nothing (see Taylor, 1945: 7–9). Although Plato's philosopher-rulers did not become a reality, the Greeks did accept the idea of rule through reason and argument. As a result, Greek citizens acquired a considerable amount of influence over the rule and direction of the state. The Athenian Greeks, in particular, ensured that they ruled their *polis* (city-state) by means of democratic decisions. In this way, they were able to ensure that political accountability replaced the use of power. Democracy provided a more cohesive form of social order than they had previously been able to achieve under a strict political hierarchy.

Hunter (1994), who examined Attic law suits to establish the means through which social order was ensured, showed that early Greek models of policing were largely limited to the execution of legal process on behalf of the communities of the *polis*. In the absence of a police who exercised extensive power on behalf of the state, the achievement of order in the Greek *polis* was characterised mainly by self-help, kinship and communality (Hunter, 1994). There were, however, proto-policing structures at certain times during the development of the Greek polity. For example, during the sixth century, Scythian archers became a police of a kind. The Scythians were non-Greek slaves purchased by Athens after the Persian wars. They were mercenaries during the authoritarian rule of Solon in the sixth century. According to Ehrenberg (1968: 78, 311), however, they also carried out a form of policing in the sixth and fifth centuries. Although they had a number of localised public order duties, they were not a 'police' in the sense in which that term has come to be understood since the nineteenth century. According to Hunter, they did not carry out patrols. They did not participate in crime prevention. Nor were they responsible for social control (see Hunter, 1994: 145–9). Also, as non-Greeks, they were widely regarded as barbarians. As such, they were eminently suitable for a role that the Greeks themselves were loath to undertake. This was far from the modern conception of an organised force as an explicit means for promoting public order (Hunter, 1994: 3–4). Later, during the so-called rule of the four hundred in the fourth century BC, 120 Greek youths were appointed as a guard, although this amounted to nothing more than an instrument of terror. Apart from these instances, formalised policing in the Greek city-states was non-existent.

In contrast to this limited form of policing, Hunter draws attention to the more community-based form of social control that characterised fifth-century Athens. She says, 'Most of the major functions of policing Athens from investigations to prosecutions fell to the citizens themselves' (Hunter, 1994: 149). The rulers and the law established collective security. However, as was the case of the trial and death of Socrates, exposure and debate in public places was the basis on which democratic decisions were invoked (Ehrenberg, 1968: 311). For the Greeks, therefore, social control was a collective enterprise. It was certainly not the role of a single policing institution. This seems to have blurred the lines of responsibility between the community and the state. However, it was certainly never the case that the control of order, in its widest sense, was simply a state prerogative.

In contrast, the Roman approach, as it developed through the Republican and Imperial eras, emphasised the controlling role of the state. Despite some evidence of self-policing in earlier times, the failure of control in Rome during the late Republic led to more concerted use of the military. During the Imperial era, in the reign of Augustus (27 BC to 14 AD), praetorian and urban cohorts were employed to keep order in the city and throughout the empire. Outside Rome, although it was not their primary function, the military were responsible for public order. This was especially the case in unpacified parts of the Empire. There, the control of serious civil unrest and fighting banditry was an important role for the Imperial military machine. The Roman model, in this sense employed the military as its disciplined public-order force. Control of the population was the aim of this application of military power.

In Rome itself, the praetorian and urban cohorts had some peace-keeping and public order duties during Imperial rule. They dealt with extraordinary incidents, such as conspiracies against the Emperor. They did duty at public games, theatres and at the circus, mainly to control hooliganism and political outbursts. In general, however, their role seems to have been a limited one. Similarly, the *vigiles*, who were a force set up under Emperor Augustus in 22 BC, also seem to have had only limited policing functions. A body of six hundred state slaves initially formed the *vigiles* but they also later recruited from among freedmen. They had some patrol responsibilities but appear to have spent more time operating as a fire brigade than ensuring public order or preventing crime. There is little evidence that their street patrolling was effective against burglary or assault. After a devastating fire in Rome in 6 AD, they formed into a corps of six cohorts. This was their final form. According to Nippel, however, there is no evidence that they ever operated as a riot police. For a comprehensive account of these developments see Nippel (1995: 94–6).

The decline of power in Rome also signalled the decline of disciplinary measures for public order and social control throughout the Empire. Of course there is controversy about whether the weakness of the mechanisms of control caused the decline or whether the decline caused the weakness in the mechanisms of control. Nippel draws on sources that tend to show that, in general, government intervention was always limited. He says:

> Protection of property and personal security were the responsibility of citizens themselves … Enforcement of general rules of law and order was the business of local authorities … The maintenance of public order concentrated on basic rules. There was apparently (even under Christian Emperors) no comprehensive policy for disciplining the lower order of society.
>
> (Nippel, 1995: 113)

Roman society, in this sense, was mainly self-regulating. This was so, even in the turmoil of the Roman political world. This also serves to confirm the limited role of the state in keeping order. Although we may tend to associate the Roman model with disciplinary measures (especially in times of dissent), it is clear that social factors modified their effect. Public order does not rely entirely on external means for its control. This is the case, even in societies that are highly authoritarian.

We should not limit our comparison of community-based and state-oriented methods for ensuring order in pre-modernity to those of Greece and Rome. Traditional authority elsewhere in Europe used local tribes to ensure social control. According to Reith (1943), this is the origin of the embedding of social control within society rather than within a specially appointed body. He says:

> …the basic conception that the people are the police and the police are the people is directly traceable to the dawn of European history, and to the customs of some Aryan tribes of the Continent, whom their leaders made responsible for securing the observance of tribal laws.
>
> (Reith, 1943: 14)

Although this may seem a little far-fetched, comparison between the different responses to the problems of the ancient world certainly indicates that, from the earliest times, there were two main forms of policing aimed at social order. The first relied more upon social control through the institutions of civil society and the second more upon the idea of external control of the population by the state. This is a familiar distinction and is not only of historical interest. It is of considerable importance to our central question, namely 'What is policing?' Alderson (1985) has argued that these competing ideas underpin the essential differences in conception of the British and continental models of policing. The British system, he suggests, leans to Athens, whereas continental systems, such as the French, lean towards Rome. In Britain, although it has always raised suspicion, particularly since the intro-duction of the new police during the early nineteenth century, the British constitution does not generally regard police power as lying at the very heart of state authority. In contrast, a large proportion of the police in France is clearly a part of the apparatus of the French state. These distinctions are well known. In the context of the police role in peace-keeping and ensuring public order, however, we should take them seriously. This is not just a matter of a preference for a particular model of policing. It affects the way we perceive democracy. It is concerned with how democratic principles have emerged and how we should apply them to this aspect of policing practice.

The rise of nation-states and their adoption of modern constitutions had an impact upon the way in which policing methods have developed. For this reason, when trying to understand the police role in ensuring order, it is instructive to examine the differences in attitude that states may take towards the role of police in the constitution. This is not just a matter of comparing policing styles. Different states will ascribe different meanings to the term 'order' and have different attitudes to the role of police in managing 'dis-order'. This will depend on their history and on their political and constitutional structure.

At one extreme, the idea of the *Polizeistaat* (police state) seems to provide the worst kind of example of the use of police for the ultimate control of the population. This idea was particularly prominent in the German states from the seventeenth century onwards. It originally related to the measures taken by a state to ensure an ordered political and social environment. We have already discussed this in the context of the diversity of meaning of the term 'police' in Chapter 2. However, according to Chapman, it was not initially a negative concept, being '... dedicated to three purposes: the protection of the population: the welfare of the state and its citizens: and the improvement of society' (Chapman, 1970). Since then it has been realised in a variety of abhorrent forms, both in fact (in totalitarian regimes) and in fiction (for example in the extremes depicted in George Orwell's novel *Nineteen Eighty-Four*

(1949)). Whatever form it has actually taken, the police state has always been highly authoritarian in character. It has never been much concerned with the protection of individual citizens. More often, it has been concerned with holistic measures for the promotion of order or for the protection of the security of the state. In the most extreme circumstances, it has simply served to promote the power of party or of political tyrants. Given the history of the twentieth century, the spectre of the police state will remain to haunt us all.

In democratic states, measures for ensuring public order should comply with the law, be accountable and respect human rights. However, there is always a clear danger that the state may play a role in maintaining public order that goes beyond the impartial application of these principles. According to Reiner (1984), the extent to which a state might be (or may become) a police state with these tendencies depends upon five criteria. These include how much power the state accords to the police; the extent of measures to ensure accountability; the degree of organisational centralisation; whether there is a military structure; and whether the organisation tends to dominate other agencies. By these criteria, Britain does not yet appear to have become a police state. Compared to the role of police in other states, in Britain it is difficult to see policing as the instrument of state power.

The distinction we have explored here between state control of order and more community-based methods is of crucial importance to peacekeeping. Clearly, their origins are in Greek and Roman models of political life. As we shall argue below, however, there are continued tensions between these underlying approaches to promoting social and political order. Many of these remain unresolved, even in the established democracies. Similarly, there are also unresolved tensions between the desire for liberty and the need for ensuring order. At the centre of these tensions is the problem of the use of coercive force, especially the use of such by police in their peacekeeping role.

Coercion: the paradox of liberty and order

We cannot explain the kinds of dilemmas faced by the British police by claiming that the rule of law and accountability is the basis upon which it operates. We need to take other factors into account, including the problems that arise from their use of discretion in maintaining order. In Chapter 1 we examined the basis for the development of the police institution. We located its origins in early modern thinking about progress and social control. For Thomas Hobbes, the only way to avoid anarchy was for people to agree to have an authority placed over them (see Hobbes, 1651, in Macpherson, 1986: 289–94). Later, however, the idea that all social and political action should aim to produce good consequences became predominant. Utility became the driver of much of the social, legal and administrative reform of the nineteenth century. This thinking emphasised the need for a police institution that (in addition to the prevention and detection of crime) would also ensure order.

Jeremy Bentham, James Mill and John Stuart Mill developed the theory of utilitarianism. They put forward the idea that actions were only good in as much as they promoted the greatest happiness of the greatest number of people. Its precise effect is still a matter for debate. However, the doctrine inspired the work of a generation of Victorian reformers. Their work included the reform of factories, relief of the poor and the development of local government and public utilities (Hampsher-Monk, 1992: 305). There can be little doubt that utilitarian thinking also had an effect upon police reform. As such, the constraints imposed upon the liberty of the few to promote the liberty of the many would have been an ample justification for social intervention by the police. This includes the application of the means to promote order by controlling public dissent.

Such restrictions on liberty, however, caused problems for liberal thinkers. For this reason, later revisions of utilitarianism, in particular John Stuart Mill's *On Liberty* (1859), argued for no restrictions to be placed on liberty, except in cases where harm was likely to be done to others. If accepted, this would place a limit on state intervention. This would restrict police interventions to cases where the infringements were specifically against the liberties of others. Cases of this kind would be limited to such things as attacks upon people or property. However, this negative sense of liberty could not account for the perceived need for wider intervention. This is particularly the case where the containment of dissent was in the public interest. As we saw in Chapter 1, the positive theory of liberty provided a potential answer to this problem. Although the context of this discussion was the role of the police in ensuring social order more generally, it also relates to their peacekeeping role. In this sense, it is possible to see the role of the police in controlling public order in the light of the goals of both negative and positive liberty.

These issues are still relevant to policing. In the negative sense, the application of police powers to control disturbances relates to the notion that they need to be controlled because they may impinge directly upon the rights and liberties of others. In this sense, obstruction of freedom of movement or direct injury to people or property justifies coercive action against the demonstrators. This is so, despite the fact that the European Convention of Human Rights protects their rights of protest and association. The idea that coercion also promotes positive liberty is more difficult to understand in democratic states. It probably has more relevance to action taken by police on behalf of the state in other types of polity. In such cases, states can argue that they place restrictions upon rights to protest against their decisions for the general good. Such arguments, however, are on very dangerous ground. Democratic constitutions do not normally rely upon them. However, governments may invoke them if there are strong grounds for suggesting that the activities of demonstrators are against the national interest. In fact, governments rarely invoke such arguments in Britain. If they do, it is usually in the context of national emergency. In such cases, legislation covers the intervention. For example, the government of the day enacted the Public Order Act 1936 to deal with the public order problems associated with the rise of Fascism. In circumstances of this kind, police do not generally deal with such problems except under the legislation.

There is another perhaps more subtle sense in which peacekeeping is connected with the idea of positive liberty. Skolnick (1966) and Bittner (1967) point to the fact that police officers do not enforce the law when it appears to them better to use discretionary methods that maintain the peace. Skolnick (1966: 33) argues that the officers he observed dealing with prostitution and minor street offences were not acting as law enforcement officers but as peace officers. Bittner's (1967) study of policing in a socially deprived area ('skid row') makes a similar point. According to Bittner:

> In general the skid-row patrolman and his superiors take for granted that his main business is to keep the peace and enforce laws on skid row, and that he is involved only incidentally in protecting society at large. Thus his task is formulated basically as the protection of putative predators from one another.
>
> (Bittner, 1967: 707)

Here, the policing of conflicting interests reflects the sense in which it tries to keep the peace rather than to promote the general good. Such peacekeeping is more concerned with maintaining the *status quo* and preventing trouble than dealing with the infringement of rights through law enforcement. The fact that peacekeeping often takes precedence over law enforcement in such localised circumstances dilutes the claim that policing is the assertion of the authority of the state. The peace, in this sense, is more a matter of 'police property' than 'state property'.

Whether engaged in law enforcement or peacekeeping, for Bittner (1970) the ability to use coercive force is the defining characteristic of the police role. These claims are clearly Weberian in their origins, following Max Weber's dictum that a crucial characteristic of the state is to guard and maintain the monopoly of coercive force. According to Weber:

> Today … we have to say that a state is a human community that (successfully) claims the monopoly of the legitimate use of physical force within a given territory. Note that 'territory' is one of the characteristics of the state. Specifically, at the present time, the right to use force is ascribed to other institutions and to individuals only to the extent to which the state permits it. The state is considered the sole source of the right to use violence.
>
> (Weber, in Gerth and Wright Mills, 1970: 78)

Reiner (1992b) concurs with Bittner's claim to this effect. Speaking of the role of the police, he says:

> Their specific role in the enforcement of laws and the maintenance of order is as specialists in coercion. This does not mean … that the police routinely invoke their coercive powers, ultimately the capacity to use legitimate force (Bittner, 1970, 1974; Klockars, 1985). The craft of successful policing is to be able to minimise the use of force, but it remains the specialist resource of the police, their distinctive role in the political order.
>
> (Reiner, 1992b: 2)

Of course, this does not mean that the police must routinely use force, or that the force used is always maximised. However, if force is used, its application should be necessary and not merely the arbitrary exercise of power. It should also be proportionate to the threat that it confronts. The European Court of Human Rights uses these principles in adjudicating cases brought under the European Convention on Human Rights. The Human Rights Act 1998 gives them effect in domestic law. They also apply to the 'continuum of force' policies adopted by many police forces. Here the amount of force should be minimised and only escalate if necessary to deal with increasing levels of threat (McKenzie, 2000: 181–3). Indeed, at the lower levels in the continuum of force, reputation or the mere possibility of the use of coercion may serve its purpose, without recourse to actual physical force of any kind.

The question of whether the monopoly of coercive force is the defining feature of the modern state is particularly relevant to democracy. According to Beetham (1991), the power of the state in democracies does not depend on what people believe about tradition, charisma of the ruler or legal-rational rules. Power is legitimate when it conforms to established rules that both dominant and subordinate accept and where there is evidence of consent to the particular power relation (Beetham, 1991: 16). Schwartzmantel (1994), who has provided an extensive account of the role of the state in contemporary society, accepts this point. He says:

> Increasingly, and perhaps exclusively in the modern world, no political system is considered legitimate unless it can claim, with some degree of conviction and plausibility, that it derives its power from 'the will of the people'.
>
> (Schwartzmantel, 1994: 17)

Participation by a majority of the people in fair elections is an important way of ensuring a degree of consent. State power, therefore, is not dependent upon coercion alone, although it may retain this in reserve. As such, however, it no longer occupies the central place in defining the role of the state. This contrasts with the views of those who take the more essentialist Weberian approach. Although this raises a number of important questions that are beyond the scope of this book, the key principle is that of the extent of the consent. In the case of policing, if the argument that practice is reciprocity is correct, the necessary conditions suggested by Beetham are in place. The element of consent in reciprocity has been set out in Chapter 2. Rights and rules are its basis. The element of consent is only satisfied by performance, namely when policing actually keeps the peace in such a way that enables the rights of all to be realised.

For a number of reasons, therefore, it is perhaps now less clear than ever that the public police can be characterised in the way in which Bittner (1970) suggests. The specialist use of force, although always present, no longer fully determines the functions and structures of policing. As discussed in later chapters, some modes of policing are characterised by agencies and forms of interaction that do not involve the use of force at all. The claim that the capacity to use force is the core of policing is not now strictly the case. This is so both at the level of individuals (who may personally eschew the use of violence or be in jobs where it simply never arises) and at the institutional level. Many policing activities are not now concerned with the application of coercive force. The public police are certainly no longer alone in being able to exercise such power. There is potential for the legitimate use of force by other bodies not part of the public police. These include HM Customs and Excise, the Security Services, the military and even security companies in some circumstances. In this sense, although the very discourse of police–public relationships seems to contain implicit knowledge of the potential for overt coercion, it no longer occupies centre stage. It is perhaps now more important to recognise the potential of hidden sources of power and influence that might affect consent and accountability. Although we have concentrated on peacekeeping in terms of action, it is worth remembering that police/public discourse may itself be power-laden (Foucault, 1972). In this sense, whatever we do, we cannot simply wish the tensions away.

Policing alone cannot resolve the paradox between the ideal of liberty and the need for a peaceful environment that might enable us to enjoy it. Peace, in this sense, remains a relative concept. The two accounts of the relationship between order and liberty that we have discussed (namely negative and positive liberty) are part of this tension. They are not, however, the solution to the problem. On the one hand, individuals, groups and organisations infringe rights and liberties. The state and public authorities themselves provide a challenge to liberty and therefore need to be constrained. In a way that seems attached to the negative theory of liberty, these aspects are matters for law and law enforcement. On the other hand peacekeeping entails a view of human interaction which takes a less legal-rational and more humanistic view. This seems more attached, in a pragmatic way, to the positive idea of liberty. Both of these ways of looking at the relationship between liberty and order are important to our understanding of policing. All they do in reality, however, is to re-emphasise the tensions between keeping order and keeping the peace as important components of policing practice. The tensions between them emerge very clearly in a comparison of different styles of policing.

Four models of public order policing

At the founding of the new police, the official text certainly made explicit its most basic assumptions about keeping order. Reith argues that the two great hostile forces of crime and mob disorder were the driving factors for the foundation of the new police. Of these, disorder was perhaps the more prominent during the period immediately preceding 1829. According to Reith:

> Of crime it could be said that the evils of its steady and rapid increase were mitigated by a lessening of offences accompanied by violence, but each successive wave of mob disorder which every few years accompanied the swing of the industrial pendulum from boom to slump eclipsed its predecessor in both violence and menace.
>
> (Reith, 1938: 239)

Indeed, the failure of the military, the existing watch and the constables to deal with these riots was an important factor in the development of the new police in Britain.

The question of the relative value of the police and the military in dealing with these problems has arisen consistently in the context of the maintenance of public order in the modern state. In Europe, military involvement in policing tasks had long been a feature of the control of civil unrest. The reason for this was because other forms of policing were remarkably unsuccessful in this respect. In both England and France, the police (*Maréchausée*, Paris guardsmen and English constables) had all proved to be incapable of dealing with major outbreaks of disorder. For example, they had difficulties in controlling order in the flour war (*guerre de farines*) of 1775 and the Gordon Riots of 1780 in London. However, neither did using the military prove to be the answer for preserving order. They also failed to control the mob in the Gordon Riots. This, and the killing by militia of protesters at the Peterloo Massacre of 1819, revealed the problems of using the military for this purpose. Despite this, governments continued to use them in a public order role in England and elsewhere in Europe well into the nineteenth century (Emsley, 1983).

The military nature of regular policing was more evident in Europe than in Britain. This was particularly so in France where '... Roman policing sank enduring roots into the Gallic world' (Stead, 1957: 13). This is certainly true of many of the policing measures that France adopted. For example, the *Maréchausée* were a military police whose origins were Royal bodyguards at the time of the Crusades. They were responsible for patrolling provincial France. They were reorganised in 1790, with the new title of *Gendarmarie Nationale*. Their role was to supply sentries and guards for courts, prisons and the National Assembly. The police of Paris, who had been in existence long before the Revolution, also had military elements. Many European police forces can trace their origins and current ethos back to the political upheavals of the eighteenth century. This was especially the case in those countries that napoleonic policies had influenced. In the Netherlands, for example, the government had also deployed *Maréchausée* for controlling order. (For accounts of these developments see Stead, 1957, Emsley, 1983, Benke *et al.*, 1997).

In Britain, in contrast, there had never been a strong military influence on policing. The decline of the routine use of the military to deal with public disorder tended further to distinguish the British system from that elsewhere in Europe. In Britain, the development of the professional police greatly decreased the incidence of calling upon the military to deal with civil disorder. In fact, the Metropolitan Police did not call for the military to support them in dealing with public disorder until 1866. Then, the military assisted the police to deal with the violent Bloody Sunday riots for parliamentary reform (see Ascoli, 1979: 132–3). In general, however, it was the regular police who dealt with all instances of disorder. Most of these were only simple disputes. However, they were also capable of dealing with serious disturbances. Although there was disquiet about the role of the new police, they proved capable of carrying out a public order role in addition to tasks relating to the prevention and detection of crime.

There is a well-established constitutional power that allows the police to call upon the military to assist the civil power when this is necessary. With the exception of Northern Ireland, it is comparatively rare for this to happen. The police have certainly dealt with all instances of public unrest in mainland Britain without the overt assistance of the military in recent years. The police did not seek military assistance during the riots that occurred in London and other cities during the early 1980s. Similarly, they did not seek assistance during the miners' strike of 1984. There have been joint exercises and planning in the field of counter-terrorism. There has also been action by the military Special Air Service against terrorists. Of course, this does not mean that there are no contingency plans for such assistance. But apart from the deployment of troops in Northern Ireland, and their use in providing cover during emergencies or industrial disputes, UK Ministry of Defence statistics detail no incident of military aid to the civil power in the past decade.

Policing in the Soviet Union and the Warsaw Pact countries has had a very different history to that in the West. Until the recent political changes, police in these countries exercised power directly on behalf of the state. Here, the police not only dealt with crime and public order but also defended the state against its enemies. The army was primarily concerned with state security in terms of external threats. The primacy of police tasks in such circumstances follows an extreme example of the Roman model. The states of Eastern and Central Europe have now incorporated police into the civilian administration. Although they still have some of the characteristics of a state police, this has started to bring them into line with policing elsewhere in Europe.

The means by which states manage their peacekeeping and public order depends on their constitution and on their political structure. How do the differences between states become manifest? We can answer this by examining the range of possibilities. First, it is important to assess the relative roles assumed by the police and the military. This includes the extent to which the police themselves are militarised. Here, the degree of centralisation, accountability and means of control appear to be the key issues. A military-style police is more likely to be centralised in its command structure. The extent to which police have a military-style rank structure or whether they are armed or uniformed does not appear to be the issue. Most police forces are militarised if these are the criteria. (For discussion of these points, see Reiner, 1984, 1992; Bayley, 1985: 53–60; and Mawby, 1990: 194–5.)

The structure and military-style trappings of the police do not allow us to distinguish them from the military in relation to their public order roles. A better alternative is to examine their roles in relation to the state. We can do this by assessing the relative extent of their powers, goals and lines of accountability. Using this approach, Wright (1998) argues that each of the following four models are evident in this state/police/ military relationship.

I. The civil police model

The context of this model is that of a civil society characterised by a plurality of state and non-state associations. Here, the constitution separates *all* powers and objectives of the civil police from those of the military. The civil police are responsible for dealing with crime and other risks and keeping the peace. The role of the military is to defend the society from external aggressors. In this model, the police do not fulfil a state function where government directly controls their actions. They operate with a considerable amount of discretion, right down to the lowest level. This is in contrast to the politically conceived objectives, orders and strict rules of engagement that characterise the military. Policing in Britain and in the Netherlands appears to follow this model. In terms of accountability, they have an arm's length relationship with government. The principle of the separation of powers is the basis for this arrangement. In some jurisdictions, national and local tiers of government ensure a degree of separation between police forces, as for example between the federal and *Länder* police in Germany. In the civil police model, police may make limited use of paramilitary methods. When these become extreme, or where objectives are pursued which are primarily for the protection of the state, the civil police model begins to shade into model 2 below.

By 'paramilitary' in this context, I mean a coordinated form of action by police units which use military-style deployments with tactical co-ordination and rules of engagement. This may include the use of special equipment, including protective clothing, shields and weapons. Such units may also use, or have access to, firearms or other military weapons. The discretion, which the police normally regard as part of their ethos, is absent. I also use the term 'paramilitary police' to distinguish those units, which remain subject to specific police regulations in most jurisdictions, from designated military units, the members of which are subject to military discipline under the Army Acts or similar legislation. Although this term remains controversial, it does not merely mean police who make occasional use of military equipment and style of dress. My use of the term 'quasi-military' refers to police units which have shared conditions of service and interchangability with the military, as is still the case in Hungary under the Service Relations Act XLIII/1996. Some aspects of this are elaborated below. (See also Waddington (2000: 87–95) for a useful debate on this issue.)

2. The state police model

The context of this model is that of a civil society characterised by a plurality of associations. The concerns of the state, however, tend to predominate. Here, the constitution only separates *some* powers and objectives of the police from those of the military. In this model, although still operating within the rule of law, many aspects of policing are considered to be within the envelope of the state rather than separated from it. This, along with the existence of police barracks, military-style service regulations and deployments, tends to locate some of the police forces of a country outside the purely civil police. For example, in France the *Police Nationale* is accountable to the Ministry of the Interior and appears to be within the civil administration. However, both they and the *Gendarmarie Nationale* are within the envelope of the French state. Like the army, they have a duty to protect it. In this model, the paramilitary character of policing is more developed. This is the case in the *Gendarmarie Nationale* and some public order units of the *Police Nationale*. Similarly in Germany, the *Bundesgrenschutz* (*BGS* – Federal Border Police) are closer to the state model. This is so, despite the fact that they are now civilianised. In contrast, the *Länder* police have a more easily identified civil function.

3. The quasi-military police model

The context of this model is that of the monolithic state where the concerns of the state dominate all others. In this model, the constitution ensures that the police and the military share *most* of their powers and objectives. Although the police are responsible for investigating and preventing crime, they are also directly responsible for the security of the state in pursuing its enemies. There is little or no attempt to ensure a separation of powers. At the extreme, in totalitarian states, the police do not need to legitimate their actions through the rule of law. The achievement of the state's political goals is their key criterion for effective action. Interchange of personnel between police and army is frequent. This is the so-called 'universal soldier' model. This policing model was widely in operation in Eastern and Central Europe before the political changes of the early 1990s. *In extremis*, the role of the police shades into that of model 4 below. When we speak of removing the military aspects of policing in the emerging democracies, we seem to be thinking of moves away from model 3 towards models 1 or 2.

4. The martial law model

The context of this model is that of total political control by the state. In this fourth model, there is *no* separation between the powers and objectives of the police and those of the military. Police are under military command and control and are subject to military law. States have only used this kind of full martial law infrequently in Europe since the immediate aftermath of the Second World War. It seems only rarely to have been realised in its most extreme form, even under Soviet rule. It was evident in British colonial rule, for example in Malaya from 1948 and in the conflict between the British and the Mau Mau in Kenya in the 1950s (Killingray, 1997). Interventions by the Serb police in Kosovo and by the Indonesian police and military in East Timor in the late 1990s are also applications of the martial law model. However, the extent to which the latter were legitimised in international law by a formal state of emergency is disputable.

Paramilitary policing or conflict management?

The increase in paramilitary policing has been evident even in those states whose policing is of the kind set out in model 1 above. In Britain, in the late 1960s and 1970s, the police were not prepared for the increase in violence during public protests. Demonstrations during the early part of this period, such as those by the Campaign for Nuclear Disarmament (CND), had mainly been peaceful. During the late 1960s, however, there were extensive protests against American involvement in the war in Vietnam. These showed greatly increased levels of violence. Police were criticised for their own violence and for lack of tactical control in the demonstrations in Red Lion Square in 1974. One police officer and one demonstrator died because of these disturbances. At a carnival at Notting Hill in the 1970s, police officers had to defend themselves with lids from rubbish bins during serious disturbances. During this period the police developed specialist units to deal with crime and disorder (Special Patrol

Group units). These units were not strictly paramilitary by the definition set out above. Nevertheless, critics regarded their focus on high crime areas and their deployment to deal with public disorder as controversial.

Until the urban riots of the early 1980s, however, the response from the police was uncoordinated. After the riots, the police deployed more personnel, vehicles and equipment to deal with spontaneous disorder. Training and command and control were improved. Thereafter, in London and most other cities, the police could deploy designated units in a paramilitary way. Now, they are available on a 24-hour basis to deal with spontaneous or unpredicted disturbances. However, the deployment of apparently better equipped police to deal with disturbances has not always been successful. The riot that took place at Broadwater Farm Estate in Tottenham during the 1980s, for example, showed severe flaws in the police handling of the situation. Here, the police failed to achieve their peacekeeping objectives. A police officer was killed during the rioting and relations with the local community were severely blighted. The increased use of firearms by the IRA and other terrorist and criminal gangs since the 1970s has also produced an escalating response from the British police. There has been an increase of armed police, compared with the early 1970s. This includes 24-hour armed response vehicles. Police armed with automatic weapons are a familiar sight at British airports (Northam, 1988). They are paramilitary in this sense but also in terms of their deployment.

There have been similar developments in most countries of Western Europe over the same period. A number of events have prompted these changes. In Germany, there were threats from the Baader-Meinhof group and the Red Army Faction. In France and Spain, attacks on individuals, buildings and transport systems have prompted the deployment of specialist anti-terrorist units. Throughout Europe, increased threats from terrorism, organised crime and civil unrest have led to the expansion of paramilitary forces. There are many examples. In Belgium, the *Gendarmarie* continues as a standing force. They retain a wide range of military arms and equipment, despite the fact that they were de-militarised in 1992. The French *Gendarmarie* is also well equipped. A standing public order 'third force' exists through the *Gendarmarie Mobil* and the *Compagnies Républicanes de Sécurité* (CRS). Despite their being part of the civilian *Police Nationale*, the CRS make use of military-style structures and tactics. In Germany, the *Bundesgrenschutz* (BGS – the Federal border police) are a paramilitary force. They have extensive weaponry. There are also specialised anti-terrorist units at both federal and *Länder* levels. In the Netherlands, the *Koninklike Maréchausée* (Royal Military Police) are a third force which deal with public disorder.

These developments go far beyond the routine arming of the police, which is a legacy of the military roots of policing in most of Europe. There has also been an increase in paramilitary policing elsewhere in the world. For example, there has also been an extensive increase in Special Weapons and Tactics (SWAT) teams in the US. Kraska and Paulsen (1997) argue that the work of elite units of this kind promotes a pronounced militaristic culture. Military-style activity also produces a preoccupation with danger and a high level of pleasure in those employed on this work. All this evidence shows that paramilitary policing has increased in the past twenty years. The wider indication is that states tend to adopt such measures when confronted by serious threats to their security. We can call this 'the paramilitary imperative'.

In democratic states, this can be in conceptualised in terms of an organism that necessarily adapts to ensure its own survival. The adaptation, however, leads to a vicious paradox. In this sense, it is a paradox for liberal democracy to try to preserve democratic values by adopting the very means that will tend to subvert them. In the British context, the shooting of civil rights marchers by troops in Northern Ireland on 'Bloody Sunday' and of terrorist suspects by British military Special Air Service operatives in Gibraltar in the so called 'Death on the Rock' are cases in point. The use of the military in such cases raises questions as to whether such deployments were in pursuance of the sanctions of criminal justice, the protection of citizens or the protection of the state. If it were the protection of the state, such action would appear inimical to liberal democratic ideals.

It would not be legitimate for a democratic government to evade this paradox by conceding its monopoly of coercive power. This would mean that democracy was unprepared to defend itself. No government has yet been prepared to contemplate surrender on this scale. A more viable option might be to follow the principle of the separation of powers. Here, a state would put measures into place that would separate paramilitary police work from other policing roles. This would inevitably lead to a two-tier police. It would lead to a public order third force, located somewhere between the police and the military. So far, the British government has firmly rejected the idea. There is an extensive literature on the subject. For a review of the development of paramilitary methods in Britain, see Northam (1988). For arguments that are critical of using these methods for public order, see Jefferson (1987, 1990, 1993). For the arguments for using a more tactical approach to public order, see Waddington (1987, 1991, 1993). There is a useful overview of the debate in Critcher and Waddington (1996).

The increase of paramilitary policing methods in the past two decades is not the only trend. Della Porter and Reiter (1998) report the use of softer and more tolerant protest policing styles. Although most democracies in Western Europe have a paramilitary capacity, there has been a tendency to use a less coercive approach against some protesters. Of course, this is always open to the argument that it is simply the state getting its way through manipulation. Clearly, this tactical approach, equivalent to an 'iron fist in a velvet glove', has its dangers. For example, according to della Porter and Reiter (1998) states are applying it very selectively in many parts of Europe. The extent to which repressive force is used depends upon the perceptions of the nature of the protesters themselves. Those considered more at the margins of society continue to be dealt with harshly.

Alongside this there is also a clear trend towards conflict management rather than the immediate use of coercion as the norm. Reference to Figure 2.1 in Chapter 2 shows the shift from the 'modern' construct of maintaining order to the late-modern mode of policing practice of peacekeeping. The shift from controlling disorder to managing conflict reflects this transition. This is perhaps a more palatable option for policing democracies. The use of this more cautious approach is certainly evident in British policing. In England and Wales, ACPO has adopted a conflict management model. This appears to recognise the extent to which policing should aim towards peacekeeping rather than simply coping with public disorder. Analysis of the political, social and economic contexts of dissent and the proximate factors which lead to disorder are being used to develop proactive measures to prevent it or to deal with it when it arises. Despite these trends, however, the use of paramilitary force remains a readily available option. This is so in Britain and elsewhere, even where states only maintain it as a reserve of coercive power (della Porter and Reiter, 1998: 30–1). We have already mentioned the events in Oldham and Bradford in the North of England during the summer of 2001, where extreme violence was used in disturbances involving Asian and white youths. Given these examples, whether policing can strike a balance between the controlling (coercive) and managerial aspects is the crucial question.

The configuration of this mode of policing practice depends upon the relationship between state, citizen and the police. In this sense, it is deeply concerned with politics. We have already mentioned that the term 'policing' does not refer to the work of the public police alone. However, because it so deeply concerned with the tensions between liberty and order, this initially seems to be an area that is likely to remain within the domain of the public police. This certainly seems true of the deployment of armed or paramilitary units to deal with the most difficult and contentious peacekeeping or public order situations. Having said that, many of the problems which we have discussed refer equally to the work of some private organisations, such as guarding companies and stewards, who are responsible for keeping order in shopping malls, sports grounds and other places to which the public have access. They face many of the same peacekeeping versus order maintenance dilemmas as the public police in this respect. Many of the above comments, therefore, also apply to them.

In fact, it is difficult to assess the role either of the police or of other organisations that are responsible for order or peacekeeping without returning to the important concept of reciprocity. Reciprocity is necessary to ensure the balance between rights and obligations. In cases of extreme disorder for example, there is a link between the accountability of the state for the safety and security of its citizens and the sense in which citizens have a right to expect that protection in a democracy. Protesters (who do not give up their rights in this respect) are entitled to believe that the police will not treat them in an exceptional and draconian manner. The use of force is not regarded as permissible unless it is necessary and proportionate. The law does not permit the police to shoot hostage-takers out of hand. Unless hostages are shot or the police foresee loss of life, negotiation should take place. There are rules of engagement through which these interactions take place, even in quite extreme circumstances. This is why we would rightly regard 'shoot to kill' policies with abhorrence. In general, however, peacekeeping applies to more mundane circumstances. It is more likely to apply in everyday street confrontations of the kind that Skolnick (1966) and Bittner (1967) describe. Here the paradox of liberty and order is at its most immediate and personal.

The idea of reciprocity is the basis for peacekeeping as a mode of policing practice in democracies. It reflects the fact that all citizens (including those of us who dissent from some decisions and express our protests) have rights both to protest and to enjoy security. However, the tension between liberty and order is always present. In reviewing peacekeeping as a mode of policing practice, we have found no satisfactory answer for those who are critical of the controlling role of the police. The subject remains full of controversy. History records no state (not even a democratic one) that has discarded its reserve capacity to impose order by force, should the need arise. That only happens on Star Trek. The reality is that in most countries, the police do take a degree of responsibility for the protection of the state. Even Britain has adopted mechanisms for internal security that mimic those of the military. In the face of international terrorism, they are increasingly likely to do so. Although peacekeeping as a mode of policing practice seems to be adopting more managerial strategies, this sobering fact is worth bearing in mind.

Chapter 4

Policing as crime investigation

This chapter examines policing from the perspective of the investigation and detection of crime. It discusses five aspects of investigative practice. First, it explores the development of crime investigation in British policing, focusing on the growth of the investigative culture. Secondly, it examines different types of investigation. It compares the so-called reactive and proactive models of investigation and crime management. It reviews the investigation of high-volume and serious crime in the light of this distinction. Thirdly, it considers the investigation of organised crime, contrasting this with other approaches in the typology. Fourthly, it reviews the critique of the police as crime-fighters. This includes the debate about whether patrolling and crime detection contributes significantly to crime control. Here, the idea of crime control relates to the suggestion that policing can control either the levels of crime or the outcomes of particular cases. It does not refer to the theory of Hirschi (1969), which suggests that individual involvement in crime depends on the extent of social bonds. Chapter 6 will examine this aspect of control theory in the context of community justice. Finally, it examines the role of the police as gatekeepers of the criminal justice system. It explores recent attempts to make crime investigation more professional. It examines the potential for the replacement of the culture of crime fighting by a more scientific and due process approach. It concludes that despite the evidence of ineffectiveness and malpractice, the logic of reciprocity ensures that investigation will remain a key mode of policing practice.

Origins of the investigative culture

There were forms of crime investigation in existence before the modern era. However, they were never systematic or defined in terms of organisational function. In Britain, the prosecution of offenders before the development of modern policing was either a matter of state or of highly localised enforcement of the common law. At the state level, in high politics, investigation and spying were never far apart. Extensive networks of informants, such as those of Sir Francis Walsingham during the reign of Elizabeth I, were an effective means of political control. The executioner's axe often dealt with its victims. There was a limited amount of investigation in localised law enforcement, but the pursuit of accused persons by sheriffs or constables seemed to be the main activity. According to Bellamy (1973):

> ... in the more lawless decades of the late Middles Ages, a felon could consider himself distinctly unlucky if he was captured by the authorities. Policing was left largely in the hands of the local community.
>
> (Bellamy, 1973: 201)

Although the use of the term 'policing' here is probably inappropriate, direct action emphasised the importance of local communities in pre-modern law enforcement. Common law arrest by citizens was an established principle. However, it required more certain grounds than if the arrest was by a constable (Bellamy, 1973: 102–3). Constables did not often make pre-emptive arrests, although they had the power to do so. Under the Statute of Winchester 1285, constables could arrest strangers at night if they behaved suspiciously. Justices of the Peace later had the authority to instigate arrests to prevent breaches of the peace or arson.

It is important to recognise that until the eighteenth century, the state did not instigate the investigation of offences such as larceny, robbery and burglary. English common law was not the King's law. The whole community, or at least the property owning factions within it, invoked it. Law enforcement and social control were personal and highly localised. According to Gatrell (1990), until the founding of the professional police:

> Control was exercised face to face, not bureaucratically ... Detection and prosecution remained at the discretion and mainly at the expense of victims or association of local farmers and businessmen.
>
> (Gatrell, 1990: 385)

Gatrell (1990: 386) also points to the fact that the word 'crime' did not appear in common usage until the 1780s and then was only used to indicate personal depravity. 'Crime' was not used to refer to an aggregate of offences until the debates about policing and law reform at the end of the eighteenth century. Thief-takers investigated offences and pursued offenders during the eighteenth century, mainly for reward. Because of the impossibility of taking action on their own account, citizens contracted them to do so (Johnston, 1992: 6–9). This was the *reductio ad absurdum* of the logic of personal responsibility that characterised earlier forms of law enforcement. As Hobbs (1988: 17–20) and Emsley (1996a, 1996b: 201) suggest, however, the activities of eighteenth century thief-takers such as Jonathan Wild and the so-called trading justices were not by definition corrupt. Their practices only reflected the commercialism of the age.

By the latter part of the eighteenth century, the problem of street robbery and the widespread commission of crimes on the Thames had become of major concern to reformers. The founding of the new police and the bureaucratisation of policing functions was a watershed in the meaning of crime. Reformers regarded the police as the means for its prevention and control. The idea of a preventative police was paramount in much of the contemporary debate (Hobbs, 1988: 29–32). The Home Office, however, played down the importance of investigation in the mid-Victorian era. Not until the formation of the London detective branch in 1842 were even comparatively small numbers of police employed as plain clothes detectives. According to Babbington:

> It was not until 1842 that the Home Secretary authorised the Commissioners to appoint twelve plain-clothes detectives to work from a small room at Scotland Yard and to operate anywhere in Britain. During the next twenty-seven years, this force was never increased to a total of more than fifteen men.
>
> (Babbington, 1969: 234–5)

In this sense, official attitudes reflected public suspicion about the political surveillance role of plain clothes police. Only after Howard Vincent's 1877 reforms was the London detective force formally re-organised into the Criminal Investigation Department (CID). It was also increased to 30 officers at Central Office (New Scotland Yard) and 250 in the London divisions to deal with rising crime (Ascoli, 1979: 149).

High-profile failures, such as that of the investigation into the 'Jack the Ripper' murders in the Whitechapel district of London in the 1880s, affected public attitudes to detectives and to the police more generally.

Arthur Conan Doyle's fictional detective Sherlock Holmes provided an image of detective work that only served to confirm the public view of 'real' detectives as incompetent bunglers. Conan Doyle's claim that, 'Detection is, or ought to be, an exact science, and should be treated in the same cold and unemotional manner', was not borne out in practice in real-world detective work (Conan Doyle, 1890 – *The Sign of Four*). The role of real detectives (then as now) was full of ambiguity. Hobbs points to the fact that:

> From the early days the detective was caught between the demands of 'the job' and the official version of his practice. The ambiguity resulted in the detective branch being pilloried for its inability to solve major crimes.
>
> (Hobbs, 1988: 41)

Even after the turn of the century, the ambiguities of the detective culture were never far away. This was so, despite measures to consolidate it within a formal framework using more rational investigative methods. Developments in the early 1900s included the introduction of the Henry system of fingerprinting. The foundation of the Detective Training School in London in 1902 improved the training of detectives. However, as Hobbs (1988: 43) suggests, detailed information regarding the development of the CID during this period is thin on the ground. Lack of evidence may indicate that there was little controversy. However, there was certainly suspicion about corruption and about the degree of autonomy that the CID enjoyed. According to Ascoli:

> It is impossible to know with any certainty the extent of police corruption during the fifty years after the CID was formed; corruption is difficult to define. But it is beyond argument that by the summer of 1922 the CID had become a thoroughly venal private army.
>
> (Ascoli, 1979: 210)

Although he was not strictly a member of the CID itself, the vice scandal that resulted in the imprisonment of Sergeant Goddard in 1929 may also indicate that there were more extensive undercurrents (Morton, 1993: 76–81).

Historians have yet to write the detailed history of investigation between 1900 and the 1950s. Lack of information continues to dog rigorous assessment of the true nature of the CID during that period. Accounts of CID work before, during and after the Second World War are usually either superficial or self-congratulatory. Certainly, the

75

extravagant claims of some commentators during this period do not impress. For example, Sir Harold Scott's suggestion that the CID provided a 'university of life' for those who followed it as a career smacks of hubris rather than of candour (Scott, 1957: 124). There is every indication, even in the 1920s and 1930s, that the truth was very different. The 1933–38 Detective Committee of Enquiry into Improving the CID was a response to a state of affairs that clearly needed attention. Although that inquiry was long-winded and was aborted at the onset of war, real issues were implied. These included the need to rationalise an institution beset with problems brought about by its own lack of accountability.

Popular accounts of detective work do not provide critical evidence of its real nature. *Fabian of the Yard*, which provided the basis for a television series in the 1960s, emphasised the skill and dedication of the detective. Some of this may have been true. The investigators who formed Scotland Yard's Central Office Murder Squad during this period certainly had a high reputation. Provincial police forces often called upon these officers to carry out investigations in serious cases. From its foundation in 1907, in 74 years this unit cleared up 90 per cent of the cases it investigated. However, by 1977, the number of cases had fallen to only seven, marking the increased ability of provincial police forces to carry out their own investigations. Although the period up until the late 1950s may well have been, as Reiner (1992a: 58) says, the 'golden age' of policing, we do not know enough to make a firm judgement about the overall nature of detective work during that time.

The lack of an extensive and rigorous literature on detective work in the earlier years is certainly not true of the period from 1960 onwards. As discussed in Chapter 1, it was clear by then that some parts of the CID, particularly in London, were in severe but self-inflicted difficulty. Malpractice in detective work seemed widespread. The 1963 Challenor case inquiry highlighted the problems that could arise from delusions about a magisterial role for police in dispensing justice. In 1969, the so-called 'Times Enquiry' into the activities of some Regional Crime Squad officers revealed corruption, collusion and cover-up of crimes between detectives and criminal gangs. Malpractice in the Metropolitan Police Central Drugs Squad, including the systematic fabrication of evidence, pointed to lack of control and a culture where kudos was more important than ensuring that justice was done. Corruption on a grand scale riddled the so-called 'Dirty Squad' of Central Office at New Scotland Yard. Instead of combating the trade in pornography, they enabled it to operate. Several detectives, both senior and less senior, were imprisoned as a result of inquiries into these activities. (See Cox *et al.*, 1977: *passim*, Reiner, 1992a: 79 and Morton, 1993: 128–61 for more detailed accounts of these issues.)

In parallel with these events, however, there was a surprising level of success against organised crime. The police could pursue important cases to a successful conclusion, as shown by the arrest of those responsible for the 1963 'Great Train Robbery' by officers of the Metropolitan Police Flying Squad. The arrest of the Richardson Gang in 1966 for shootings, assaults and fraud indicated that organised crime and gang warfare would not be permitted to continue unchecked (Hobbs, 1988: 50–2). It is worth noting, however, that the detectives who dealt with the Richardson gang were specially selected. They were not from a single division or regular squad but came from the Metropolitan Police and provincial police forces. Assistant Chief Constable Gerald McArthur, a senior officer who had worked on the Great Train Robbery and had later moved from London to a provincial force, led the inquiry. In the period from 1967 to 1969, the police mounted a similar operation against the Kray gang, again with specially selected officers. This was led by an officer who had also worked on the Great Train Robbery investigation earlier in his career, namely Detective Chief Superintendent Leonard 'Nipper' Read. At its height, the Kray investigation employed 240 selected officers, with no established instances of corruption or malpractice. These operations contrast strongly with the activities of the squads which were the subject of the fall of Scotland Yard cases discussed by Cox *et al.* (1977). Either there were two totally different sets of operating mores in the CID at that time (a 'firm within a firm') or the role ambiguity suggested by Hobbs (1988: 41) had penetrated to a very deep level, both psychologically and organisationally.

The appointment of Robert Mark as Assistant Commissioner in the Metropolitan Police in 1967 did not, at first, signal his eventual role in the battle against corruption. It was not until his appointment as Deputy Commissioner responsible for force discipline that he was able to make an incursion into the autonomy of the CID, which until then was the sole authority for dealing with criminal conduct among its own ranks. The return to uniformed duty of any CID officer who could not work un-supervised was the first step taken by Mark to limit CID power. The second step was the setting up in 1971 of A10 Branch. To this unit he gave the task of proactively investigating complaints and corruption, reporting directly to himself as Deputy Commissioner. In 1972, on his appointment as Commissioner, he immediately instituted changes to the CID chain of command. He introduced interchange between uniform and CID, whereby CID officers returned to uniformed duties on promotion. He appointed uniformed officers with no previous experience as detectives into the CID as supervisors. An account of these developments appears in Mark (1979: 115–25). Hobbs (1988: 64–79) provides a useful summary.

This, in common with the whole of Hobbs's opus on detective work, provides an exemplary analysis of these events and the development of the detective culture.

Mark was clearly committed to the demise of the Metropolitan CID as an autonomous entity. However, he was careful to continue to support the practice of investigation, including work against organised crime. He appointed trusted officers to the Serious Crimes Squad under Detective Chief Superintendent Bert Wickstead and a number of successful investigations were carried out during the 1970s (Mark, 1979: 172). This was clearly within Mark's own span of control and was worth celebrating. An indication of the extent of Mark's distrust of the parts of the CID that he did not previously control is to be found in the fact that no mention is made anywhere in his autobiography of the arrest of either the Richardson or Kray gangs. This is surprising, given that the Kray inquiry did not start until well into 1967. By March 1967, Mark was in a very senior command position in the Metropolitan Police. The work of the Kray squad did not finally conclude until 1970, when it became the model for the formation of the later Serious Crimes Squad. Mark's omission of all mention of the successful Kray investigation is all the more surprising, given the fact that they engineered the escape from Dartmoor prison of 'Mad Axeman' Frank Mitchell (Hobbs, 1988: 55). Mark must have had a very deep interest in this investigation, having assisted Lord Mountbatten in the 1966 inquiry into prison security following the Mitchell escape. However, he confines his reference to the Kray connection to the statement that, 'Mitchell's gangland associates simply collected him by car when he was outside on his own and brought him to London' (Mark, 1979: 81–3).

Despite Mark's optimism that the tide had turned, changes to the accountability, supervision and promotion of detectives did not provide a long-term antidote to corruption. The success against the gangs in the 1960s and 1970s indicated that not every officer in the Metropolitan Police CID was corrupt. The fact that officers drafted into the CID after Mark's reforms proved equally susceptible to corruption and other malpractice tells us something about the corrosive nature of detective work itself. As Sherman (1974) and Punch (1985) have shown, corruption is not just a matter of rotten apples in the barrel. The barrel itself may be rotten. Anything put into it may also rot. Mark's mistake was to see the rotten barrel of the CID primarily as a problem of organisational autonomy rather than of investigation and its culture. It is the ambiguity of detective work and the very opportunity for malpractice that it provides that are potentially corrupting. More recent failures, including a number of miscarriages of justice, such as the Carl Bridgwater murder case and the failure of the investigation into the death of Steven Lawrence, show that the problems of the investigative culture have not disappeared. Without a change to the whole ethos of investigation, they are likely to continue.

A typology of investigation

What is it that police investigate in crime investigation? Do they investigate crime or the criminal? What methods do they employ and to what extent are they effective? These are difficult questions. Crime investigation is a seriously under-researched field. For this reason, before moving on to consider the crime-fighting or gatekeeping roles of investigators in the criminal justice system, it is necessary to say more about types of investigation. It may seem obvious to say that categorisations of crime, burglary, robbery, assault and so on are the lines along which types of investigation are fragmented. This is certainly important, however, because these classifications are the primary means through which crime is recorded and classified for the purposes of statistical analysis. This is an area of considerable controversy, particularly where police have creatively manipulated crime figures to show their performance in a good light. The nature and number of offences, however, have also influenced investigative methods and the organisation of investigation in a more structural way. For this reason, it is necessary to review types and methods of investigation and to draw some important distinctions between them.

In the past three decades, crime investigation has not been the sole prerogative of the CID. During the 1960s in London, because of increases in the numbers of crimes reported per detective, uniformed officers began to investigate so-called minor crimes such as theft, criminal damage and less serious assault. Detectives continued to carry out investigations of cases of the more serious crimes of robbery, burglary and serious assault. In fact, this was already the pattern in some police forces outside London. Most of these investigations were reactive, in that they were concerned with *post hoc* investigation of reported crime. Increasingly, however, during the late 1960s and 1970s, specialist squads at both force headquarters and on some busy divisions began to deal more holistically with aspects of robbery, burglary and drugs cases. In doing so, they often focused upon the activities of target criminals rather than upon reported crime. Some police forces employed standing central squads for this purpose, especially in the larger cities. Many of these units approximated to the model of the Metropolitan Police Flying Squad, which had been set up in 1920 to deal with serious crime and gangs in the metropolis (Frost, 1948: ix). In the 1960s, Regional Crime Squads were set up primarily to deal with series of robberies that crossed force borders. In 1986, the Regional Crime Squads were consolidated by the formation of specialist drugs wings to tackle increasingly organised drugs trafficking. (Association of Chief Police Officers, 1986; Wright *et al.*, 1993). Squads of this type investigated gang activity in a more proactive manner, with the assistance of criminal intelligence units, rather than on a reactive case-by-case basis.

Cases of homicide and other serious crime (such as kidnapping and rape) continued to the dealt with reactively. Senior detectives investigate these cases. Officers seconded from routine divisional CID work usually assist them. Although some forces have now adopted a dedicated pool of officers to carry out such investigations, the principles remain the same. The investigation unit sets up an incident room. It deploys teams to deal with enquiries, usually generated by information from the public. Although on a much smaller scale, perhaps only involving one officer, all reactive investigation theoretically follows a similar pattern.

Many criminologists are sceptical about this pattern of events. Bayley (1996: 35–6) claims that investigators begin with identification then collect evidence but rarely collect evidence and then make an identification. The role of the public in detection rather than that of investigator is also strongly emphasised. For example, Coleman and Norris (2000) maintain that:

> There now seems to be a general consensus of research findings that the public is primarily responsible for the detection of between 83 and 85 percent of cleared-up offences (Steer, 1980; Mawby, 1979; Bottomley and Coleman, 1981).
>
> (Coleman and Norris, 2000: 124)

Although it is right to say that the public plays a crucial part in crime investigation by providing information, the sense in which the public can be said to be 'primarily responsible' for detection (especially in the case of serious offences) is misleading. Whether the identification or the search for evidence comes first (and there are many examples of both) even in minor cases it is comparatively rare for a member of the public to initiate an investigation without police involvement. Indeed, the investigative process does not place the primary responsibility for detection upon the public at all. The criminological consensus, in this respect, is far from the mark. So far, there is no mechanism, apart from often grossly incomplete media speculation about who may have committed an offence, through which the public could exercise such responsibility. Indeed, in England and Wales, the Police and Criminal Evidence Act 1984 assumes that the primary responsibility for investigation lies with the police, with HM Customs and Excise or with the investigators from the Armed Services. Similarly, the Prosecution of Offences Act 1985 places the primary responsibility on the Crown Prosecution Service (CPS) for prosecutions rather than upon individual members of the public. The truth is, as critical-path analysis of the reporting and investigation of most offences shows, reactive crime investigation plays an important gatekeeping role in this respect. Of course, this does not mean that it is effective or that it is free from malpractice. Nor does it deny the fact that the public is the primary source of information that supports investigation (McConville *et al.*, 1991). However, we should certainly not confuse this fact with a proper assessment of the logic of the investigative role.

The investigation of serious crime is the paradigm case of the reactive model of crime investigation. Although major crimes such as murder are always included, the police usually define serious crime in terms of the gravity of the case and difficulty of investigation rather than simply by offence type. Some forces categorise serious crimes according to a descending hierarchy, namely from cases of grave public concern, through major crime where the offender or victim is unknown to major crime where the identity of the offender is known. The police also consider cases to be serious on subjective criteria, for example where the head of crime operations thinks special staffing or finance is required. With some scandalous exceptions, such as the Steven Lawrence murder and other racially motivated crimes, the police have been comparatively sensitive to public and media views about the seriousness of particular crimes. The degree of seriousness also determines (at least in principle) the amount and experience of the police resources that are deployed on a particular case. From a resource viewpoint, serious crime has been defined as:

> Any crime which in its investigation demands and requires the allocation of additional resources over and above normal divisional responsibilities.
>
> (Berry *et al.*, 1995).

High levels of resources have been increasingly difficult to achieve because of the wide range of demands on the police. There has also been a shortage of experienced senior investigating officers (SIOs), large numbers of whom have left the police service in recent years. The increased complexity of serious cases has exacerbated this problem. Increased demands posed by greater accountability and by measures for disclosure of evidence to the defence have also done so.

Types of serious crime vary widely, from so-called domestic murders of husband, wife or partner, to death resulting from fights or affray, murder in the course of other crime, contract and gangland killing, sexually motivated assault, child killing and terrorist offences. The investigation of random serial killing is comparatively rare. Large squads of detectives, mainly drawn from the police area upon which the killings have occurred, generally carry out the investigation. Where the killings go beyond the borders of a single force, the forces involved now make concerted efforts to coordinate the investigation. Serial murders, such as the so-called 'Yorkshire Ripper' case in the later 1970s, have brought about considerable changes to the management of murder investigation. The US Federal Bureau of Investigation (FBI) definition of a serial murderer is 'one who has murdered three or more victims with a cooling off period between the homicides' (Egger, 1998). According to Brooks *et al.* (1988):

> Often the motive is psychological and the offender's behaviour and the physical evidence observed at the scene will reflect sadistic sexual overtones.
>
> (Brooks *et al.*, 1988: vii)

This was certainly true of two cases that caused police in England the greatest difficulty and damage to reputation. These were the 'Jack the Ripper' murders of the late 1880s which resulted in the deaths of at least five prostitutes and the 'Yorkshire Ripper' case some ninety years later.

The Yorkshire Ripper investigation was an important watershed in serious crime investigation in Britain. In particular, it opened up the important debate about the denial of justice for victims. The failures in the Yorkshire Ripper case were a product of the investigative culture and of the lack of effective systems for managing the huge amount of information generated during the inquiry. Police did not arrest the perpetrator, Peter William Sutcliffe, until 1981, by which time he had killed 13 women. An inquiry accepted that at least four lives were lost due to the failure of the investigation. The abandonment of major leads for resource reasons, concentration upon hoax letters and tape recordings and the failure of the manual system for analysing information on suspects were major flaws. After the conviction of Sutcliffe, an inquiry under Sir Lawrence Byford made a number of recommendations to avoid failures in the future. These included the standardisation of major incident room procedures and the appointment of an overall commander for series crimes. The introduction of the computerised Home Office Large Major Enquiry System (HOLMES) supported the new incident room procedures. Berry *et al.* (1995) carried out a further study of serious crime investigation on behalf of the Home Office. This study predicted the shortfall of experienced SIOs that seriously affected police capabilities in this field in the late 1990s. A degree of secrecy has surrounded these problems. However, ACPO have now consolidated the procedures by the introduction of a national Murder Manual and by efforts to improve the skills of SIOs.

Interestingly, the arrest of Peter Sutcliffe was the result of police action during routine patrol rather than of the investigation itself. In 1981, a police sergeant and a probationer constable were on a motor patrol in the South Yorkshire Police area, away from the area where the majority of 'Ripper' victims had met their deaths. Because the constable had not previously completed a 'prostitute' file (a file leading to the cautioning or prosecution of a street prostitute), the sergeant suggested that they should look for an opportunity to do so. During their patrol, they found a car that contained a man and a woman who they suspected might be a prostitute. In making a routine check of the car, they found that its registration was that of another vehicle. They arrested the driver for stealing car registration plates. The driver was Peter William Sutcliffe. The officers became suspicious of Sutcliffe's reaction to his arrest. When they returned next day to the place where they had arrested him, they found a hammer and a knife, weapons of the type Sutcliffe used on his victims. At this stage, they finally realised that they had arrested the Yorkshire Ripper.

This case demonstrates one important lesson. It is one that critics of the effectiveness of patrolling or detective work often overlook. The lesson is that the application of resources to meet objectives is not always commensurate with outputs and outcomes but often exhibit a form of loose coupling between them (Chatterton *et al.*, 1995). The officers who arrested Sutcliffe were not on patrol to tackle specific forms of crime. It was the fact of this very flexibility that led to an important arrest. Conversely, arresting the Yorkshire Ripper and thereby solving the crime was the entire focus of the investigation team. A number of variables intervened to confound their intentions. In addition to the need to improve investigative methods, the Yorkshire Ripper case tells us much about the supposed functionality of investigation. In this sense, the problems of loose coupling raise fundamental questions about whether it is ever logically possible to make crime investigation entirely effective.

The investigation of high-volume crime provides an indicator of the gate-keeping role of police in crime investigation. It also highlights the difficulties of ensuring the achievement of planned outcomes. Rises in reported crime since the 1960s have meant that police have increasingly been unable to respond to crime on an incident-by-incident basis. Consequently, the reactive paradigm has broken down. One police response to these increasing demands has been formal and procedural. Unless there are reasons for doing otherwise, in some forces, police consider minor cases to be of low priority and they are screened out from further investigation (Eck, 1982). In this system, police make decisions on a rational basis. This includes the allocation of points to each aspect of the case to see if it reaches the threshold for investigation. On the other hand, there is evidence that the way in which the police actually make investigative decisions is still subject to a great deal of discretion. In a study commissioned by the Home Office, the findings of which (regrettably) were not more widely circulated, it was shown that investigative methods were subject to decisions which depended primarily upon moral considerations. These were often based on the psychological impact of the victim's predicament. Criteria, such as that of an objective assessment of the seriousness of the crime, the existence of official

Source: Irving *et al* (1996) *Reacting to Crime: The Management of Police Resources, London, Home Office*

Figure 4.1   Crime investigation process: decision flow

policies or cost rarely had an effect on the investigator's decisions (Irving *et al.*, 1996: 25). Investigators deployed resources according to their subjective judgement of the morality of the case, including assessment of the relative value of the loss. There was little reliance upon on any rational rules of engagement.

This research also distinguished between reactive and proactive models of investigation, suggesting that both are relevant to crime investigation. Figure 4.1 (on p. 84) illustrates the difference between them and the extent to which they may be connected.

In this model, it will be noted that reactive investigation is regarded as a sequence of decisions from action at the initial scene of a crime through to case disposal. Proactive investigation, in contrast, is a sequence of decisions that begin with pattern analysis of a series of crimes. The use of intelligence packages and the deployment of resources lead to the conclusion.

During the 1990s, the Metropolitan Police carried out a long-term operation to reduce burglary and other crime. This operation was given the code-name of Bumblebee. Gloucestershire Constabulary used a similar approach to reduce crime in an operation which was code-named Gemini. Research by Stockdale and Gresham (1995) recognised the importance of both the reactive and proactive modes of investigation to these operations. It also recognised the importance of publicity and of community initiatives to the success of these strategies. Other researchers carried out an evaluation of other crime-management schemes that made use of the combination of reactive and proactive strategies. In a study for the Home Office, two such approaches (at Thanet in Kent and Gateshead in Northumbria) were compared (University of Kent 1995; Amey *et al.*, 1996). Police at both sites made use of proactive methods, including crime pattern analysis, targeting of offenders and measures that mobilised policing through a tasking and coordinating group. This complemented the initial action that the police took in respect of reports of individual crimes. The police prioritised individual cases through a crime desk that dealt with incoming reports. The crime desk decided what type and level of resources the police should apply. However, except in cases of emergency, they gave the proactive approach priority over the reactive. In some cases the identification of a suspect preceded the gathering of evidence. In other cases, the police gathered intelligence and evidence before they identified the suspect. However, the evaluation of these models of investigation shows that the claim that the public has the primary responsibility for detection is not the case. It is certainly not the case where the police apply rational crime management methods.

Organised crime

Proactive strategies have long been the key to dealing with organised crime. There is certainly a notable lack of success in tackling criminal gangs by reactive methods. For example, the murder of George Cornell by Ronnie Kray in the Blind Beggar public house in the East End of London in 1966 was not solved by the reactive investigation set up immediately after the event. It was not until the police had arrested the Krays for substantive offences as a result of proactive inquiries that witnesses felt confident enough to break their silence. From an investigative perspective, it is difficult to see how the police can deal with organised crime in any way other than through proactive, intelligence-led investigation. Proactive policing, making use of surveillance methods, informants, 'supergrasses' and 'sting' operations, has characterised most police efforts against organised crime in the past two decades. Unfortunately, this kind of policing sometimes mirrors the very criminal activity that it seeks to confront (Dorn *et al.*, 1992). Maguire and John (1995) have suggested that such methods have a high cost for the police organisation. This is true in terms of surveillance costs. It is also true in terms of both the economic and human costs of running informants, especially where officers feel forced to lie to protect their lives (Dunnigham and Norris, 1999).

There is no doubt that the stakes involved in organised crime are high. Reports in the press suggest that organised criminal activity produces a turnover of around $500 billion per year. It could be as high as $1,000 billion. Estimates of money laundering activity suggest that it amounts to between $250 and $500 billion per year (Boland, 1997). The UN Drugs Control Program (1998) estimated that organised drug trafficking is worth around $400 billion or about 8 per cent of world trade. This is equivalent to the world's textile industry. In addition to trafficking in drugs, organised crime includes such things as protection rackets, kidnapping, terrorism and maritime piracy. Trading in stolen vehicles, arms, illegal immigrants, nuclear materials, women and children, protected animals and birds, stolen art, cultural objects and body parts all provide lucrative rewards for criminal gangs. Types of organisation include predatory gangs and those (such as smugglers and bootleggers) that are parasitic on legitimate commercial activity. Some have close relationships with legal business or with the holders of state power (Lupsha, 1996).

Despite the availability of popular accounts about the nature of organised crime, researchers are only now subjecting it to more rigorous scrutiny. (For example, see Williams, 1997 on Russian organised crime.)

Certainly, organised crime has been hard to define. To date, there is no universally agreed definition of the problem or of the investigative measures which should be deployed to tackle it. For example, Article 1 of the Joint Action of the Justice and Home Affairs Council of the European Union in 1998 states that:

> A criminal organisation shall mean a lasting, structured association of two or more persons, acting in concert with a view to committing crimes or other offences which are punishable by deprivation of liberty or a detention order of a maximum of at least four years or a more serious penalty, whether such crimes or offences are an end in themselves or a means of obtaining material benefits and, if necessary, of improperly influencing the operation of public authorities.
>
> (European Union, 1998)

Others seek to emphasise both its social consequences and the violence that is constitutive of the activity. For Fijnaut et al. (1998), organised crime is what ensues:

> … when groups primarily focused on illegal profits systematically commit crimes that adversely affect society and are capable of successfully shielding their activities, in particular by being willing to use physical violence or eliminate individuals by way of corruption.
>
> (Fijnaut et al., 1998: 26–7)

The first definition was in the context of the legal and political responsibility of the European Union. The second was in the context of a Commission of Inquiry for the Dutch Parliament carried out by criminologists. The differences between the definitions represent the different terms of reference of the bodies that created them. Both are valid within their own context.

Lack of agreement about the extent to which criminal organisations have rational structure and purpose means that it is difficult to agree on the definition of organised crime. Cressy (1972) and Skolnick (1990) suggest that criminal organisations have a rational structure. There are well-defined roles for leaders and members. There are underlying rules and goals that determine their behaviour. Other research indicates that some gangs are loose confederations, lacking in persistent focus. There is comparatively low cohesion between members. They define their goals expressively rather than instrumentally (Klein et al., 1991; Klein and Maxson, 1994). Some of these findings seem configured by the research methodology. This is especially so where an interview cohort is that of gang members who are serving prison sentences. In such cases, it is not surprising that people try to give rationality and structure to their actions.

What does seem to be common to all of the research, however, is that most organised gangs are characterised by violence or the threat of violence. Their cultural or locational origins also affect their attitudes to the types of crime that they prefer. Although they sometimes adopt a cellular structure, in other cases they have more dynamic patterns of association. They also vary in their degree of task specialisation, planning, direction and control, risk-taking and the availability of significant funds for investment (Hobbs, 1994). Like a legitimate business, organised crime works to develop its own competitive edge. For this reason, it needs to have capital available to undercut its competitors and to purchase expertise. There are no jurisdictional, bureaucratic or legal limits on the action it may take. It often uses corruption to facilitate action, to acquire influence, to gain access to rule-makers and rule enforcers, to penetrate opponents' operations and to set up targets. When we add this to its global network of contacts, organisational secrecy and expert covert operation, there is little doubt that organised crime provides a formidable problem for crime investigation (Lupsha, 1996; Wright, 1996).

We can contrast the flexibility of organised crime with the restrictive regime faced by the investigative agencies. Unlike organised crime, if they are operating under the rule of law, they have no extra-legal sanctions to deal with the competition. As a result, the investigation of organised crime is very different from that either of other serious crime or of high-volume crime. The investigation of organised crime also shows the limitations of reactive methods. For this reason, the agencies that investigate organised crime in all jurisdictions have adopted squad, task force or security-service style deployments to deal with it. They have introduced 'supergrass' informants and witness protection programmes to ensure the availability of evidence at the trials of gang members. They have increasingly used intelligence systems to map the associations between actors, events and activities. By these means, they evaluate the vulnerability and power of individuals and groups. Investigators often make use of specialised technical resources to aid these methods. In England and Wales, for example, the number of warrants issued for the interception of communications rose from 515 cases in 1990 to 1,776 cases in 1999 (Home Office 2000a). These figures do not include warrants issued in respect of Northern Ireland nor those issued by the Foreign Secretary (MI6 and GCHQ).

Organised crime is not an area where it is easy to explain away the need for investigation as a mode of policing practice. The numbers of investigators employed in these roles in the UK is comparatively high. For example, as long ago as 1987 in England and Wales there were 1,300 investigators employed full time in the investigation of drugs trafficking, in police forces and in the (then) Regional Crime Squad Drugs Wings (Wright *et al.*, 1993). This did not include a large number of officers from HM Customs and Excise who were also employed full time on tackling international aspects of this trade. Nor did it include officers from local police forces employed on drug investigations part-time or in the course of routine policing. Because the above data was the result of a specific research project, no directly comparable figures are now available. However, the concentration of officers doing similar work has not decreased in recent years. Mandated under the Police Act 1997, the National Criminal Intelligence Service (NCIS) complements the operational capability of the National Crime Squad (NCS) in tackling cross-border crime and in working with policing agencies from abroad. Not including officers who are employed on tasks related to drugs and organised crime in police forces, as at 31 March 2000 there were 1,389 police officers employed in the NCS. On the same date there were 248 police officers employed in the NCIS. In addition, there were 361 civilian staff employed in the NCS and 287 in the NCIS (Home Office 2000b). The NCIS and police forces have increasingly used specialised civilian intelligence analysts to work alongside detectives. Although beyond the scope of this present volume, the activities of these agencies highlight the extent to which investigation of organised crime is an important issue in policing.

So far, there is little sign that crime investigation is likely to wither away. For high-volume crime such as burglary and theft, a certain amount of reactive investigation continues. This focuses on cases where there is a higher probability of detection. However, police are increasingly making use of proactive crime management methods to deal with high-volume crime. This involves a higher degree of analysis and problem-solving than was hitherto the case, concentrating on local hotspots and likely offenders. As yet, there are no national figures available to quantify this activity. The police continue to use reactive methods for the investigation of most serious crime. This is so, unless specific information is available before the crime is actually committed or unless it is part of the activity of organised crime. The investigation of organised crime appears to be increasing. Such investigation is almost entirely proactive. Agencies are increasingly using intelligence evaluation to set their priorities in this respect. Patterns across the typology show that crime investigation will remain a key mode of policing practice. However, it is already no longer the sole responsibility of the police as a single institution. Of course, whether investigation is actually able to control crime, either in the aggregate or in individual cases, is quite another question.

The myth of crime-fighting

The role of the police in fighting crime is frequently criticised by criminologists. There are two predominant theses that deny the efficacy of police in crime control. The first of these suggests that neither police patrolling nor investigation of crime significantly influence crime levels. The second suggests that police are mistaken to adopt a crime control approach rather than due process in dealing with individual cases. We will examine each of these aspects of crime control in turn.

The debate about the problematic role of policing in relation to crime has been building strongly since the 1960s. It now represents a critical consensus among a large number of criminologists. There are many examples in the literature. Wilson (1968) argues that crime is a social phenomenon and that police activity such as patrol or investigation does not significantly affect crime rates. Maguire (1982) found that fingerprint evidence was responsible for less than a half of one per cent of detections of house burglaries. Banton (1986) found that police action did not affect robbery rates in London over a 50-year period. Mayhew et al. (1994) point to the problems of attrition in the criminal justice process. From 100 per cent of actual crimes, 47 per cent are 'reported', 27 per cent are 'recorded', 5 per cent are 'cleared-up' and only 2 per cent result in conviction (Mayhew et al., 1994, quoted in James and Raine, 1998: 10). Waddington (1999: 6) points to the propensity among many police officers to regard crime-fighting as the primary role of the police. However, he also points to the comparatively ineffective nature of their crime-fighting, both in terms of patrolling with the aim of preventing crime and of detecting criminals after the event. The investigation of crime, both in its reactive and proactive forms, is generally ineffective (Waddington, 1999: 6–9). This applies, he says, as much to *post hoc* investigation through 'sleuthing' and forensic science as to the new idea of proactive intelligence-led policing. Nothing the police do, it seems, can make much of a difference. Reiner (1992a) and Morgan and Newburn (1997) also question the effectiveness and legitimacy of the crime control thesis.

Arrests through patrolling, if successful, would be an important component of investigation. This would be true in respect of any individual cases but also in the sense of making a contribution to controlling crime at the aggregate level. Random patrolling, however, has been widely criticised as a means of controlling crime on both counts. In the US, Wilson

(1968) showed that only 10 per cent of patrol time directly concerned crime and law enforcement. The Kansas City Preventative Patrol Experiment (Kelling *et al.*, 1974) demonstrated that even if types and levels of patrolling are varied, there is little impact on crime. In the UK, Ekblom and Heal (1982) found similar results. Hough (1985: 9) found that the chances of a patrol officer intercepting crime were very small. Of calls to police to attend incidents, only one-third related to crime. Morgan sets out similar arguments, showing that crime amounted to 35 per cent of the work of his sample (Morgan, 1990: 1–9). The 1988 British Crime survey revealed that only 18 per cent of public contact with the police involved crime incidents (Skogan, 1990). There were similar findings in the 1992 British Crime Survey (Skogan, 1994) and in subsequent surveys (Mirrlees-Black and Budd, 1997; Yeo and Budd, 1999; Sims and Mynhill, 2001).

Bayley (1994: 1996) confirms many of the above findings in studies carried out in 28 police forces around the world, including the US and Britain. He says:

> Very little of the work patrol officers do has to do with crime. British and US studies have consistently shown that not more than 25 per cent of all calls to the police are about crime; more often the figure is 15–20 per cent.
>
> (Bayley, 1994: 17)

According to Bayley, rarely do police act proactively in anticipation of crime and most of their work is about restoring order and providing services (Bayley, 1994: 20). This follows the earlier claims of criminologists such as Ericson (1982: 5–7) which suggest that police work is mainly about reproducing order. The implication of these findings is that the crime-fighting model is totally inappropriate to the police of the future. For Bayley, when the work that police actually do is analysed, it follows that:

> Modern police perform two major functions: authoritative intervention and symbolic justice. Most police officers are engaged in one or the other of these most of the time.
>
> Authoritative intervention is what patrol and traffic officers are primarily responsible for. It is almost wholly reactive, rarely anticipatory. Crime is involved only occasionally or ambiguously. The purpose of authoritative intervention is to restore order. Almost no attempt is made to correct underlying conditions that have led to the need for police intervention.

Symbolic justice is the realm of detectives and traffic officers. Also largely reactive, it is achieved through law enforcement. Its purpose is demonstrative, to show offenders and the public that a regime of law exists (Silberman, 1978, Reiss, 1971). The success of police in rendering symbolic justice is almost entirely dependent on information supplied by the public, just as the mobilisation of patrol officers is for authoritative intervention.

(Bayley, 1994: 34)

Although appearing to have the character of a knock-down argument, there are some problems in this analysis, at both the empirical and logical levels. A wide range of evidence is available but we need to take care in its interpretation. Indeed, even empirically, evidence has emerged to suggest that the amount of crime-related police work is greater than is believed by those who think it marginal (Greene and Klockars, 1991). Misclassification of activities that are actually deeply ambiguous may also be a factor in underassessing the degree to which police are involved in crime-related work (Kinsey et al., 1986). In this respect, local victim surveys have revealed higher levels of crime-related contact than those in national victim surveys. As we have already mentioned, Shapland and Vagg's (1988) analysis of contacts with the police showed that 53 per cent involved potential crime.

There is also something logically strange in the claim that because an activity is not predominant in terms of time commitment, it is relatively unimportant in the practice as a whole. On the contrary, it may still be a defining characteristic of the practice. Although crime investigation is clearly not the only mode of policing and perhaps not the one that takes the most time of patrol officers or detectives, this does not imply that it is merely of symbolic significance. A simple analogy illustrates the point. Under the rules of the game of golf, the apparent function of the golfer is to hit a golf ball and get it into the hole in the least number of shots on 18 occasions in a full round. A round of golf may take anything from three to five hours. During that time, the actual hitting of the ball and observing its flight towards and into the hole may take no longer than ten minutes. Does this imply that for the remaining time the golfer is not playing golf? Perhaps discarding that ten minutes of activity would not seriously affect golfing practice? Perhaps hitting the golf ball has only symbolic significance? Both golfers and logicians would rightly this claim as ridiculous. There are an almost infinite number of activities that make up the practice of playing golf. A golfer may do any one of them well or badly. These include selecting a club, hitting the ball, thinking, planning, walking, discussing and so on. Some criminological assessments of police work imply that because the time they spend on activity relating to crime is not 100 per cent or because they may do it badly, it has no relevance as a mode of policing practice. Criminological research about time spent on patrol and investigation tells us very little about the role played by crime investigation in policing practice, or about the logic of the way in which it contributes to the criminal justice process. Arguments from analogy should warn us that we cannot so easily dispose of the real presences of a practice by such claims.

Perhaps a more compelling critique of crime-fighting is that suggested by Young (1991) who describes the extent to which the construction and presentation of performance within the detective culture is pervaded by the detection rate and by crime control. He says:

> The whole ambience of 'prevention' is nebulous to detectives, for it speaks of events that do not happen and cannot be identified or counted, while the 'detection rate' tells of 'captures' and the process of law and prosecution: of the creation of crime files and the punishment of offenders.
>
> (Young, 1991: 255)

This tendency leads to the manipulation of the recording of crime to maximise estimates of police performance. Apart from any subsequent investigative activity, police certainly play a role as the initial recorders of crime by receiving information about offences from the public. If recorded as a crime, the incident becomes part of official crime statistics declared annually by the Home Office. Over the past twenty years, there has been controversy about the extent to which these figures are correct (see Bottomley and Coleman, 1981; Burrows and Tarling, 1982; Young, 1991; Bottomley and Pease, 1993; Coleman and Moynihan, 1996). There is no doubt that in some cases, police have deliberately manipulated the figures. The practice known as 'cuffing' has been widespread. Figuratively speaking, this means using the magician's trick of making an object (the crime) disappear up one's cuff or (alternatively) jotting the details on a shirt-cuff rather than in official records. Such crimes never appear in the official statistics, thus attenuating levels of recorded crime and inflating the percentage of crime that has been cleared-up.

According to Young (1991: 323–6, 385), the reasons for this are deeply embedded in the detective culture. For example, it was revealed by a Kent police officer that detectives from that force had falsified clear-up figures by getting prisoners to admit to crimes they had not committed, knowing that no additional sentence would be imposed

(Young, 1991: 378). These practices have themselves been labelled 'performance crime' and it has been suggested that they are 'structurally coerced' by the nature of the police organisation and the requirements of the performance culture (Sharpe, 1995). What damage these tendencies have done in the longer term to effective crime analysis is difficult to gauge. They do, however, say a great deal about the investigative culture, particularly the belief that it is important to present police crime-fighting activities in a good light. However, as Young maintains, this leads to a serious paradox in upholding the rule of law. He says:

> To admit that 'bending' and 'fiddling' the account is the norm would be to acknowledge the fact that irreverence, disorder, and potential chaos sustains an institution which is allegedly geared to prevent its occurrence.
>
> (Young, 1991: 390)

In addition to the detectives' belief in crime-fighting, there is also evidence to show that some aspects of investigative practice demonstrate a symbiotic relationship between detectives and those they police. This provides a very different critique of detective work to that set out in the work of Young (1991), Bayley (1994), Waddington (1999) and others. For Hobbs (1988), the entrepreneurial trading relationship between detectives and criminals is a reflection of this culture. This has some similarities with the trading outlook of the thief-takers of the eighteenth century. The relationship between detectives and their criminal contacts illustrates the fallacy of assuming that detective work is simply concerned with the control of crime through detection. According to Hobbs (1988), it is about how entrepreneurial investigators and perpetrators maintain the balance of power. Both sides are interested in 'doing the business'. For Hobbs, the very discourse of the practice of investigation indicates the logic of the relationship by mirroring aspects of the discourse of criminality itself. Quoting Van Maanen (1978: 322), he notes that:

> ... 'deceit, evasiveness, duplicity, lying, innuendo, secrecy, double-talk and triple talk mark many of the interactions in police agencies'. This description accurately describes many of the characteristics of the 'working personality' (Skolnick, 1966) of detectives.
>
> (Hobbs, 1988: 197)

This applies not only to Britain. How deeply the culture is embedded is shown in the widespread nature of this kind of discourse. From the use of informants through to the role of detectives in clearing up crime, the key question is not about their effectiveness. It is about the normative aspects of influence and manipulation of the social conditions within which justice and injustice are decided. In other words, it is about what goes on between the 'cops' and the 'crooks'. It is about negotiating who gets what in a process which is more political than legal. There can be little doubt that this provides constant role ambiguity and challenges, even for honest detectives.

Aspects of police work in which the potential for control-oriented strategies can operate are continually expanding. It is worth bearing in mind that the community to which Hobbs's research refers is that of the East End of London, which at the time of his research still had a degree of social cohesion. This may not be the case elsewhere, particularly where police have lost touch with those engaged in criminality. In the case of pervasive youth crime or in neighbourhoods with populations with no basis of mutuality with police, the symbiotic trading relationship is missing. Consequently, other control discourses have sprung up. These include focused policing and zero-tolerance policing (see Chatterton and Rogers, 1989: 64–81; Dennis, 1997; Weatheritt, 1998). Both methodologies are a form of crime-fighting. Indeed, this is explicit in some accounts of zero-tolerance policing (Dennis and Mallon, 1997: 70–3). While broadly agreeing that crime-fighting by the police is probably ineffective, we will further discuss these methodologies in the context of policing as the management of risk in Chapter 5.

Investigation as gatekeeping

If police are generally unsuccessful in crime-fighting at the aggregate level, to what extent are they effective in their efforts to produce successful outcomes in individual cases? Here, the idea of crime control is a particularly dangerous concept. It can lead to gross distortions in the administration of justice, from police bias in defining suspect populations to actual miscarriages of justice. Mayhew et al. (1994) clearly shows the degree of attrition in the criminal process with only 2 per cent of all crimes likely to result in conviction. At this rate, the police are certainly losing the war on crime – a fact that may or may not entirely be concerned with investigative effectiveness. However, in all cases where they exercise powers of arrest or where they invoke legal process through other means, investigators play an important gatekeeping role in the criminal justice process. Investigation is the primary logical filter that categorises and evaluates events before the rest of the system can play its part. This is all the more reason why it should be free of bias and prejudice. If the gatekeeper of the city is corrupt, who then is safe?

When operating in the investigative role, however, as Packer (1964, 1968) and Skolnick (1966) suggest, the police regard crime control as more important than due process. In contrast to their failure to be able to control the aggregate of crime, this affects individual cases. It involves assumptions of guilt, belief in the necessity of ensuring convictions and avoidance or evasion of legal controls. It also produces distortions to the application of sanctions provided in law. As Coleman and Norris (2000) claim:

> Whereas the primary focus of the due process model is the acquittal of the innocent, the crime control model prioritises the punishment of the guilty.
>
> (Coleman and Norris, 2000: 141)

The research evidence, even after the enactment of PACE 1984, shows the predominance of the crime control model in investigation and in the prosecution process. For McConville *et al.* (1991), the role of police in case construction is pernicious from the very outset. Social factors define the suspect population. The police seek out particular categories of people and subsequent investigations aim at getting them convicted. Investigation is not a search for truth. Inevitably, detention places a suspect in a hostile environment. Police dictate the terms of interviews. This dominance distorts the records of interview. Informal rules affect charging decisions, not the requirements of due process. Police manipulate the paper reality in order to authenticate cases. Consequently, although the CPS appears to be independent, it is, in fact, subordinate to police. Conviction or acquittal is determined early in the process by informal rules, not in the criminal justice system by due process (McConville *et al.*, 1991: *passim*).

Of course, there are many cases where this does not apply but these telling criticisms are borne out by a number of examples. The literature of miscarriages of justice, from the Maxwell Confait case, through the Birmingham Six and Guildford Four cases to the Carl Bridgwater murder case, seems to support the argument (Rose, 1996: 1–9; Ashworth, 1998: 11–15; Walker and Starmer, 1999). While there is little doubt a damaging crime control attitude has influenced investigative work in recent years, the extent to which it is generalisable to all cases of crime investigation remains open. The potential for damage to the criminal justice system as a whole certainly seems to have been recognised. Legislators, judges and police themselves have put measures into place attempting to curb its worst effects. PACE provides a number of effective controls. Reflecting on judicial decisions, Zander (1994) emphasises the increasing need for police to adopt due process attitudes. The increasing application by judges of the doctrine of 'the fruits of the poisoned tree', where all evidence is excluded if some flaw is found, means that cases will be lost unless due process is followed. There is evidence that the police have recognised the need for change. Although not conclusive, new approaches to investigative professionalism show that the police have recognised that crime-fighting and crime-control attitudes to investigation are mistaken and counterproductive.

What are the prospects for improvements in the investigation of crime? Is there evidence of a move towards a new approach to professionalism? The arguments of this chapter show that a 'thick' sense of professionalism has formed the investigative culture. This is characterised by the exercise of power, by hunches rather than analysis, by loyalty to colleagues and by attitudes oriented towards crime control. Although more research is yet required, recent developments indicate that a 'thinner', instrumental sense of professionalism is emerging. This is characterised by the adoption of competencies and standards, by transparency, science and the acceptance of principles, especially the principle of due process. Although the Stephen Lawrence murder demonstrates vividly that this is by no means a convincing transition, there is evidence that crime investigation has the potential to be a very different world to that described by Hobbs (1988) and Young (1991).

Despite the justifiable criticisms that remain, there is evidence that the police are now making serious efforts to improve their professionalism in the investigation of crime. Although its long-term effectiveness is not yet proven, the National Crime Faculty (NCF) based at the National Police Training College in Bramshill, Hampshire appears to be developing into useful resource for investigative best practice. It provides advice for investigators, especially for those who are working on serious and serial crime. It is making efforts to review the evidence in previously unsolved cases. It is attempting to improve the skills of senior investigators by means of a new training and development programme (Smith and Flanagan, 2000). Elsewhere, psychologists are helping to develop new techniques, such as preparing profiles of offenders in murder and other serious crime cases (Canter and Alison, 2000). DNA analysis is adding strength to the identification of suspects by forensic science. Better technology is making possible a more corporate approach to the use of information and intelligence. This should enable investigators to avoid the problems identified in the failed Yorkshire Ripper inquiry. Police and psychologists have developed new techniques for interviewing in an attempt to move the ethos of police questioning away from an adversarial approach towards a search for the truth (Milne and Bull, 1999). More scrutiny of these developments is needed if they are to convince critics that crime investigation can become more objective. If successful, however, they will erode the old cultural values and promote a more scientific approach. As a result the whole process of investigation should become more transparent.

Ensuring a reasonable degree of transparency in crime investigation is important for the way in which the public perceives the legitimacy of the police. We have established that the public provides the bulk of the information to the police leading to detection (Morgan, 1990: 3–4, McConville *et al.*, 1991: 19). The media, the public and the investigators play key roles in the investigative process. According to Innes (1999a), the police often seek to use the media as an investigative resource, especially in murder inquiries and other serious and difficult to solve cases. Television information-gathering programmes such as *Crimewatch UK* show that this is the case, although such programmes also satisfy the interests of the broadcasters. Publicity, in this sense, is a two-way process. It provides fast access to information held by the public that might not otherwise be forthcoming. It provides a degree of public ownership of the investigation but also confirms the gatekeeping role of investigators. Similarly, we should welcome early involvement of the CPS in investigations and the review of cases by other police forces. If properly managed, the closer involvement of the CPS following the Glidewell Report (1998) should lead to more commitment to due process, not to less. In the longer term, increased transparency will help improve both the quality and effectiveness of crime investigation.

Of course there are dangers in too much reliance upon the 'techno-fix' or upon publicity. Technology does not provide a total key to investigation nor reduce it to a machine-like operation. Publicity does not overcome the problems of investigation of the kind that Hobbs (1988) and Young (1991) identified. Perhaps more important than the trend towards instrumental professionalism is the extent to which investigation plays a pivotal moral role in the criminal justice process. The empirical evidence discussed in this chapter shows that crime investigation has often failed in its duty to follow the rule of law. The claims of police to be able to control crime through investigation in any direct sense are doubtful. Indeed, the attempt to promote effective crime control has sometimes produced the gravest distortions in the criminal justice system. However, we need to take its very existence into account in understanding the role that ethical concepts play in making investigation meaningful to practitioners. If, as this chapter has claimed, crime investigation does have an indispensable logical place in policing practice and in criminal justice as a whole, what should replace crime control as the key concept that endows investigation with meaning? The answer to this question is the reassertion of the role of the investigator as gatekeeper. As such, investigators have particular kinds of moral duties. They should be impartial, quasi-scientific agents. They should be servants of the law and of scientific and legal processes, rather than of institutional performance or government anti-crime policies. Here, we do not conceive of the idea of professionalism in instrumental terms. It is a matter of rights and obligations rather than of effectiveness. We have already mentioned this in the context of Zander (1994) who emphasised the legal and ethical reasons for the adoption of the due process approach to investigation.

The primary logical support for crime investigation as a key mode of policing practice is the argument from reciprocity. If the citizen has a right to the protection of the state in return for recognition of an obligation to abide by the law, there is a parallel right to have crimes (as failures of the state to provide that protection) investigated. This is not an enterprise transaction, concerned with commercialism of the kind practised by Jonathan Wild or by security companies on behalf of specific clients. Even if privatised companies on behalf of victims carried out investigations with direct access to the courts, it would still not be an enterprise association. It remains a 'practice' in terms of the argument set out in Chapter 1. If the anti-statist answer to this question is that there is no such right or obligation, then there is no requirement for investigation at all, beyond the power of an individual to use any means (legal or otherwise) to redress their own grievances. By this token also, the rights of suspects would also eventually disappear. Justice, in this sense, would tend towards personal or corporate retribution, rather than towards the restoration of rights through legal process and arbitration.

However, if the answer is that if a state does have a responsibility to assist a victim to obtain justice, then that victim has the right to have the offence properly investigated by a competent public authority. Indeed, this is precisely the way in which investigation is currently being interpreted in the European Court of Human Rights and elsewhere. This is the key finding in the case of *Osman* v *UK* 1998 (*The Times*, 5 November 1998), and the inquiry into the death of Stephen Lawrence. *Osman* successfully argued that the rule based upon public policy that does not allow actions for negligence against police investigators violates the right to have the matter resolved before a court. This is contrary to Article 6 of the European Convention on Human Rights (see Wadham and Mountfield, 1999: 89–90). The Steven Lawrence inquiry accepted the principle that negligence in investigation should also be subject to public scrutiny. In both cases, investigative failures breached victims' or family rights. They are not merely examples of technical incompetence.

We have argued in this chapter that investigation is a key mode of policing practice because it is part of a reciprocal mechanism that enables citizens to realise their rights. As will be evident by referring back to Figure 2.1 in Chapter 2, these developments mark the transition from controlling crime in the individual by means of crime detection to the use of crime investigation in a more managerial way which respects due process. Rights are recognised either directly (in the case of reactive investigation into specific crimes) or indirectly (in the case of proactive investigation into criminal activity). Investigators (of all kinds, not just the police) play an important gatekeeping role in this respect. Although it may be important to a government, as a matter of policy, to limit the amount of crime, this is not the role of crime investigation. Indeed, policy thinking is increasingly accepting the idea that investigation and law enforcement alone cannot have an influence upon crime. The role of investigation is quite different. We will discuss the question of whether investigation is structurally compatible with strategies for reducing offending in Chapter 5 in the context of the management of risk. We will extend this debate in Chapter 6 in the context of policing as the promotion of community justice.

Chapter 5

Policing as the management of risk

This chapter examines the management of risk as a mode of policing practice. In particular, it explores the way in which policing applies the concept of risk to the problems of community safety and crime reduction. First, it discusses the concept of the risk society, reflecting upon the social conditions of late modernity. It argues that recognition of cultural diversity and differences in risk perception are important to the management of risk. Secondly, it reviews the development of crime prevention and community safety as ways of dealing with crime risk. This includes a discussion of a number of theories of crime prevention. The third section examines the specific trajectory of policing methods in relation to the management of risk. It compares policing which aims at the solving of problems with the more disciplinary 'zero-tolerance' approach to the reduction of crime. It also reviews claims which suggest that risk-communication is the primary function of policing the risk society. Fourthly, it discusses efforts to develop a more holistic model of crime risk management. It reviews crackdown theory and other crime reduction strategies in the light of evidence-based practice and the 'what works' thesis. Finally, this chapter explores the role of partnerships and of public participation in community safety. It examines the impact of the Crime and Disorder Act 1998 alongside a wider consideration of the objectives of central and local government. It discusses institutional methods for the management of risk and compares them with the ways in which citizens might manage risk.

The risk society

Pre-modern societies regarded both natural calamities and unpleasant social events as the result of sin. According to Douglas (1992):

> Most little cultures develop some common term that runs across the gamut of social life to moralize and politicize dangers. In the pre-industrial West, Christianity used the word *sin* ... A major sin would be expected to unleash dangers on the community at large, or to affect the sinner's nearest and dearest ... The public discourse on sin's dangers mobilized a moral community.
>
> (Douglas, 1992: 25–6)

The rise of industrialisation and science, however, led to the predominance of other forms of explanation. Science and commerce adopted explanations based upon the theory of probability. For example, no longer could sin or fate be regarded as a suitable explanation for the sinking of a ship. Secularised communities could no longer explain disease by sin in this or a previous life. As technology improved, Western medicine became a scientific activity, far removed from the casting out of devils. Measures to deal with crime moved from blame for individual depravity to control by a functional bureaucracy, namely the police. As we have seen in Chapter 1, modernity was the ground upon which such developments were possible. Crime in the individual could be 'detected' and thereby 'controlled' (see Figure 2.1). Crime in the aggregate could be rationalised through social explanation. Such crime could be 'prevented' if only the variables were fully understood. In late modernity, however, contingency and uncertainty in both the natural and social environments have shown that it is not possible to control all the variables. As a result, we have increasingly used the concept of risk to express the limitations of control theory. The management of risk is replacing measures of control as the predominant means by which we can foresee and neutralise both natural and social disasters.

Risk assessment seeks to identify and evaluate risks from a variety of threats to health, safety and social well-being. Much risk assessment involves evaluating the risk by estimating the probability that an adverse event will occur. This is especially the case in making assessments of risk for insurance purposes. This has long been the case in insurance against death, personal injury, loss of property and risks associated with motoring. Such risk assessment depends to a great extent upon the availability of long-term actuarial data. This enables insurers to make predictions and to match the premium to the risk that they face.

Engineering also makes extensive use of quantitative methods for risk assessment. At the design stage, engineers calculate whether components, machines and structures may be subject to potential failure. They test models and prototypes to determine whether these calculations are sustainable. In this way, technology (one might suppose) can provide an ever-increasing degree of safety and confidence that the risks are tolerable.

Although actuarial assessment of risk continues to predominate in some fields, in recent years, events have called into question the probabilistic basis upon which it relies. In turbulent economic conditions, some insurers have found it increasingly difficult to guarantee their products to provide a return upon investment. House buyers have not had their mortgages completed due to shortfalls in profits from endowment policies. In the BSE crisis, it has not been possible for science to produce convincing enough answers to restore widespread public confidence in the beef industry. In the flooding in England and Wales in 2000, explanations about what appear to be extraordinary changes in natural phenomena have not satisfied those affected by the loss of home or business. Railway accidents have led to radical reassessment of the extent of risk. Railtrack (the British company which owns and maintains the national rail network) has replaced a large quantity of track-work in an attempt to reduce risks far below levels which, fifty years before, railway companies might have regarded as tolerable. Failure to deliver justice in specific cases and to deal with crime in the aggregate has produced a crisis of confidence in the effectiveness and legitimacy of policing and the criminal justice system. We can frequently observe the public anger across this range of concerns. The public invariably transfers the blame to agencies who fail to predict and prevent negative consequences. Governments or the agencies themselves seldom manage to assuage this anger by giving reassurances.

The problems of risk are not just about a lack of accurate actuarial data or incompetence on the part of public agencies or private sector organisations, although these may sometimes be factors. They are also deeply concerned with changes in belief about the ability of management and technology to control the social and physical environments. For Young (1999), this awareness of risk produces its own tensions. He says:

> The fears come and go: carjacking, BSE, AIDS, road rage. They flicker on the screen of consciousness, something is going on but we are not sure who or what to believe ... The awareness of risk generates an actuarial attitude in the citizen of late modernity.
>
> (Young, 1999: 70–1)

For Beck (1992), the obsession with finding solutions to the problem of risk is exceptionally pervasive. Someone, the argument goes, must be able to provide a technological solution. There are many examples. In medicine, no argument can account for failure, whether it is about lack of resources, training or skills, or even about the deeper intractability of the medical problem itself. Biological and genetic engineering must be capable of dealing with both risks to life and to lifestyle.

Medical science must be capable of replacing virtually every organ in the body to preserve life. We blame teachers not only for low standards of education (which evidence may show is sometimes a justifiable complaint) but for every failure in learning. The police are held responsible (in a direct sense) for crime: for failures to contain its volume and for failures in individual investigations, regardless of the non-availability of effective means of control or of credible evidence that might lead to arrest and conviction. Some commentators suggest that policing, the criminal justice system or even criminology itself produces crime as a social artefact (see, for example, Pavarini, 1994).

The trajectory of this plethora of claims and counter-claims is that we have projected risk, rather than the substantive concepts of safety, health or crime, into the foreground of popular and theoretical speculation. As Beck (1992) rightly claims, this indicates a society obsessed with risk – the 'risk society'. For Giddens (1991):

> … no one can disengage completely from the abstract systems of modernity: this is one of the consequences of living in a world of high-consequence risks.
>
> (Giddens, 1991: 142)

Late modern social theory has both generated and taken advantage of this agenda. It has ratcheted up the intensity of the debate in ways closely connected with the development a new, supposedly emancipatory, life-politics (Giddens, 1991: 212). In this sense, risk has become a political as well as an actuarial concept.

There can be little doubt that during the latter part of the twentieth century, the concept of risk shifted from the assessment of threat or danger (real or perceived), to the idea of risk as blame, liability and accountability. Initially, this emerged from the emphasis on individualism. In early modernism, society made rules to protect the collective from the excesses of individual appetites. Now, in late modernism, individuals need to get protection from the effects of the collective: particularly from the state and its institutions. We do not protect the environment for its own sake. We do so for the sake of the harm that a damaged or polluted environment may do to individuals and groups. According to Douglas (1978), this emphasis has led to risk becoming a tool of the legal system. In traditional, hierarchical societies, sinning or breaking taboo meant that the individual was deviant. In an individualist, highly pluralist but global culture, being at risk means that society is out of line with the individual or group whose rights are in need of protection. This has inverted the meaning of risk. It calls in question earlier methods of calculation. Actuarial and quantitative methodologies no longer support risk assessment in a direct and unequivocal way. Perception competes with calculation in the discourse of risk. According to Pidgeon et al. (1992):

> From the perspective of the social sciences, risk perception involves people's beliefs, attitudes, judgements and feelings, as well as the wider social values and dispositions that people adopt, towards hazards and their benefits … risk perception cannot be reduced to a single subjective correlate of a particular mathematical model of risk, such as the product of probabilities and consequences, because this imposes unduly restrictive assumptions upon what is an essentially human and social phenomenon.
>
> (Pidgeon et al., 1992: 89)

Neither the social nor the natural sciences are immune from disputes about the nature of risk. Quantitative and qualitative judgements of risk compete with one another for position. Engineers, scientists and academics involved in studying the uncertain business of risk employ terminology that is itself marked by uncertainty. The very term 'risk' itself has been the subject of dispute between different academic disciplines. Psychologists' views have been criticised by anthropologists for failing to take account of the cultural dimensions of risk perception.

A major challenge to orthodox psychological approaches to risk perception over the past ten years has come from cultural theory. (For a discussion of the origins of cultural theory, see Douglas (1978, 1992), Douglas and Wildavsky (1982) and Thompson et al. (1990).) Cultural theory argues that in society, there are four distinct cultural archetypes. Although one must be careful not to misrepresent the subtleties of cultural theory, we can paraphrase the traits of these archetypes as follows:

Individualism: This is the culture of entrepreneurial professions, often in the market place, in entertainment business or in brokerage. It is expansionist and robust and is found on the entrepreneurial edge of any profession or business.

Fatalism: Fatalists or 'isolates' are people who have had their autonomy withdrawn by the predatory expansions of other cultural types. They are naturally capricious and are often in the most victimised part of the social structure.

Hierarchy: This is the 'central community' of society. The authority of the established professions is accepted, as is the ranking they generate. The social demands they make on each other are also cultural demands to conform. They are robust within limits, but severe pressure may take them outside their cultural frame of reference.

Egalitarianism: This culture rejects the knowledge base of the central community along with its authority. Often forming into enclaves which give them their reasons for dissent, they accept the affinity that this gives them with other enclaves. However, this is by nature a fragile state.

(See Douglas, 1992: 102–10, 263–4, *passim*)

Each of these positions reflects a coherent cluster of attitudes, beliefs and ways of life. These four ways of life inform the perceptions of participants and determine their behaviour. Participants also use them to justify the validity of their social situations.

From this perspective, therefore, risk is a cultural, rather than an individual perception. As Warner (1993) puts it, for the anthropologist, risk is:

> ... threat or danger whose perception will depend on the prevailing culture in which there are four major groups: hierarchists, egalitarians, fatalists and individualists.
>
> (Warner, 1993: 7)

On the other hand, the psychological dimension of risk perception suggests that different people perceive risk in entirely different ways. This perspective remains methodologically individualist in outlook. In contrast, the social or anthropological approach is collectivist in its methods. It suggests 'that people select certain risks for attention to defend their preferred lifestyles and as a forensic resource to place blame on other groups' (Royal Society 1983). No single measure of risk, therefore, can represent the perceptions either of individuals or of the disaggregated cultural types. Risk assessment and risk management, therefore, must take account of the relative balance of all cultural types within the relevant domain. This means adopting holistic methods of analysis and recognising that the management of risk is the management of diversity.

What is the relevance of all this to the analysis of policing practice? The distinction between the four cultural biases represented above highlights the need to manage risk of any kind in a way that recognises its plurality. This is particularly relevant to community safety and to the prevention of crime. For example, Frosdick and Walley (1997) have applied the lessons of cultural theory to the analysis of the problems of stadium and arena safety. Following Douglas (1992), they argue that the evaluation of risk in public assembly facilities such as football grounds is concerned with risk perception across groups with different cultural biases. The right way to assess risk is by means of a holistic review of activities to generate an understanding of the disaggregation of attitudes and cultural bias of the participants across the domain as a whole. The institutions involved should design their activities to take account of this diversity. Similarly for Mars (1983: 1–20), crime at work can be understood by distinguishing between types of crime and linking them to types of occupation. Using cultural theory, Mars shows that there is no monolithic way of dealing with the diversity of crime risk in the workplace. Following Douglas (1970, 1978), he argues that workgroups are characterised according to their cultural bias: by individualistic and entrepreneurial activity; by isolation and subordination; by their tight knit structure; or by loose configuration. Crime will manifest itself in different ways according to these biases (Mars, 1983: 29). Institutions need to develop diverse strategies of crime risk management according to these patterns. Cultural theory, therefore, provides important insights into safety and crime risk. These are areas where further research would be beneficial.

If we accept the importance of risk perception, we can never control crime risk by instrumental means that take no account of diversity. O'Malley (1992) has pointed out the problems of the effects of contingency on the management of crime risk. Neither actuarial or 'social risk' methodologies can rely upon linear patterns or definitive answers on the nature and direction of specific developments. Crime risk management, therefore, is not simply a matter of controlling crime by reducing the crime figures. Good crime risk management requires knowledge of the context within which the problem has developed. It requires the recognition of a diversity of cultural attitudes. It also requires widespread participation in order to plan for reducing risks. In this sense, policing as the management of risk again confirms practice as reciprocity. Here, it also begins to add recognition of the importance of diversity. Policing has a responsibility to manage risk fairly. The public has the right to protection and an obligation to assist in the process. Undoubtedly, because there are no right or wrong answers, the climate of risk as blame means that policing constantly will be called to account over the adequacy of its arrangements for dealing with crime and public safety. We will discuss these issues in the last section of this chapter. First, however, it is necessary to show the way in which the policing role in crime risk management has developed.

From crime prevention to community safety

As discussed in Chapter 1, crime prevention was the key objective of the modern police from its inception. Policy and circumstances have increasingly modified their involvement. However, the police still continue to play an important role in crime prevention going into the twenty-first century. The objective of this chapter is not to provide an extensive analysis of the development of crime prevention and community safety strategies. Although it is necessary to allude to some aspects of their development, we introduce them here only to illustrate the extent to which they support the thesis that the management of risk is a key mode of policing practice. Readers who require more extensive analysis of crime prevention theory and practice should refer to Gilling (1997, 2000).

History has much to tell us about the way in which modern policing has changed its approach to crime prevention. The unfocused methods of the 1960s gradually evolved into a more integrated approach to crime reduction by the turn of the century. Development by the Home Office of crime prevention panels and the Crime Prevention Centre at Stafford in the 1960s was an early recognition of the connection between crime and risk. This did not, however, signal a revolutionary change in police attitudes. The police still regarded crime prevention as a poor relation to patrol and detective activity. We have discussed the problem of controlling crime by traditional methods of patrol and detection in Chapter 4. In contrast, however, research since the 1960s shows that some crime prevention activities do have local or cumulative effects, especially where policing efforts are combined with those of other agencies. The difficulty is in deciding which of a range of crime prevention activities has most effect on the amelioration of risk.

There are a number of theories that support the prevention of crime by means of environmental measures. Criminologists still regard some of these as controversial. Oscar Newman argued that a defensible space around an area and building would deter potential offenders from attacking the premises (Newman, 1973). While Newman's work was primarily concerned with architecture, Felson argued that it is the wider spatio-temporal organisation of routine social activities that provides the means through which crime can be understood (see Cohen and Felson, 1979 and Felson, 1994). Also drawing upon both spatial and psychological concepts, Brantingham and Brantingham (1991) argued that place is a major determinant of crime. However, analysis also needs to consider other factors such as the law, the offender and the nature of the target. Their research in environmental criminology showed that factors such as street layout could affect local levels and patterns of crime (Beavon *et al.*, 1994).

These theories are based on the idea that criminality is concerned with rational choice. Rational choice, in this sense, is a combination of the situation in which a crime may be committed and the disposition of a person to commit the crime. It is a weighing of costs and benefits by someone with a pre-existing disposition to commit crime (Clarke, 1983; Gilling, 1997: 61). The perception of opportunities and risks affects such choices. These in turn are moderated by physical factors such as the hardness of the target (locks, alarms, design, etc.). Situational factors such as location, degree of natural surveillance, street lighting and so on also affect them.

Situational crime prevention, therefore, is concerned with modifying the opportunity in such a way that the commission of crime becomes less attractive. There are, of course, several objections to rational choice theory, in terms of an objective understanding of the risks and the opportunities that it provides. For Bottoms (1994), it is difficult to reconcile the ideal of choice upon which the theory relies and the reality of the opportunities as they actually present themselves. Environmental factors may affect the extent of an opportunity to commit crime. Psychological and social factors may also do so. It is difficult to provide a holistic analysis that combines both. Nor is it clear that rational choice is the predominant factor in expressive crime (Trasler, 1986, 1993). In crimes of violence in particular, emotional factors may be more important. There is also a political and moral case against situational prevention. Gilling (1997) says:

A frequently expressed worry is that situational measures tend to be oriented largely towards social exclusion: strangers or outsiders are the objects of an array of surveillance and security technology intended to exclude them, but in doing so they generate a mutual suspicion and a profoundly anti-communitarian fortress mentality. This is socially devisive and renders the integration of offenders and other stigmatized groups increasingly problematic, but it is also extremely inconvenient for the law abiding, and a potential infringement of their civil liberties (Clarke, 1980).

(Gilling, 1997: 186)

However, Gilling concedes that situational crime prevention is '... obviously a start' in seeking to reduce crime, even if not to eliminate it altogether. For this reason, it is therefore '... a criminology for the real world and one that understandably finds favour therein' (Gilling, 1997: 65).

There has been extensive research on crime prevention using these theories over the past two decades. Initiatives have covered a wide spectrum. Most of this research has drawn upon rational choice theory. The Home Office has funded much of the research and has published the output in Crime Prevention Unit Papers and in the Crime Detection and Prevention Series. This has included initiatives aimed at police operations against crime, crime prevention and the management of offender behaviour. Many of these studies have been influential. For example, research on the Kirkholt Estate in Greater Manchester was particularly influential in developing new multiple strategies for crime prevention (see Forrester *et al.*, 1988; Forrester *et al.*, 1990; Tilley, 1993a). In this study, the local authority and police improved security at burgled residential premises on the basis that these premises had a higher chance of further victimisation. Phase II of the project included analysing the motivation of offenders through the help of the probation service and other agencies. Researchers have also carried out extensive work on so-called 'repeat victimisation' in the 1990s. This has included action research into burglary and other high-volume crimes in conjunction with local police (see Farrell and Pease, 1993; Anderson *et al.*, 1995; Chenery *et al.*, 1997). Lloyd *et al.* (1994) also studied repeated victimisation of women in cases of domestic violence. Sampson and Phillips (1995) studied the phenomenon in cases of racially motivated crime.

We should not forget that policing as the management of risk involves activities other than crime prevention. These include the management of risks from traffic accidents and other risks associated with the use and condition of the streets or the built environment. These matters are grossly under-researched because of the prominence that the Home Office has given to policing and crime risk in recent years. The role of the police as an emergency service, however, implies a need for a large amount of contingency planning in conjunction with other services and agencies. Policing also has a regulatory role in these fields, not least in relation to their role in dealing with moving traffic violations. However, *contra* Bayley (1994: 34), this does not only amount to authoritative intervention by the police or to a symbolic representation of justice. It also implies a wider preventative role in dealing with risks and public safety. We can see a good example of this in the work of accident prevention units. Although such units do make use of exemplary enforcement in enforcing speed limits and dealing with other traffic violations, such activity is not an end in itself. The police carry it out for the purpose of risk management, often in consultation with local communities.

Crime remains at the core of risk management. Research has now broadened its focus beyond that of situational crime prevention and rational choice theory. The recognition of the importance of the psychology of the offender and the social context within which crime takes place has changed the focus from that simply of crime prevention. The broader concept of community safety is the result. This underlines the need to develop a more holistic approach to crime that combines social, psychological and environmental factors. As Bottoms (1994: 586) suggests, environmental criminology will need to take into account both the spatial distribution of offences *and* the social production of offenders. Without a holistic approach that recognises that both localism and mobility influence the commission of offences it is unlikely that crime risk management will be successful. Here there is still a mismatch between policing practice and criminological theory. For these reasons, we should assess the initiatives that the police have put into place for the management of crime risk in terms of the extent to which they contribute to this holistic approach. We should not see them merely as instrumental ways of controlling crime.

Policing the risk society

In parallel to the development of crime prevention theory, other changes are evident in the relationship between policing and risk. Influenced by Sir Kenneth Newman, who in 1982 became the Commissioner of the Metropolitan Police, the police began to adopt new problem-solving methods, especially in relation to crime. The seminar on new departures in crime prevention held at Bramshill Police College in September 1982 and visits to New Scotland Yard and the Home Office by both Herman Goldstein and George Kelling fostered new thinking about the way that the police should engage with crime risk. Toch and Grant (1991) have alluded to the adoption of problem-solving strategies of all kinds during this period both in the UK and in the US. Not surprisingly, the approaches advocated by Goldstein and Kelling produced very different effects. On the one hand, they reinforced a more community-oriented style of policing which recognised the importance of the contribution that the public and other agencies make to local crime prevention. On the other hand, they produced a more disciplinary model of crime control, namely so-called 'zero-tolerance policing'.

Goldstein (1990) argued for a problem-oriented approach to police work. This approach was subject to extensive experimentation in Britain in the 1980s and early 1990s. According to the problem-oriented policing (POP) model, policing should be about identifying and solving under-lying problems within communities. It is not simply a matter of respond-ing to individual incidents. Incidents are only symptoms of the deeper problem. Active involvement of the community and other agencies is vital to both defining the problems and to identifying the strategies to deal with them. It requires intensive commitment from the whole police service and is not the task of specialist squads (Leigh *et al.*, 1996). A number of factors have hampered the development of this approach, including the lack of reliable data and the means to analyse it. Perhaps more critically, British policing has not yet developed the mind-set and the infrastructure for problem-solving. Although promising long-term solutions, rising demands and lack of resources have meant that the requirements of problem-oriented policing could not easily be satisfied. All too often for this reason, policing has reverted to a reactive 'fire brigade' mode in dealing with crime and other risks.

In an influential article, Wilson and Kelling (1982) suggested that damage, rubbish and graffiti have a profound effect on crime in local neighbourhoods. If the police and other agencies deal with these so-called 'broken windows', they suggest, it signals a wider interest in neighbourhood improvement. It leads to better conditions in the com-munity and reduction in levels of crime. As was the case with Goldstein's problem-solving approach, the broken windows thesis attracted con-siderable interest on both sides of the Atlantic. In New York in the early 1990s, Police Commissioner Bratton and Mayor Giuliani instituted an initiative that drew upon these ideas and aimed to reduce crime. Police officers were set clear goals and provided with the infrastructure to achieve them. This included an increase in police officers and some reorganisation of the force. The initiative also included the development of crime reduction strategies. At their heart was a computerised system for managing and analysing crime data (COMPSTAT). Bratton also im-posed direct accountability on police precinct commanders for levels of crime in their area. There was also more extensive contact with local com-munities and more cooperation between the police and other agencies (Bratton, 1997). There is a widespread belief among some New York

Police Department officers and academics that these measures produced the considerable decrease in recorded crime in New York City and on the subway over a number of years during the 1990s (see Kelling and Coles, 1997; Bratton, 1997; Allan and Wright, 1997; Gorta, 1998; Kelling, 1998). This claim remains controversial. Certainly, the removal of beggars, 'shakedown artists', unlicensed street pedlars, squeegee pests, graffiti and other so-called 'incivilities' was very much in line with the Wilson and Kelling's (1982) broken windows thesis. This earned for the initiative the name of 'zero-tolerance policing', although Bratton himself did not use the term. However, its ethos was reflected in the slogan adopted by his force on official handouts, namely 'We do not just take the reports – we are the police' (Allen and Wright, 1997).

In Britain, the reaction to zero-tolerance policing was (and remains) varied. In places where community-oriented strategies were already in place, or where crime was not exceptionally high, police did not regard its adoption as viable. Even where this was not the case, some police officers thought it had dangerous implications. One chief constable who was opposed to the concept maintained that:

> That part of the 'Zero Tolerance' principle characterised by aggressive policing, confrontational management, opportunistic short-termism and undue emphasis on 'the numbers game' poses an enormous threat for the future. If this culture is not tackled, then – on the basis of the British experience – the risk of serious corruption and inner city disorder in the future is real.
>
> (Pollard, 1997: 60)

In Hartlepool and Middlesbrough in the mid-1990s, however, zero-tolerance methods were adopted to turn around an environment that had suffered from dereliction and a long-term rise in crime. The intention of the police was to 'return peace to the streets'. According to Dennis and Mallon (1997):

> A central intention of the strategy in Hartlepool was to break into the vicious spiral of a deteriorating situation of personal safety, defacement and dereliction of the streets: a reduction in the law abiding citizen's confidence in his own capacity and the capacity of the police to control the situation; a further deterioration as the confidence of the unruly elements increases; and a further loss of public confidence in itself and the police.
>
> (Dennis and Mallon, 1997: 65)

This initiative focused upon anti-social behaviour, burglary and the so-called 'quality of life' crimes of the kind that had an effect on the environment. The police focused on the latter because they believed that such behaviour was the precursor to more serious forms of crime. In this sense, zero-tolerance policing was a disciplinary and enforcement-led approach to crime and other risks. As Johnston (2000: 65) has noted, however, the police later softened their rhetoric to reflect a longer-term move towards a problem-oriented approach. Despite this, zero-tolerance policing remains a strategy that aims at dealing with crime in a disciplinary way. It is, as Innes (1999b) has shown, an 'iron fist within an iron glove'. As such, it marks a regression to control-oriented methods rather than to those based on improvement in social or economic conditions.

As is the case with crime prevention measures based upon rational-choice theory, the key issue in relation to these two types of policing strategy is not the extent to which they are successful. This is a matter for a much more extensive evaluation. The suspicion, taking account of Leigh *et al*. (1998) and Pease (1998), is that the effects of both POP and zero-tolerance policing are probably limited. In any case overall reduction in crime is not a sophisticated enough measure to determine success. The key issue for the current argument is not effectiveness but the underlying logic of these strategies as means of dealing with crime risk. For better or for worse, this certainly seems to be the direction in which they are aimed. As Johnston (2000) argues:

> Whether these two operational philosophies are compatible with one another remains to be seen. The significant point for present purposes, however, is that the philosophy of POP accords fully with the risk-orientated and intelligence-based modes of policing ...
>
> (Johnston, 2000: 66)

These tensions should alert us to the ambiguity of risk and to its role in triggering different kinds of responses to crime in late modernity. Nevertheless, the involvement of police in community safety and in these other initiatives shows that the management of risk has become a key mode of policing practice.

Ericson and Haggerty (1997) have rightly identified the management of risk as a key activity of policing. However, their thesis goes far beyond this modest claim. Suggesting that much of the literature on policing is redundant and stagnant, they put forward a comprehensive theory of policing (*sic*) that argues that the police play a key role in risk communication. According to Ericson and Haggerty:

Policing and the society in which it takes place are best understood in terms of a model of risk communication ... Our point is that policing consists of the public police co-ordinating their activities with policing agents in all other institutions to provide a society-wide basis for risk management (governance) and security (guarantees against loss).

(Ericson and Haggerty, 1997: 3)

Police, they argue, have become 'knowledge workers' in the field of risk communication, serving a range of other organisations including the insurance and security industries. Police have always gathered information on people and events and have kept surveillance on suspects. Now, however, they carry out these tasks for a different purpose. The whole focus of policing has changed. It no longer serves the ends of criminal justice. It has moved from deviance to risk, from control to surveillance and from order to security (Ericson and Haggerty, 1997: 19–38, 39–48). Police intersect with all other major institutions and their primary function is to communicate risk to them (Ericson and Haggerty, 1997: 127).

There is little problem with the general claim that police have become increasingly involved in risk management in late modernity. However, considerable difficulties arise in assuming that risk is the category that defines their role. We will not revisit here the arguments about the poverty of functional explanation but there are several objections to the thesis they propose. First, it is difficult to sustain a meta-narrative of such global proportions on such limited empirical evidence. Research only in a single jurisdiction that may not be typical does not support generalisation. Limited observation and a small number of interviews with a disproportionate number of information-handling specialists (48 out of 155) does not help to justify their claims. Above all is the danger that the reification of risk simply ignores its diversity and ambivalence. It makes no concessions to plurality or to the patterns of connection between risk and cultural bias (both inside and outside the police organisation) of the kind identified by Douglas (1992). They seem to have formulated their theoretical claims around a preconceived political anxiety about a new panopticon where the police play the controlling role. This one-track thesis both places too much weight on an unequivocal notion of risk and gives too much credence to the idea that the police have the controlling influence. A little more reflection upon the substantive aspects of other modes of policing practice would have served better. Research in other jurisdictions, if not in Canada, shows that risk is important, but it is not the sole factor in the structuring of policing roles, tasks and modes of practice. The debate about policing is configured less by an overarching rationale of risk communication than by endless controversy about its methods and strategies. As the following sections will claim in relation to the relationship between policing and other agencies in Britain, the situation is far less rational and much more 'messy' than that feared by Ericson and Heggarty (1997). This is true, both in terms of crime risk management and of inter-agency cooperation.

Crime risk management: identifying 'what works'

As argued above and in Chapter 1, we have yet to see convincing unified theoretical models of policing in general or of crime risk management in particular. On the contrary, what more often confronts us is a sceptical catalogue of 'what does not work'. In Chapter 1, in relation to policing, we characterised this as a form of 'epidemiography'. More recently, however, there has been a trend towards the development of evidence-based practice. This draws on the more encouraging aspects of empirical research. The idea of 'what works' has been central to such evidence-based approaches to practice in the public sector services. These include applications in medicine, in social work, in the Probation Service, in policing and crime reduction (see variously Chapman and Hough, 1998; Goldblatt and Lewis, 1998; Jordan, 1998; Sheldon and Macdonald, 1999; Trinder and Reynolds, 2000). Sheldon and Macdonald (1999), who have promoted the idea of evidence-based practice in social work services, define it as follows:

> Evidence-based social care is the conscientious, explicit and judicious use of current best evidence in making decisions re-garding the welfare of those in need of social services.
>
> (Sheldon and Macdonald, 1999: 4)

Here the emphasis is upon the commitment to ethical obligations, to explicit solutions and sound judgement in applying the best available evidence. For Sheldon and Macdonald, these are all deciding factors in maximising performance.

An extensive study by Sherman (1997), commissioned by the US Department of Justice, reviews the state of the art in policing and crime-reduction techniques. It identifies a range of techniques that are not effective. This concurs with much of the evidence provided in the epidemiography discussed in Chapter 1. Perhaps more interestingly, Sherman identifies a range of techniques that did prove to be successful.

These were subject to as much evaluation as those that did not work.

Jordan (1998) reviews the findings. He argues that the research evidence shows that some approaches to crime reduction are viable, even without enthusiastic implementation by highly skilled personnel. Table 5.1 lists the strategies by which the police may play a significant role in reducing crime outlined by Jordan (1998: 65–6). (For details of the supporting research, please refer to the original publication.)

According to Jordan (1998), the research literature shows that in certain circumstances the police can make a significant impact on local crime rates. He says:

> In general, success follows on selection of the appropriate tactic for the problem under attack: effective management and good targeting of resources... Where there is still uncertainty about particular police strategies there is an obvious need for rigorous evaluations that would include a series of studies to refine our understanding of what works, for whom and in what circumstances.
>
> (Jordan, 1998: 74)

Other studies also suggest that policing work on crime reduction is not as ineffective as sceptical criminologists believe. For example, Pease (1998: 39) has looked at the phenomenon of 'fast crime reductions' that had hitherto not been linked to any particular policing activities. He found many cases not previously recognised as such by higher police management and others where the police had quickly forgotten the rapid reduction in crime. Most importantly, even where the change was recognised and recalled, there was reluctance to undertake extra data-gathering to clarify the mechanism that had brought about the reduction in crime. It was clear 'what' had happened: the mechanism (the 'how') was missing. For Pease, this evidence suggests that crime levels are not intractable, provided that suitable strategies are applied.

How can the police take advantage of this syndrome? Research by Sherman (1990) has shown that police crackdowns work to reduce local crime rates in the short term. Sherman defines a crackdown as '... sudden increases in officer presence, sanctions, and threats of apprehension either for specific offenses or for all offenses in specific places' (Sherman, 1990: 1). Crackdowns are usually implemented for a comparatively short period of time, during which, as Sherman shows, they invariably have the have the effect of reducing offending. However, they do not last. The initial deterrent effect erodes as time passes, as enthusiasm wanes, as

Table 5.1 Police strategies for crime reduction

Strategy	Underlying hypothesis	Summary of research implications about the underlying hypothesis
1. Increase the numbers of police	The more police a city employs, the less crime it will have.	Effect of overall numbers is unclear.
2. Random patrol	The more random patrol a city receives, the more a perceived 'omnipresence' of the police will deter crime in public places.	Not effective.
3. Increase the use of police power of arrest	The more arrests police make in response to reported or observed offences of any kind, the less crime there will be.	Effective in some domestic violence situations: counterproductive for juveniles.
4. Contact with the community in general	The greater quantity and better quality of contacts between police and citizens, the less crime.	Not generally effective except where the objective is to increase police 'legitimacy' with the public.
5. Informal contact with children	Informal contact between police and young people will dissuade those likely to offend from doing so.	Not generally effective.
6. Respond quickly to emergency calls	The shorter police travel time from assignment to arrival at a crime scene, the less crime there will be.	Mixed evidence. US research finds it ineffective, but indications from UK work are that it may yield a marginal improvement in clear-ups for burglary.

7. Target high profile crime or criminals	The higher the police-initiated arrest rate for high-risk offenders and offences, the lower the rate of serious or violent crime.	Targeting repeat offenders appears to be worthwhile, but targeting drugs markets is less effective.
8. Directed patrol	The more precisely patrol presence is concentrated at the 'hot spots' and 'hot times' of criminal activity, the less crime there will be in those places and times.	US evidence is that this is an effective strategy for dealing with local problems.
9. Targeting repeat victims	Crime can be reduced by protecting victims from further crime.	UK research indicates that this can effect a significant reduction in certain types of crime.
10. Inter-agency working	The police can prevent crime by working in partnership with, or providing crime-related information to, other agencies, mainly local authorities but, with the intention of informing the national effort to reduce crime, perhaps also the DETR, DfEE, Probation Service, etc.	UK evidence is that this can be a very useful mode of working for the police.
11. Problem-oriented policing	If police can identify specific patterns of crime and analyse the underlying problems in the community, they are more likely to come up with solutions that reduce the number of criminal incidents.	The main tenet of this rational approach has been tested on a small scale, but formal evaluation of the impact of crime in a wider implementation is awaited.

(Reproduced with the authority of HMSO.)

organisational constraints set in and as prolific new offenders take over. Because offender perceptions of risk are heightened not only during the crackdown but beyond, a further residual deterrence is also evident which lasts for about one-third of the length of the crackdown (Sherman, 1990; Wright, 1994). The transience of the effects of crackdowns is no reason to forgo the respite they afford, however temporary. Wright and Pease (1997) therefore proposed the use of crackdowns as the first part of a cycle of change, while recognising that they are transient, vulnerable to criticism and more concerned with thief-taking than with community protection. Wright and Pease (1997) proposed the use of an iterative crime reduction strategy, using a 'crackdown–consolidation' cycle. If the initial crackdown was successful in reducing crime to the target level (as the evidence showed it could be) and this level did not again start to rise, then a variety of consolidating community-based measures would be put into place to keep it there. If crime levels again started to rise, police would repeat the crackdown–consolidation cycle until they achieved the planned target crime levels. In implementing such a strategy, publicity is as important as police action. As Sherman (1990) found, because offender perception of risk is the basis of the crackdown principle, keeping potential offenders guessing may help to keep them honest. Action by other agencies and the community is also crucial to the consolidation of the gains.

Although this approach has not yet been subject to large-scale evaluation, police have successfully used the crackdown approach on many occasions (Sherman, 1990). Of the occasions on which it has been evaluated, police used it successfully to target prolific burglars at Toller Lane in the West Yorkshire Police area (Pease, 1998). Pease also reports a markedly successful crackdown–consolidation cycle at Boggart Hill in the same police area. There, burglaries per household dropped by 62 per cent over the period of the research (Pease, 1998: 41; Farrell et al., 1997: 5). Of course, these are not 'quick-fix' methodologies but painstaking, focused and highly intensive local strategies where a number of agencies work together. They are more than a reworking of zero-tolerance policing. So far, this idea has not been extensively debated. With the exception of Waddington's concession of the possible application of Sherman's crackdown thesis to designated areas relating to terrorism, the work of the sceptical criminologists discussed above does not mention this approach (Waddington, 1996: 17; see also Johnston, 2000: 40). Given the obvious political agenda, that the *cognoscenti* choose to ignore this form of strategic crime risk management is not surprising. However, unless other agencies and citizens are involved with the police in the management of crime risk, it will simply remain a form of 'police property'. A more inclusive model would clearly require more public participation and partnership with other agencies.

Partnership and participation

It is difficult to identify precisely when the debate on policing and crime prevention first used the concepts of participation and partnership. Participation, in the sense in which we use it here, refers to the question of whether the public has an obligation or an opportunity to take part in the management of crime risk. Partnership refers to a purposeful relationship between the police and the public or between the police and other agencies in this field. The debate on policing does not appear to have mentioned either concept until the rise of community policing in the early 1980s. They did not merit a mention in Sir Robert Mark's auto-biography (Mark, 1978). From the early 1980s, however, the idea that the police could no longer tackle crime alone became something more than a slogan. Alderson (1979) sets out the principles that form the basis of community policing. These focus on the priorities of local communities in peacekeeping and in crime prevention. Most police forces in the UK adopted these themes during the early to mid-1980s. However, civil unrest and other factors adversely affected the ability of the police to achieve progress in this direction. The 1984 miners' strike, continued inner-city unrest and pressures upon police resources from rising crime meant that they were often only able to meet current demands.

Despite these problems, the Home Office continued to encourage the police and other agencies to cooperate. The Home Office promoted a number of initiatives during the 1980s. These included the formation of the Home Office Crime Prevention Unit (1983). Home Office Circular 8/84 encouraged all agencies to get involved in crime prevention (Home Office 1984). They supported the launch of Crime Concern in 1988. From 1988 onwards, the government supported the development of the Safer Cities initiative. This was especially the case in cities which were in need of regeneration and therefore likely to be subject to social unrest. The government provided central funding for these schemes but also insisted on parallel local funding. The details of the initiatives varied from city to city. No specific strategy was identifiable and there was no fully self-sustaining structure in place to develop one or to take it forward (Tilley, 1992: 35). However, the involvement of police, local government, and other statutory and voluntary agencies in a form of partnership was a common factor in each scheme. The fourth Safer Cities Annual Progress report argued that the partnership approach was a sound basis for generating effective community safety and crime prevention work (Home Office, 1993c). Home Office research also identified the reasons for success or failure in particular initiatives under the programme. These included studies of efforts to reduce motor vehicle crime, to combat crime against small business and to reduce the incidence of burglary (Tilley, 1993b, 1993c; Tilley and Webb, 1994).

The Home Office continued to encourage the trend by proposing a more coordinated approach to partnership in the early 1990s. Home Office Circular 44/90 set out a number of examples of successful partnerships. It invited police, local government, probation services, fire services, social services and education to consider ways in which the good practice identified in these examples could be taken forward. In 1991, the Independent Working Group of the Standing Conference on Crime Prevention presented its report (the Morgan Report – Home Office, 1991). It made proposals for the generation of safer communities and for local delivery of crime prevention. This report fully supported the partnership approach. It also argued for a lead agency to coordinate efforts. It suggested that a cohesive local structure should be set up, with full-time coordination. It maintained that this should relate to the local democratic structure and should therefore be statutory. According to the report:

> … in the longer term the local authorities, working in conjunction with the police should have a clear statutory responsibility for the development and stimulation of community safety and crime prevention programmes, and for progressing at a local level a multi-agency approach to community safety.
>
> (Home Office, 1991: 29)

As Gilling (1997) suggests, the government had its hopes dashed if they simply wanted a technical report from the independent working group (Gilling, 1997: 98). In the event, however, they rejected much of the report. Cost undoubtedly was also a factor in the decision. The fact that both the Labour Party and local authority associations had lobbied for a statutory role for local authorities, and the longer-term Conservative policy of limiting their functions, also meant that the Morgan proposals were ripe for rejection.

Despite this rejection, the Conservative government continued to give general support to the principles of partnership. In their research on the subject, however, Liddle and Gelsthorpe (1994a, 1994b, 1994c) found that there were continued difficulties in working in partnerships. These included problems of structure and coordination, and of lack of leadership and evaluative insight. As a result, partnerships were only making patchy progress. They also noted that the police continued to play a central role in multi-agency crime prevention work. However, they also found that the police did not have their effort evenly distributed across all force areas. While partnership principles were finding increasing acceptance, there was still a degree of scepticism among the police about the benefits. Liddle and Gelsthorpe (1994) also reopened the key issue that Morgan had identified, namely, the question of whether a lead agency would be preferable to a more corporate approach.

The change of government in 1997 enabled New Labour to reverse the decision that the Conservatives had taken on the Morgan Report. The Crime and Disorder Act 1998 for the first time placed the coordination of community safety and crime prevention on a statutory basis. Section 5 of the Act makes local authorities and chief police officers the 'responsible authorities' for setting and implementing strategies aimed at achieving a reduction in crime. The Act expects them to do this with the cooperation of local probation and health services. To help set strategic priorities, section 6 of the Act provides a statutory requirement for an audit of local crime and disorder. The intention is that the provision of baseline data will lay the foundation for future monitoring and evaluation. It will also promote ownership of the outcomes among the partners (Hough and Tilley, 1998). The implication for police primacy in dealing with crime and crime prevention is significant. According to Loveday (2000):

> By its introduction, the legislation ends the traditional police monopoly of responsibility for crime control within the local authority area. Under provisions within this Act this is now a responsibility shared with the local authority.
>
> (Loveday, 2000: 224)

Loveday (2000) also points out the implication for Local Police Authorities who are responsible for the setting of local policing plans. In many places, the local crime reduction strategy has totally eclipsed them. Giving a statutory responsibility of this kind to local authorities will substantially increase their policing role in the wider sense of that term. The Act also affects the independence of chief police officers in the direction and control of their force. Local political control of operational policing now seems more likely than at any time since the 1980s, when local authorities in London (GLC), Liverpool and Derbyshire tried to gain control.

At the time of writing, whether this will be the ultimate effect is uncertain. Partnerships have carried out much of the initial audit and objective-setting in most local authority areas. As yet, however, there is no consolidated evaluation of the implementation of the Act. Partnerships may have their benefits. In general, however, we are entitled to be sceptical. This is especially the case where crime is again beginning to rise. Sceptics may also be less than sanguine about the inertia implied by bureaucratic committee-defined strategies and whether they are likely to lead to effective action on the ground. The limits of cooperation revealed in the Safer Cities initiative and in other projects under Single Regeneration Budget funding should warn us against too much optimism. Statutory intervention alone is unlikely to provide long-term solutions to crime reduction.

The participation of the public in schemes aimed at the reduction of crime has also been difficult to stimulate. This is so despite the fact that the mobilisation of active citizens has been the goal of both Conservative and New Labour neo-liberalism. These problems were evident in neighbourhood watch and other schemes that were introduced as part of Conservative crime reduction policies from 1982 (Brake and Hale, 1992). The extent to which these have been successful as a measure for dealing with crime-risk continues to be controversial. According to Gilling (1997):

> There may be good grounds for suspecting that, beyond the erection of signs and placement of stickers in windows, a large proportion of schemes are in fact dormant, if not entirely lifeless. In theory, however, among other objectives, Neighbourhood Watch is intended to prevent crime both by enhancing surveillance and other opportunity reducing measures, and by building or exploiting other informal social controls, essentially a combination of situation and social crime prevention. In practice, neither objective may be realized as the implementation of the idea falls short of the ideal that accompanies its enthusiastic promotion.
>
> (Gilling, 1997: 143–4)

Watch systems may provide some benefits, such as giving the police more opportunities for intelligence-gathering. However, they have certainly had difficulty in maintaining their momentum without a considerable input from the police or other agencies. They have failed to become free-standing mechanisms for crime reduction. Consequently, these schemes have either failed or have remained within the ambit of 'police property'. Only rarely have citizens genuinely taken ownership of them.

New Labour's crime reduction strategies have so far been visible mainly in the development of agency partnerships. In general, there has not been a widespread development of active citizenship to confront risk, except in popular action on some housing estates to register disapproval about drugs misuse or about paedophiles who are resident there. Indeed, the very need to provide legislation to compel institutional partners to do what they had hitherto been unwilling to do voluntarily does not augur well for citizen involvement at the individual level. The general apathy for local politics exemplified in the extremely low turnout of voters in local elections should also caution against high expectations in this respect. Despite the reality of public apathy, we can find plenty of theoretical support for public participation. We find it in the idea that drives much social-democratic thinking in late modernity, namely in the notion of an emancipatory politics. For Giddens (1991), who has been influential in New Labour policy thinking:

> Liberty is to be achieved through the progressive emancipation of the individual, in conjunction with the liberal state, rather than through the projected process of revolutionary upheaval. … Emancipatory politics makes primary the imperatives of justice, equality and participation.
>
> (Giddens, 1991: 210–12)

For Giddens, emancipatory politics removes oppressive forms of power relationships and empowers citizens to deal with the problems of risk and justice. However, risks and their consequences are unavoidable in the conditions of late modernity. Giddens maintains that:

> The notion of risk becomes central in a society which is taking leave of the past, of traditional ways of doing things, and which is opening itself up for a problematic future.
>
> (Giddens, 1991: 111)

But who should deal with risks? For Giddens, reverting back to the comfort of traditional ways of thinking (which would include the idea that it is the police that deal with crime) is not a viable option. The answer is that active citizens will need to deal with risks, including, presumably, the risk of crime. For Giddens, therefore, active participation is ultimately necessary to enable citizens to confront risks and their consequences. It is a form of self-therapy, but one that also questions the ability of professionals to deliver the service.

Where is the evidence of such public participation? So far there is little sign of a widespread public acceptance of such a doctrine. To be sure, single-issue pressure groups are increasing. There is also an unprecedented amount of civil litigation against public sector organisations for negligence in the delivery of their services. However, this is far from using active citizen participation to provide any kind of replacement for the external delivery of services. In this sense, the kind of emancipatory politics proposed by Giddens seems utopian. The role of neo-liberalism in cutting the cables that anchored people and societies in culture, tradition and history has added to the feeling of being adrift with little hope of a satisfactory landfall. As Beiner (1992) suggests, 'If modern experience of citizenship is largely incoherent, liberal theory … tends to reflect this coherence rather than to help resolve it' (Beiner, 1992: 116). As a result, the very idea of citizenship has been fractured. All too often, all we have in relation to dealing with risk are the experiences of consumers of commercial products or the dissatisfied 'customers' of beleaguered public institutions. It is hardly surprising that many citizens regard themselves as trapped between the predatory extremes of global commerce on the one hand and public sector incompetence on the other. We can find few answers to this in any significant differences between Conservative and New Labour law and order policies. Both have retained strong disciplinary measures for dealing with offenders. Both have been highly interventionist for the purpose of managing crime risk. Both have adopted the rhetoric of active citizenship as a means of combating crime.

Despite the fact that the Crime and Disorder Act 1998 has now placed it on a statutory basis, the partnership approach continues to have a chequered career. Its promotion by the police themselves during the early 1980s was not altruistic. The need for cost-reduction in the face of cash limits was one part of its rationale. Spreading responsibility to other agencies and to the public to ease demands upon police was another. These were imperatives, both in terms of public perceptions of police effectiveness and the effects of rising crime, which was then starting to be overwhelming. Of course, the partnership idea was also in line with other developments in governance under the then Conservative administration. The development of Regional Government Offices decanted some power away from the central ministries. The drive to roll back the boundaries of the state claimed to promote the responsibility of citizens for self-protection. To a great extent, New Labour has continued this myth. Only the institutional mix has changed.

The extension of policing beyond the public police recognises the importance of developing broadly based institutions capable of managing risk in late modernity. It also supports the idea that has been central to this book, namely that citizens stand in a reciprocal relationship with policing in each of the key modes of policing practice. In this sense, Young (1999) is right to claim that citizenship is a relationship:

… of reciprocity between all citizens which fully recognises the necessity of reciprocity between citizen and state in the enactment of social goals and institutional change.

(Young, 1999: 199)

The management of risk, therefore, is not limited to the kind of self-therapy that Giddens (1991) seems to support. However, an inclusive form of citizen participation is still important in the sense that it contributes to the partnership between the public and the institutions that are involved in promoting community safety and crime reduction. An emphasis on wide participation also recognises the diversity of risk perceptions of the kind argued by Douglas (1992) and others. The relevant social goal is that citizens can live in safety and security. Of course, this still leaves unanswered the question of whether the Crime and Disorder Act 1998 is about political control or about effectiveness in risk management. Of course it could be about both, but without a more clearly defined debate to reveal government strategies for the future of policing, the jury is still out.

Chapter 6

Policing as community justice

This chapter discusses the promotion of community justice as a mode of policing practice. In particular, it compares the use of authoritative intervention by means of law enforcement with the role of the police alongside other parties in negotiating justice in diverse communities. First, it discusses the implications of different models of justice, law enforcement and social control. It examines three models of justice, namely the retributive, the consequentialist and the restorative. It assesses the implications of these models for policing. It explores the relationship between social control and justice in the light of the discussion of the problems of crime control in earlier chapters. Secondly, this chapter examines the concept of community, suggesting that we need to re-evaluate the term in the light of debates about individualism and cultural diversity. Building on these distinctions, it explores the idea of community justice, suggesting that it is associated with the ideas of fairness and communication. Thirdly, it begins to explore questions about the kinds of policing which might be most appropriate to the delivery of community justice. Here, it addresses the question of whether the 'professional' (expert) model of policing is sustainable in this regard. It also examines the so-called 'service ethos' of British policing in the light of the fact that the police continue to be heavily involved in traditional enforcement activity.

The fourth section extends this debate to develop a critique of community policing, which we briefly introduced in Chapter 5 in the context of the management of risk. This section also puts forward a critique of the conception of social control that community policing would require if we were to regard it as a sustainable mode of policing practice. The final section discusses the policing of communities that consist of a variety of cultures. This includes an examination of the tension between the need for an impartial and universal application of law and the ever-increasing pressures to meet the needs of diverse communities. It draws contrasts between the policing styles that may be appropriate to these differences. It concludes that the key activity of this mode of policing practice is communication and negotiation under conditions of fairness. The arguments reflect the transition from law enforcement to community justice that was introduced in Figure 2.1 in Chapter 2. It will be suggested that security in communities is more likely to be ensured by effective normative measures designed to reduce offending than by the un-reflective and routine use of enforcement controlling deviance in individual offenders.

Justice, law enforcement and social control

Although it is tempting to discuss concepts such as community policing from the outset, there is a need first to clarify the background to the concept in the light of theories of justice and social control. Again, as was the case with crime prevention and community safety, this is not an exhaustive account of these theories. We introduce the contrast between retributive, consequentialist and restorative approaches to justice here primarily to locate the concepts that are crucial to this present work within their wider context. Community justice may have more to do with normative social control than with the disciplinary approach. For this reason, we need to evaluate the connection between justice, law enforcement and social control in the context of the conceptual models that configure them.

The notion of retributive justice has a long history in western political and legal thought. It is primarily associated with conservative theorists who emphasise that there is a strong connection between the rights and the obligations of citizens. For Hegel (1770–1831), for example, there are logical connections between our use of reason and what we must expect from a system of justice. Reason both explains the crime and establishes the justification for its punishment. According to Hegel, unless there are circumstances that demonstrate that the action was not voluntary, committing a crime is the action of a rational being. As such, in acting to commit the crime itself, the criminal also wills his own punishment. Punishment, therefore, is a right. Far from being an externalised im-position, retributive justice provides the 'annulment of the crime' and serves to confirm the ultimate freedom and autonomy of the criminal

(Hegel, in Knox, 1952: 70–1). Similarly, for Bradley (1846–1924) retributive justice establishes that crime is not a disease to be treated but a reassertion of rights. He says:

> Punishment is the denial of wrong by the assertion of right, and the wrong exists in the self, or will, of the criminal.
>
> (Bradley, 1927: 27)

For Hegel and Bradley and for retributivists generally, a failure to punish is degrading both of the individual and of the human condition in general because it does not respect the autonomy of the perpetrator.

The logic of the retributive theory of justice also implies the idea of 'just deserts', namely that offenders should get what they deserve proportionate to the gravity of the offence. The crime control model that we discussed in Chapter 4 has strong connections with this theory of justice. As Skolnick (1966) argues, we may think of professional police officers as 'craftsmen' who emphasise their own expertness in the field of crime and criminal justice. As expert craftsmen they suppose that they have the ability to distinguish between guilt and innocence (Skolnick, 1966: 196–7). For this reason, they focus on trying to control crime rather than simply carrying out law enforcement according to due process principles. Where they do take law enforcement action, however, there is a direct connection with punishment as 'just deserts'. Skolnick's 'craftsmen' in this sense, are logical retributivists. Indeed, for some police officers, the dislocation of their belief in the connection between law enforcement, guilt and just deserts is a primary cause of 'noble cause corruption'. It appears equally, as we have already discussed, in erroneous assumptions about the magisterial role of the police. It appears as much in the reality of the Harry Challoner case as in that which is represented by the fictional 'Dirty Harry' Callaghan. For a compelling analysis of the so-called 'Dirty Harry' syndrome, see Klockars (1980). Readers interested in pursuing the arguments for and against the concept of 'just deserts' should refer to von Hirsch (1969) or to Sher (1987).

In contrast, liberal social theory provides the basis for consequentialist theories of justice. For example, we can find extensive arguments for the consequentialist theory of justice in John Stuart Mill's *Utilitarianism*. (Mill, 1861: 43–67). Consequentialists believe that we can justify punishment only if good ends are the result. For utilitarians, such punishment should tend to promote the greatest good of the greatest number of people. Criminal justice may achieve this in various ways: by social rehabilitation of the offender, by absence of further offending or redress of the victims' rights. However, opponents of consequentialism argue that it is not possible to tell in advance whether or not good ends will result. Retributivist claims against consequentialism argue that treatment-based sentencing often does not work. In cases where it does not recognise the autonomy of the offender, it is definitively unjust. Positive retributivists believe that the system should punish the guilty, even if this does not achieve good consequences. Negative retributivists make some concessions to consequentialism in suggesting that the system should only punish the guilty if their punishment will benefit them. However, neither form of retributivism can say why punishment itself is justified.

Not all police work is retributivist. Their involvement in schemes that try to divert young offenders from crime exemplifies consequentialist thinking within the police. In such cases, the police undoubtedly have a role in this kind of work, albeit one that may be distinctly secondary to that of the Probation Service or social workers. In some areas, police are not only concerned with retributive applications of justice but are increasingly involved in so-called 'restorative justice' programmes. Such programmes define an offence in terms of its moral, social, economic and political context and consequences. The criminal justice system invokes procedures to restore the rights of the victim to the *status quo ante*. Restorative justice removes the stigma of crime by repentance, forgiveness and restitution, rather than simply by punishment. In this way, it focuses on the fact that the offending has caused harm, not only on the breaking of laws (Williamson, 1996: 37–8). For Nicholl (2001), this is an important distinction that opens up possibilities for a new form of local policing and community justice. It builds upon the confirmation and restoration of rights. It does not simply ensure punishment for their violation. She says:

> A restorative understanding of justice explains that the victim, offender, and the community, all have crucial roles to play in establishing justice. While the criminal justice process is authoritarian, technical and impersonal – focusing on blame and guilt – restorative justice offers more participatory arrangements – focused upon needs and obligations. The processes under the new model encourage victims and offenders to understand each other, and require the offender to take responsibility.
>
> (Nicholl, 2001: 7)

In effect, these principles are an extension of the so-called 'republican theory' of criminal justice. According to White and Haines (1996: 172–90), this endorses the idea that offenders are responsible for their actions.

However, it also holds that the response to those actions should be constructive. It is 'republican theory' because it restores the 'personal dominion' of both victim and offender through both symbolic and substantive measures. These include restitution, compensation and reparation in recognition of harm. It may also include the reassertion of victims' and community rights through so-called 'reintegrative shaming' (Braithwaite, 1989; Braithwaite and Pettit, 1990).

As discussed in Chapters 3–5, police are involved in many interventions where they act as gatekeepers to the criminal justice system. However, the extent of social control implied by this form of professional law enforcement is problematic. If it is effective, it demonstrates an authoritarian influence. If it is ineffective, it fails to support the rights of individual victims. Either way, we need to question the extent to which crime control through law enforcement and punishment alone can provide a satisfactory account of the role of policing (especially the public police) in promoting justice in communities. Garland (1996), for example, highlights the predicaments that rising crime rates have created for governments in Britain and elsewhere. In pursuing the myth of sovereign crime control, states have reverted to punitive strategies (which are easier to deliver), rather than sacrificing their economic or social objectives. The result, according to Garland, is an ever more divisive and exclusionary project of 'punishment and police', which reiterates the flawed control policies initiated during the nineteenth century. It is the very failure of this approach that shows the extent to which sovereign states are limited in their ability to control crime.

This does not mean, however, that all forms of social control are irrelevant. For Cohen (1985, 1994: 67–9), criminal justice has been characterised by its use of four distinct styles of social control: firstly, the punitive style, which is coercive rather than voluntary; secondly, the compensatory style, which leads to the repayment of a debt by the offender; thirdly, the conciliatory style, which implies that the parties work together to negotiate a mutually acceptable outcome; and fourthly, the therapeutic style, which is aimed to help change the personality of the deviant. Generally, however, each of these strategies leaves untouched the normative social conditions within which the crime took place.

For Hirschi (1969), it is the extent of the social bonds that tie an individual to society that determines whether or not he or she will follow society's rules and values. These social bonds consist of attachments, commitments, involvement and beliefs. They determine whether people (the young in particular) will uphold social values or follow the paths of crime and anti-social behaviour. However, recent trends in promoting justice by means of increasing social control have tended to expand and to intensify their disciplinary dimensions. For Cohen (1994), these include the expansion of agency roles. There has been a 'dispersal of discipline' to a number of agencies. This has led to the broadening of professional knowledge and power. Risk management, control of populations and privatisation have all played a part. For these reasons, Cohen remains sceptical about the critical discourse that surrounds this debate. As a result, he is reluctant to recommend one particular form of social control rather than another. However, he points to the need to establish successful social control at both the instrumental and the normative levels.

On the one hand, instrumental social control measures are able to communicate the ability of the community to impose sanctions, to give rewards and to increase the 'interactional costs' of crime. In doing so, they can change the behaviour of potential deviants. The increased focus on the treatment of offenders in the community reflects this tendency (Vennard and Hedderman, 1998: 103). The so-called 'new penology' provides similar means of social control through structural measures. According to Feeley and Simon (1992):

> ... community based sanctions can be understood in terms of risk-management rather than rehabilitative or correctional aspirations. Rather than instruments of reintegrating offenders into the community, they function as mechanisms to maintain control, often through frequent drug testing, over low-risk offenders for whom more secure forms of custody are judged too expensive or unnecessary.
>
> (Feeley and Simon, 1992, in Muncie *et al.*, 1996: 372)

This includes forms of social management such as incapacitation, tagging and surveillance in and by the community. Similar ideas seem to underlie the extension of the use of the youth curfew in the UK. If they are to work, these measures need a high degree of community or parental co-operation. Cohen claims that these preventive control systems are most effective within small, closely knit and homogeneous groups. They are part of the community in the microcosm. However, they do not simply rely upon enforcement by a 'professional' institution, such as the police.

On the other hand, normative social controls affect the very nature of the community itself. Normative controls apply as much to the agencies involved in 'policing beyond the police' in the field of community justice as to the police themselves. He says:

By 'normative success' I mean the extent to which social control generates a symbolic arena in which value choices can be clarified. The criteria here are oriented to means rather than ends. Or the ends themselves – social justice democracy, human rights – are themselves subject to normative rather than empirical evaluation.

(Cohen, 1994: 84–5).

Cohen clarifies the kinds of issues that are involved. They include methods that result in social integration rather than exclusion. They are concerned with means that develop active citizen participation rather than the provision of services. They include measures that reduce the power of professional and bureaucratic monopolies. They are concerned with the promotion of human rights and with measures that provide for accountability and democracy in participating agencies.

Of course, this leaves a number of important questions unanswered. To what extent should the pursuit of community justice involve activity by policing agencies? What role should policing have in developing the normative side of social control? How does policing stand in relation to the promotion of active citizenship? These questions are particularly problematic in the light of public attitudes to the role of the public police in peacekeeping, crime investigation and the management of risk discussed in Chapters 3–5. However, before addressing these important questions, it is necessary to examine the concept that may be overlooked in debates on justice and social control, namely the idea of community and its implications for justice.

Deconstructing community

The concept of community is as important to the idea of community justice as is the idea of justice itself. As we have seen, individualism has played an important part in the development of neo-liberal theories of crime and justice. For some thinkers, the idea of community provides an antidote to the more extreme consequences of individualism. While continuing to speak from a liberal perspective, in the sense that he wishes to limit the role of the state, Etzioni has been a leading proponent of the communitarian thesis as an alternative to individualism. He argues that only a community-based approach can provide the moral ground for social and political justice (see Etzioni, 1995). However, such claims assume a high degree of cohesion within and between communities. Clearly, this is not always the case. The values and interests of some communities can be in conflict with others and with wider affiliations and obligations. The existence of different cultures, sub-cultures and modes of association inevitably produces problems for the notion of community. These problems derive from the variety of social, political, economic and aesthetic values held by different groups. In this sense, the very concept of community itself is intensely problematic. Because of discontinuities in the range and scope of the term, we should no longer think of it as denoting a single, homogeneous entity.

There are a number of reasons why we should now regard the term 'community' as essentially non-homogeneous. First, the increased mobility of populations has put increased pressure upon community cohesion. This is not new. It was also the case in Britain during the migration from the countryside to the cities during the Industrial Revolution. Indeed, the later tendency to restabilise into more heterogeneous local 'communities' may have been one of the factors why modern policing appears to have had a 'golden age' until the 1950s. In late modernity, however, there has again been a tendency for comparatively large groups of people to move from one area or from one state to another for economic or political reasons. This has often led to difficulties of integration into a host community. This can be observed for example, in negative indigenous attitudes to Turkish and other *Gastarbeiter* in some parts of Germany and to people of Afro-Caribbean, Arab or Asian origin in Britain, France and elsewhere. This militates against the formation of large-scale cohesive communities that are nationally or regionally defined. Increased individualism on the one hand and the diversity of cultures on the other have led to a less homogeneous social mixture. In the short to medium term at least, the 'mixing bowl' metaphor does not describe the reality. The idea that societies now consist of comparative strangers is not simply a matter of geographical distribution. It is also a matter of social disconnection. As Bauman (1993) argues:

> The massive entry of strangers into the living space has rendered the pre-modern mechanisms of social spacing obsolete – but above all woefully inadequate.
>
> (Bauman, 1993: 159)

In the social conditions of late modernity, this is simply the inevitable product of the increased mobility of people and the globalisation of the commerce and information. As a result, there is no possibility of a 'miraculous triumph of communal togetherness'. Indeed, in highly developed pluralist societies such as Britain, for the most part it may be increasingly difficult to identify communities at all. Although people always live somewhere, place is not necessarily defining of the community to which they belong.

To claim that the term community is problematic is not equivalent to denying the existence of society, which was famously associated with Thatcherite thinking. The term 'community' implies some degree of cohesion and shared purposes and values, whereas 'society' is a universal general name of a more amorphous entity. The reality of social and geographical dispersion shows that we should not use the term 'community' as a synonym for 'society'. For example, in British and Dutch 'society', there are Chinese communities that have closer social links with similar communities elsewhere in the world than with other communities in the host countries. Communities from the Jewish and Moslem diaspora have links that define their communities in ways that may be stronger than residence or domicile. The Roma of Eastern and Central Europe have links which cross national boundaries. Unless representative associations are taken as the key channel to communities (which would perhaps be a more democratic approach) there is a need to define communities on grounds which are not necessarily spatial.

Identification of the range and scope of a community is required, if it is to be the focus of 'community justice'. However, the lack of social network analysis often means that there are no effective tools through which public services can plan to meet exact community needs. Indeed, in the field of policing there is a danger that such systematic analysis might produce a degree of antagonism from members of the 'communities' themselves. This is particularly the case if they suspect that it is serving the ends of state security or a dominant political, ethnic or religious group. In a general sense, therefore, mobility and social fragmentation of populations blur the extent to which we can simply define communities by where they are located. Despite this, we often talk as though they we could define them according to agreed administrative boundaries. For example, we may talk about the community in Portsmouth, or in Notting Hill, or in Moss Side, Manchester without considering the wide range of cultures that these areas include. However, it is difficult to see how community justice can work effectively if doubtful geographical criteria or administrative convenience are the primary basis of our definition of community.

The distinction between wider society and 'community' also provides a problem in determining the range and scope of the administration of justice. On the one hand, justice in liberal democracies seems to imply an impartial approach based upon the rule of law and its universal application. On the other hand, community justice seems to imply a diffusion of power so that both judicial decision and social action can serve particular communities with particular needs. How is this apparent dilemma to be resolved? There are three arguments that might serve to clarify the problem, namely those derived from globalisation, from contract and consent and from the concept of fairness.

Arguments for cultural relativism seem to imply that cultures have their own logic and values. These help to define the boundaries between one culture and another. According to this view, we can establish no universal principles that apply across a range of cultures. Each culture or (where they can be empirically identified, community) has its own set of values which order its actions and render it internally consistent (Winch, 1958). In late modernity, however, especially where there is a diversity of cultures in the developed countries, there are some logical connections. According to Eriksen (1997), the globalisation of commerce and com-munication mean that cultures have some goals and benefits that are common. For this reason, it is intellectually and morally indefensible to seek refuge in the fiction of assuming that cultures are isolated and committed to their 'proper logic' (see Eriksen, 1997: 49–53). If this is true, multiculturalism is both universal and diversified in its very nature. The danger in policing is that this ambivalence is not recognised. The police may simply be serving the dominant culture.

Liberal democracy recognises that there are tensions between the obligations of citizens to the law and their cultural preferences. Its response is to use the idea of a contract between citizens and state as the means to resolve them. Taking benefit from common 'goods' entails a tacit acceptance of contract (Locke, 1690). Alderson (1998) emphasises the need for principled policing based upon such a contract. Here, the universal principles of human rights provide the key driver for an ethical approach for police in handling disputes and disorder, including those involving conflicts with the authority of the state. For Alderson, the solution to the problem of operationalising universal rights is in the application of ethical principles. The ideal is a just police working in a just society. The use of coercion is authorised only in cases where it is necessary to protect the rights of others. Such action is justified only within the rule of law, which is itself a universal principle (Alderson, 1998: 29–35). The primary strategy for a professional police, therefore, should be the impartial application of the rule of law within universal principles of human rights. In the case of Europe, this refers to the rights specified in the European Convention on Human Rights and in domestic law where it is compatible with those rights. This implies a need for fairness in the application of the law, regardless of cultural, racial or ethnic background. In this way, the contractarian theory of justice provides a principle that enables the system of justice to achieve cohesion and to overcome partiality.

Contract, however, only provides a starting point for justice. Society consists of groups and individuals from different cultures who have different characteristics and ways of life. Contract, therefore, cannot explain how a system of justice can deal equally with people who are unequal in some ways (for example, in property, education, health or life chances). This applies to criminal justice as much as to justice in terms of the distribution of social goods. Rawls (1972) argues for a principle of justice as fairness that asserts higher order procedural principles to resolve this problem. Fairness, in the sense that Rawls intends it, does not simply mean impartiality or equality of distribution. For Rawls, it is first necessary to agree the principles of justice so that the procedures will be fair and just. We derive these fair procedures from what he calls the 'original position'. The nature of the original position is such that it disregards all the differences between individuals, cultures and communities (Rawls, 1972: 17–22). Rawls proposes a logical device whereby the principles of justice are those chosen by a rational agent situated behind a so-called 'veil of ignorance'. Of these rational decision-makers, he says:

> They do not know how the various alternatives will affect their own particular case and they are obliged to evaluate principles solely on the basis of general considerations. It is assumed, then, that the parties do not know certain kinds of particular facts. First of all, no one knows his place in society, his class position or social status; nor does he know his fortune in the distribution of natural assets and abilities.
>
> (Rawls, 1972: 136–7)

From such a position it is rational to maintain that each person should have an equal right to the most extensive basic liberty compatible with a similar liberty for others. Citizens of a just society, therefore, have the same basic rights. In this way, we can make decisions which are fair but which also respect, and in some cases ameliorate, the differences between citizens.

Although Rawls' proposals for treating unequals equally provides a framework for fairness that seeks to overcome cultural or positional characteristics, it has not been without its critics. From a libertarian perspective, Nozick (1974: 160) has argued that Rawls procedures are not appropriate because (historically) entitlements to social and cultural goods are what they are. No amount of logical sleight-of-hand can 'bracket off' this fact. People have rights to what they have and what they are which the state should not seek to remove. For Nozick (1974) and for liberal thinkers generally, any single goal or set of social goods does not determine the good society. Rather, it is a 'framework of rights or liberties or duties within which people may pursue their separate ends, individually or in voluntary association' (Kukathas and Pettit, 1990: 93).

Theorists arguing from a communitarian perspective have also objected to Rawls' theory of justice. For Walzer (1983), it is always unjust to override the rights implied in the substantive way of life adopted by a community. The conversation about justice can only take place within the context of social meaning, not universal principle (Walzer, 1983: 313–14). Similarly, for MacIntyre (1985), justice is a matter of establishing the common good. It is also about respecting the ends of particular communities, not simply responding to universal ethical or legal principles. For these reasons society cannot reach moral consensus. The '… rival and disparate concepts of justice, and the moral resources of the culture allow us no away of settling the issue between them rationally' (MacIntyre, 1985: 252).

If this is correct, we cannot subsume the idea of community justice under any particular moral principle. Disputes and value conflicts will continue to arise within and between communities. If this is the case, what sort of policing is appropriate to community justice? Are the professional police worth saving in this respect? Does professional policing remain inexorably linked to the disciplinary modes of social control identified by Cohen? Or is it necessary, as some commentators suggest, to abandon professional (expert) policing altogether and to adopt some form of community policing? Can community policing operate in support of both instrumental and normative social control measures? How can policing meet the needs of the 'communities' it serves? Before discussing these questions and the strategies that might be appropriate to the delivery of community justice, it is necessary to discuss the viability of 'professional' policing in the light of these challenges.

Saving professional policing

In Chapter 1, we suggested that a crisis in policing is to be found in many jurisdictions, indicating a more general and endemic failure to prevent malpractice. Many of these failures relate to particular practices in modern policing, especially to crime control and keeping order. Given the extent of failures of police integrity across the world in the past two or three decades, these problems raise the question, is professional policing worth saving? To get a general sense of the trajectory of this question, we need to assess where the professional police stand in relation to other failures of integrity in public life. Public sector integrity has been one of the most pressing problems of the past decade. There are many examples. In the United Kingdom, the 1996/7 Nolan Committee investigations into standards in public life opened up a range of issues, bringing into question the probity of parliamentarians and ministers (Nolan, 1998). Corruption in the European Union and failures of integrity in high office in the United States indicate the extent of the moral degradation of public life at the very top level. Criminal justice systems have been widely destabilised by malpractice and their reputation and legitimacy have suffered. Police misconduct has led to miscarriages of justice. A more general failure to underpin systems of justice by a moral groundwork to complement the positivistic application of law has brought this about. In both the UK and the US, there is public scepticism about the law and the integrity of lawyers. In the UK, some lawyers have brought the system of fees and legal aid provision into crisis by lack of restraint and excessive charges. Power and greed have devalued the reputation of legal proceedings as much as their failure to promote justice as a search for truth (See Leigh-Kyle, 1998: *passim*; Boon and Levin, 1999: 227).

These challenges to the moral context of public life generally suggest that we should evaluate problems of police integrity against a more wide-spread pattern of failure of public morality and standards. This does not mean that it is wrong to target individual police officers or police organisations as examples of failures of integrity. Nor does it mean that we can explain away police misconduct by the fact that moral dilemmas often affect their work. Because they occupy a unique position in relation to the exercise of the coercive power of the state, they are always likely to be primary candidates for scrutiny and criticism. In fact, the critical debate about the integrity and professionalism of the police has been accelerating in most jurisdictions. Controversies over police corruption and other malpractice from the 1960s onwards in the US and UK have brought the issue of police professionalism more into the public gaze. In the US the Knapp Commission (Knapp, 1972) and the Mollen Commission (1994) reflected the problems of corruption in some parts of the American police. In the UK, a number of inquiries from the Royal Commission on the Police of 1962 to the Macpherson Report (1999) reflect an ever-deepening concern for the way in which professional police conduct should be controlled.

According to Walta *et al.* (1999), we need to question the paradigm of a paid 'professional' police that has predominated since the early nineteenth century. They argue that the relationship between the police and the public has an influence on police integrity and effectiveness. This is not just a matter of the way the police performs its role. The very role that the public police perform is the problem. They argue that a basic change in role is necessary to halt the decline of the reputation of the police, particularly among minority communities. They propose the adoption of a community justice approach to resolve the problems of integrity and ineffectiveness that are endemic in the professional model of policing. Concurring with Bayley (1994), they suggest that a more community-oriented model of policing and justice will help to mobilise community resources.

Is it possible to resist a full-scale change from a professional police to a community police? Or is the latter the only means of resolving the crisis? Would the end of professional policing undermine the system for the impartial administration of criminal justice within the democratic state? In the light of extensive malpractice by some elements of the so-called 'professional' police, some might regard this question with a justifiable degree of scepticism. On the other hand, although there are undoubted failures *in* police professionalism these are not necessarily failures *of* police professionalism. The latter is a much stronger claim. If we were to sustain it, we would need to support it by more than the current spate of failures of police integrity and effectiveness. We would require evidence of a more radical disintegration of the paid, public policing model that has sustained the existence of the professional police since the nineteenth century. Whether there is evidence of this deeper disintegration is still a matter for debate.

Any critique of the professional police needs to take serious account of the lessons of the empirical research. Two things are evident. First, to understand failures of police professionalism we should consider the wider moral, social and political contexts within which the malpractice takes place. The relationship between the police and the public has changed significantly in the past three decades, influencing both the appearance and the reality of policing. There have been shifts in the rhetoric and the substance of personal and organisational responsibility. There have been realignments in the power and status of the police in communities.

Secondly, there have been changes to the very meaning of professionalism. The 'thick' sense of the term often has a pejorative meaning. The so-called 'professional' foul in sports indicates an intention to win at all costs. Professionalism of this kind is also characterised by the oppressive application of power, consolidated by defensive closure and other measures. It shows an intention to ensure autonomy and to survive.

Perhaps the greatest support for the claims that the police are 'professional' in this sense is the extent to which external measures to ensure accountability have often been resisted with a heavy preference for self-regulation. Foucault is the key theorist of this sense of the professional in developing the idea that all professions adopt discourses that consolidate their power (Foucault, 1972). The second, 'thinner' sense of professionalism is that of competence and the achievement of standards. We discussed this in Chapter 4 in the context of criminal investigation. In the UK, perhaps not surprisingly, these two senses of police professionalism have been in conflict.

It is not surprising that there is confusion and ambiguity about police professionalism. The 'thick' sense of professionalism through professional closure has been both encouraged and discouraged. The 1929 Royal Commission on the Police considered that the constable was only acting as any member of the public would act if they had the time and inclination. As such the constable could be personally liable for civil torts. Section 48 of the Police Act 1964 changed this balance. In effect, the Act placed constables into a master-and-servant relationship with chief constables. This was a retrograde step and encouraged closure. For the first time, the law gave the constable effective protection under the umbrella of the police organisation by making the chief constable liable (see Marshall, 1965: 98–9). However, the Human Rights Act 1998 may reverse this effect, especially if constables are held to be 'public authorities' in their own right. This possibility has clearly been in the minds of police officers in the UK. Many have insured against public liability claims to cover this eventuality. In addition to these influences, other factors have consolidated professional closure. These include structural isolation from the community through the ready availability of back-up support through radio communication systems. Professional closure has also been a side effect of the increase of paramilitary policing.

On the other hand, so-called new public management has severely challenged this 'thick' sense of professionalism. The tensions are evident. In health, education, local government, policing and other parts of the public sector, government has increasingly held the professions to account. Measures that have brought this about include financial audit and increased legal and administrative accountability. We will discuss this further in Chapter 7. Apart from barristers, no profession in Britain is now immune from tortious liability. As a result, the 'thinner' sense of professionalism has been encouraged in public sector management. Here, a failure of professionalism is a failure to conform to norms or agreed standards of conduct and performance. It is in this area that difficult dilemmas arise for professional policing. Although as Stephens and Becker (1994) rightly argue, it is possible to conceive of policing as a matrix relationship that represents a symbiosis between 'care' and 'control', there are also unavoidable tensions between them. On the 'care' side of the account, research has identified that the police tend to operate on some occasions as another 'social service' (see Punch and Naylor, 1973; Punch, 1979). On the 'control' side of the account, the disciplinary aspect of policing continues through law enforcement and peacekeeping activities.

In contemporary conditions, however, the extent to which either of these forms of professionalism represents moral commitment to communities is questionable. The thicker sense of professionalism has emphasised the use of power for the maintenance of order and crime control. The thinner sense has led to a crass managerialism. The idea of policing as moral duty, which had at least a residual echo in policing discourse up to the 1960s, is not evident in either model. The implication of this changed context is that a new instrumental paradigm of professional policing has emerged. It is one that sits uncomfortably alongside the concepts of duty and fairness required in policing diverse communities. Although it may still have a role in instrumental social control, it seems unlikely that it can influence normative aspects of social control in communities. As Cohen (1994: 85) argues, sensitivity to both the instrumental and normative aspects of social control are necessary if we are not just to be talking about effectiveness but about justice. The central question for this chapter is to what extent either professional or community policing can contribute to them.

Community policing

If professional policing cannot provide normative social control, can community policing do so? Community policing seems best understood as a range of specific techniques that the police and the public use to work in partnership at a local level. Used in this sense, community policing is a micro-level concept. It is a concrete effort to promote community justice and social control by mobilising social resources within an identifiable group of people.

John Alderson has for many years been an eloquent advocate for community policing. For Alderson, a social contract between police and people provides the basis for community policing (see Alderson, 1979, 1998: 131–2). Community policing is about preventing crime, reducing fear of crime and reinforcing trust in local neighbourhoods. He says:

The community police organisation provides the root for the sound growth of effective policing. The trunk and branches represent more familiar police functions of emergency patrols, public order maintenance and criminal investigation … The public, perceiving that the police care for and respect their own group and culture, are encouraged to – and if given information and trust will – help the police to achieve their goals. It is important that the simple formula of community policing becomes part of the police culture and of their general understanding.

(Alderson, 1998: 132)

He insisted on the importance of these elements in his evidence to the Scarman inquiry (Home Office 1981). He also emphasised the importance of the participation of the public and other agencies in policing decisions. He said:

Community policing requires three elements, Community Police Councils (Consultative Groups), interagency co-operation, and community constables appointed to localities, and this arrangement in turn requires committed leadership and wide dissemination of information to the public at large – a truly participative scheme of things.

(Alderson, 1998: 128)

For Alderson, therefore, community policing is both a principle and a form of policing practice that puts police officers back into the community. It is particularly relevant to local policing. It serves to refocus policing efforts upon the needs of communities rather than on abstract notions of crime control and 'law and order'.

For Bayley (1994), the growth of community policing which was stimulated by pioneering innovators such as Alderson marked a sea change in police thinking. He says:

Community policing represents the most serious and sustained attempt to reformulate the purposes and practices of policing since the development of the 'professional' police model in the early 20th Century.

(Bayley, 1994: 104)

However, he also points to the problems of getting agreement about an exact definition of community policing, despite the huge amount of study to which it has been subjected by scholars and researchers. He also points to differences in opinion among practitioners about its real character. For Bayley, however, the amalgam of experience enables community policing to be defined in terms of a number of characteristic activities. He says:

> When police departments take the challenge of crime prevention seriously enough that they begin to break with the practices of the past, four elements recur again and again: *consultation, adaptation, mobilization and problem solving*. Since nothing can be discussed in policing without using an acronym, I shall refer to the new crime-prevention strategies as CAMPS. Consultation, adaptation, mobilization and problem-solving are what I shall be referring to from now on when I use the phrase 'Community policing'.
>
> (Bayley, 1994:105)

However, in order to recognise its other key characteristics, it is important not to equate it with problem-solving alone, despite the clear importance of the latter concept. Bayley says:

> The phrase 'community policing' has more popular appeal than 'problem-oriented policing'. It sounds less technical and more friendly. On the other hand, 'problem-oriented policing' draws attention to the programmatic implications of policing for improving crime prevention; it concentrates attention on concrete activities that police need to undertake. Since community policing and problem-oriented policing cannot be untangled in practice, I prefer to use the more resonant phrase 'community policing' but to insist that community policing be understood to include problem solving.
>
> (Bayley, 1994: 168)

The strong alignment of community policing with activities associated with crime prevention and the idea that it is a local activity are the cornerstones of Bayley's blueprint for policing. There are three kinds of activity which correlate with three levels of organisational structure. At *Level 1* are neighbourhood police officers who are responsible for local community-based crime prevention. At *Level 2* are basic policing units who are responsible for devising appropriate strategies to accomplish local police objectives. These are miniature police forces but they cannot provide what *Level 3* provides, namely the support, organisation and evaluation resources of the police force itself (see Bayley, 1994: 143–57).

This blueprint provides a rational solution for policing, within their '... unique mission to reduce crime and disorder within particular localities and drawing up plans for the utilization of all community resources' (Bayley, 1994: 161).

In fact, policing in England and Wales has adopted this arrangement, or something very like it, in the relationship between three tiers of policing, namely:

- Sector (geographical) policing;
- Basic Command Units (BCUs);
- Force-level (and Headquarters) resources.

The latter two tiers of this arrangement have been consolidated in Home Office policing policies and in the Audit Commission paper *Best Foot Forward* (Audit Commission 2001). Local policing has become the prime focus for reducing crime and disorder, building upon local partnerships under the Crime and Disorder Act 1998. Crime figures will be published at BCU level and HM Inspectorate of Constabulary will carry out inspections of local BCUs. The importance of local control was emphasised by the Audit Commission, although it was acknowledged that there was sometimes duplication of effort or 'service gaps' between the work of Headquarters and BCUs. It was also acknowledged that geographical variations meant that there is no exact 'blueprint' for all locations. The extent to which these measures will be effective across the whole range of policing practice in the longer term remains to be seen. They also need to be evaluated in the context of the centralising tendency of 'new public management', which is discussed in more detail in Chapter 7.

It questionable, however, whether these predominantly structural measures amount to 'community policing' without a more intensive direct involvement of citizens. Both Alderson and Bayley have been influential in setting out a number of theoretical and practical arguments to encourage the adoption of community policing at the local level. In doing so, they have provided a rational basis for the achievement of many of the normative aspects of social order. This is particularly the case in respect of their emphasis upon consultation with the public and the mobilisation of community resources. Alderson emphasises the moral basis of policing in his citation of the optimum conditions for a 'high ethical police' in liberal democracies. These include a healthy and vigorous civil society, a general sense of justice and fairness, tolerance and the rule of law, a realisation of the endemic propensity for ethical problems in policing and acceptance of the principles of human rights (see Alderson, 1998: 66–7). This implies a greater public involvement than that which is entailed in the current framework for interagency cooperation.

It is important to remember, however, that the concept of community policing assumes an underlying consensus on the correctness of liberal democratic principles. They assume that these extend right down to the roots of the social structure of the communities in question. They pre-suppose a degree of moral and cultural cohesion, especially in relation to property ownership, which not all communities may have. Bayley's claim that 'macro-social solutions can be left to governments as a whole' in particular does not recognise that community values may be deeply affected by disagreement, by value conflicts and by moral ambivalence about the existing social order. It does not recognise that for some communities, the solutions represented by some kinds of governance are not necessarily acceptable. Those communities may regard policing, especially in its public order and peacekeeping roles, simply as an agency of political control. Unless it adopts measures which recognise this dilemma, community policing will fare no better than more disciplinary measures for social control. If this analysis is correct, policing is increasingly likely to have to respond differentially to address different circumstances. This will depend on the kind of community it finds, not on a preconceived notion of the policing that it requires.

On the other hand, we should also certainly question whether local welfare agencies and the community itself can promote justice and local social control without reserve 'police' powers being available. It is very questionable whether we should leave action to redress such things as racial, homophobic or xenophobic attacks, or serious crimes such as murder, rape and paedophilia, to local community control. It is hard to see how very high levels of self-policing (vigilantism) could deal with them justly. These matters cannot be resolved in partisan environments. There are many examples of divided communities. The examples that spring to mind are those of Northern Ireland, Bosnia-Herzegovina, Kosovo and South Africa, where disputed enclaves, sectarian murder and gang warfare entitle an observer to be sceptical about the community as the sole form of social control. Put simply, there is no reason why we should trust unaccountable community-based groups in such cases any more than we should have trusted the unaccountable and unjust regimes that preceded them.

The idea of 'community policing', therefore, although it has a great many benefits, will only take a certain amount of weight. Properly understood, it is an approach that depends on the willingness of the professional police to relinquish some of their power. It depends on the ability of the public to participate in the development of justice within their communities. It also depends upon attempts to develop shared values between police and public. This is necessary to overcome the 'disciplinary' aspects of the relationship between police and the community. The degree of public participation will in turn depend upon the extent to which social, political and economic conditions have developed to make it possible. Society however, may need to retain some aspect of the disciplinary element to deal with some kinds of crime and disputes between cultures and communities. Policing practice is not just a matter of adopting community policing, however well operationalised it may be in terms of crime prevention and negotiating activities. What is required is a better understanding of the relationship between the different modes of policing practice and the actual conditions in the working environment. This requires more of a strategic approach to the problems implied by diversity than one based upon a doctrinaire acceptance of community policing.

Policing diversity

In comparing these forms of policing, it is clear that no single approach is totally appropriate for policing across the board. This is particularly the case at the macro (force or national) level. Conversely, neither is it possible to disregard any particular approach at the local level. According to Johnston (2000):

> Late modernity is characterised less by 'community policing' than by 'policing communities of risk'. Late modern policing should not, however, be seen as a mere reflection of some overbearing risk-based rationale, for in practice, risk-based approaches are combined with disciplinary ones.
>
> (Johnston, 2000: 51)

The key question is whether the dilemmas that these different forms of policing imply can be resolved or whether it is necessary to live with the tensions between them. We should seek the answers to this question in three areas. First, as argued above, we should seek them in a more critical and focused definition of the concept of community and one that recognises its limitations. Secondly, we should seek them in an appropriate mix of policing strategies and in a clear distinction between the 'control' and 'care' functions of policing. Policing will need to customise these according to both the needs of the impartial enforcement of law and the needs of specific communities. Thirdly, we should seek them in a contextual analysis of policing that goes beyond the listing and condemnation of its various pathological forms. In this sense, it is not sufficient to identify the failings of the police or of policing more generally. Analysis of this kind will also need to recognise the role of policing in its wider cultural, social and political contexts. Each of these contexts will require specially focused policing strategies to meet the conflicting goals of universality and diversity which they imply. The inevitable tension between these strategies and their specific goals suggests that a mixed model of policing is required. Such a model should serve both the needs of the law and of diverse cultures and communities. However, the existence of coercion as a reserve power seems likely to be a continuing characteristic of some aspects of the work of the public police, although not a function of policing generally. Highly developed communities may use coercion more sparingly. More managerial strategies may increasingly replace it.

In a study of appropriate structures to ensure effectiveness with integrity, Allen and Wright (1997) proposed a three-level model, based upon the extent of the integration of policing into the social fabric (see Figure 6.1).

At the top of the diagram, coercive, control-oriented policing attempts to deal with crime and other social problems through both reactive and

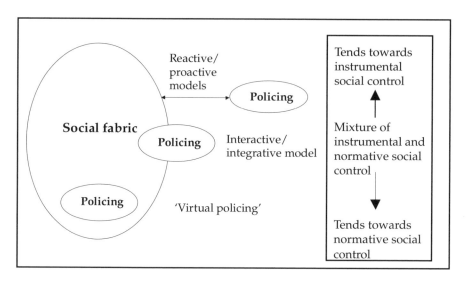

Figure 6.1   Effect on policing styles: extent of integration of policing into social fabric.

proactive activity. Where communities are fragmented or in deep conflict, authoritative intervention may be the most appropriate method of policing, with reactive and proactive elements, depending upon the type of demand. Where the state function remains very strong, the public police working under such regimes is likely to be under highly centralised control. Where the state adopts a more 'managerial' (guiding) role, less authoritarian methods are used.

In most jurisdictions, it seems likely that the police will continue to tackle organised and 'serious' crime by means of reactive or proactive professional policing. At this level, society delegates the responsibilities for investigation to a professional 'expert police', characterised by high levels of skill and knowledge. However, they do expect the professional police to operate strictly within the rule of law. Strategic plans and management styles are set accordingly. Structures are set up to ensure accountability. In such cases, the degree of integration between the professional police and society remains limited. Police forces working primarily on law enforcement at this level will generally stand outside the local social fabric. Their effect upon it is indirect. Bearing in mind the importance of the public for providing information and intelligence, they will retain strong links with the more integrative 'community' level. We should note, however, that some communities might require more interventionist methods than others in the management of risk or community safety. In such cases, a proactive professional stance may be the best response by the police and other agencies. This level aims mainly at instrumental social control.

Some communities, however, will want to participate in policing activities to a greater extent then others. Such communities will be keen to be involved in both the instrumental and normative aspects of social control. This may include involvement in the prevention of crime, diversion of offenders from crime and participation in the administration of justice. Here, the terminology of reactive or proactive policing is outmoded. At the second (interactive or integrative) level, therefore, police will work closely with other agencies and with the communities they serve. Although policing may retain a degree of professional autonomy, it will identify itself more closely with community goals than at Level 1 above. Depending upon the level of integration, some 'policing' agencies may maintain a degree of the instrumental social control function. They may well operate in a 'disciplinary' way, but this will often be with the specific agreement and cooperation of the community. At this level, communities and agencies are able to work together and to achieve high levels of partnership activity. As we have argued above, however, it is not sufficient simply to identify a community by means of its geographical location. Policing must interact with a variety of 'communities' or 'publics' that define themselves in a variety of ways (Bradley, 1998).

At the third level, that of 'virtual' or minimum policing, the degree of integration is far more extensive. The idea of the virtual is a powerful metaphor. Virtual products, in this sense, effectively mirror the demands of the environment. How might this apply to policing in the widest sense? Here, stable and relatively crime-free communities would only need to import such policing services as they need to maintain already high levels of normative social control. They would not need extensive instrumental social control. They would respect the rule of law and universal human rights as overarching principles. In many cases, as is indeed already the case, many aspects of community life have the controls embedded within them. In such cases, few additional resources will be necessary. Presumably, such a community would have already benefited from an emancipatory politics of the kind that Giddens described. However, where there is risk or economic deprivation, any community will require additional resources to ensure its stability. In such cases, elected local authorities, health authorities and education will seek to improve or maintain social conditions so that crime becomes less likely. These agencies will work directly with communities to establish the groundwork for normative social control. They may enlist the help of the public police for assistance in some cases but this will be rare. This level is more about social development than community policing. It is 'virtual' policing, in the sense that normative social control is the ultimate goal.

If the analysis across these three levels is correct, policing strategies will need to encompass a range of measures for instrumental and normative control. All three levels of strategy shown in Figure 6.1, therefore, could appear within the same jurisdiction. This extends across the modes of policing practice which we have explored here. A single policing system or a two- or three-tiered strategic approach (including 'private policing' and voluntary and statutory agencies) could deliver these strategies. The latter seems more likely. This will depend upon the degree of accountability and strategic control that is necessary within a given jurisdiction. For example, it may be necessary to retain high levels of reactive and proactive professional policing in one part of a jurisdiction where analysis shows rising levels of crime and disorder. That same sector may also require a more negotiated form of community policing. Some sectors may require community policing to deal only with minor problems. In other parts of the jurisdiction, there may be an occasional use of commercial security, for which residents associations or the local authority would provide the funds. A wide spectrum of problems at each level would require the use of problem-solving methods. This method is similar to the organisationally structured approach proposed by Bayley (1994). The main difference is that the above approach provides the means of specific targeting of the available resources. The distribution of resources, however, is a matter for local negotiation.

In summary, the promotion of community justice as a mode of practice of policing reflects a high level of reciprocity between the agencies and individuals involved. It is likely to concentrate upon normative social control and restorative justice, although it will need to retain other more disciplinary methods. It will always be subject to the dilemma of satisfying the need for universality in the application of law and the need to respect cultural and ethical difference. In deciding between these competing principles, policing must apply the principle of fairness. In doing so policing agencies should act to maximise the recognition of citizens' rights in any decision. In this way, community justice can draw upon the universal principles of human rights, upon the rule of law and upon the sensibilities of local communities. It will need to reflect upon its role in attempting to influence local social bonds, as much as in the methods that it adopts after crimes have been committed. As such, policing as community justice is as much a communication-based model of policing, where the key role is to explain and negotiate, as one which is concerned with disciplinary measures. Although law enforcement remains important in the delivery of some modes of policing practice, its role is not overriding here.

Chapter 7

The politics of policing

The analysis in Chapters 2–6 emphasises the transition from policing as the activity of a single institution (the police) to a more fragmented and diversified model of policing practice. In one sense, these changes serve to confirm the linkage between policing and politics that is implied throughout this book. There is a conceptual link between them at the level of meaning and discourse. There is a practical link in the relationship between policing institutions and the state. Where these factors are subject to change, policing will also change. The changes, however, are not simply matters of theoretical interest. Changes in the meaning and role of public sector institutions such as the police reflect deeper disturbances in the meaning and role of the state itself. In particular, they raise the question whether we should regard the institutions of state or the associations of civil society as primary providers of certain public goods. Of course, these matters are not uncontroversial. The extent to which state intervention is desirable still characterises some of the differences between the main political parties. For policing, however, this *realpolitik* reflects a yet unresolved question. That is the question of the future of the public police in the light of a redistribution of responsibility for social control to other policing agencies. This chapter examines the politics of policing in terms of the influences that are moulding its character. These include government policy and the influence of so-called 'new public management'. It also explores changes to the social, economic, political and technological contexts of policing and the increasing importance of communication.

The arguments of this chapter are set out in five parts. The first discusses the importance of policing as a public policy issue, including competing visions of the means for dealing with crime and disorder. It raises questions of how the governance of policing stands in relation to levels of state intervention and how its institutional and constitutional foundations may change. It examines public and private responses to policing problems and the idea that policing is a public good. The second section examines the extent to which policing has been seen by successive administrations as a practice which should be guided by the regulatory techniques of rational management. It explores this aspect by reviewing the pressures on the police and other public sector organisations to carry out, monitor and evaluate their role within so-called 'new public management'. This includes the ever-increasing requirement to ensure effectiveness by measuring 'performance' and more recently to achieve 'best value'. This chapter argues that these pressures are symptomatic of deeper (more ideological) attempts to control and reform public institutions.

Changes to the political, economic, social and technological contexts within which policing works will lead to changes in policing itself. For this reason, the third part of this chapter examines a number of 'futures studies' that examine these contexts. They illustrate the extent to which change is bringing ever more contingency into the policing environment. Clearly, there are linkages between internal and external influences for change in this respect. We need to understand these influences in the light of rapidly changing political, economic, social and technological contexts. The fourth section explores the extent to which communication mediates the reciprocity that we have argued is constitutive of policing practice. This is an important aspect of the debate. It relates especially to the legitimacy of policing agencies and to their relationship with communities and individuals.

Finally, this chapter questions whether current conditions herald a further radical fragmentation of the public police and of policing more generally. This includes a discussion of a more generalised disintegration of meaning that may already have served to undermine the certainties of modernity, especially those underpinning the role of the state. In response to these questions, we will compare two scenarios. The first scenario suggests that policing will be able to redefine itself in the new millennium, making use of new approaches to management and communication to consolidate its role in relation to the state and civil society. In this case, it would be able (as some theorists suggest) reflexively to draw on the best of the past and to recast it in the light of new conditions. The second more sceptical scenario suggests a radical decline in policing in the face of the globalisation of information and the post-modern fragmentation of culture, the state and its institutions. Which of these scenarios will predominate is a matter of speculation. This debate marks a shift from the descriptive and critical perspective in the earlier chapters to the normative, posing the questions: 'What *should* the police do? What is the future of policing?'

Policing, civil society and public policy

Although no serious debate yet suggests that the public police will disappear, challenges to the previously accepted certainties of its role and the hiatus of purpose into which it has fallen raise a number of questions about its future. This is equally true of policing in its wider sense: of the public and private sector agencies that have taken over some of the tasks hitherto regarded as 'police property'. What is the future of policing? What will be its place in the political structure? We need to assess these questions against the background of the approaches to state intervention and crime control that characterise the main political parties. The first thing to recognise is that all political parties have an intense interest in crime control and policing methods. The success of their crime control policies is important to all governments. Levels of crime and disorder are widely regarded by the public and politicians alike as an important measure of the competence of an administration. In recent years, the Home Office has played a major role in research and development in a number of initiatives towards this end. These include research into police operations against crime, crime prevention, reducing offending and penal policy. Often embedded in these initiatives have been moves that have sought to expand the range of participants in crime control, including partnerships between public sector agencies, commercial security and communities themselves. We have discussed many of these initiatives (and the limitations of the role of the sovereign state in crime control) in Chapter 5, in the context of policing as the management of risk. All administrations have been eager to highlight successful initiatives and to emphasise the role that government has played in initiating, funding and controlling them. It has certainly never been the case in recent years that public sector agencies such as the police have been provided with funds for carrying out their tasks without governments taking a high level of interest in the outputs and outcomes and the means through which they were obtained.

This has important implications for the supposed differences on state intervention between the major political parties. For example, a key aim of successive Conservative administrations was said to be reducing the role of the state in a number of fields (particularly in areas which are better served by enterprise transactions and market forces). However, they have not generally applied this principle to crime and disorder or to other forms of social control. All Conservative Home Secretaries since 1979 have sought to maintain a centralised grip on this field. Since 1997, centralised control of law and order objectives has continued under New Labour. Their abandonment of the doctrine of public ownership of the means of production has not reduced the degree of control considered necessary in this field. In particular, the left-realist criminologists' acceptance of the need for measures to control crime has provided a rationale for intervention because crime impacts most on the more deprived sections of the community (see Kinsey, Lea & Young, 1986; Young, 1997).

As was the case for the Conservatives, successful outcomes in dealing with crime and disorder are crucial to the reputation and future of the New Labour government. The necessity for all governments to deal with these problems illustrates what Gray (1989) has called '... the fallacy of the minimum state and the mirage of *laissez faire'*. As Gray makes clear, when asking how governments are constrained, we need to look at their positive responsibilities, including law and order and beyond. He says:

> In the British tradition ... the primordial obligation of government is to make and keep peace, where this encompasses forging and maintaining in good repair the institutions of civil society whereby persons and communities with different and incompatible values and perspectives may co-exist without destructive conflict. It is evident that discharging this duty will commit government to activities that go well beyond the provision of the public goods of national defence and law and order. It may ... entail government supplying families and communities with the means whereby their distinctive values and ways of life may be affirmed and renewed across the generations.
>
> (Gray, 1989, in McKevitt and Lawton, 1994: 26–7)

In Britain, the advance of neo-liberalism has not yet affected this principle. Rolling back the state through deregulation and privatisation was not applied to institutions with responsibilities for defence or law and order. On the contrary, Conservative governments exerted an ever-increasing degree of control over the police. They aimed this towards reducing public misgivings about increasing levels of crime and social disorder. Substantive problems have required governments to maintain control over law and order policies and objectives. The spending of taxpayers' money has meant that governments have kept a tight rein on the cost of dealing with them.

Since 1979, governments with supposedly different political principles have been in charge of law and order policies. All, however, have exemplified an ethos of social and political control. The term 'policies' in this sense includes the measures adopted, their goals, actions and effects. Many of the measures introduced in the field of policing and community safety during this period demonstrate convergence of policy across the main political parties. For example, there was a good deal of consensus over the need for wider partnerships and participation in community safety and crime prevention, as recommended in the main findings of the Morgan Report (Home Office 1991: 29). As far as the author is aware, there was no insistence from any political faction for continued functional primacy of the public police for community safety and crime prevention. The extent of this consensus raises the question of whether it represents a deeper shift in thinking about the role of police in late modernity.

One indicator of a shift from modern to a post-modern thinking about organisations such as the police is the extent to which their roles and functions are being redistributed. In a modern organisation, each unit and subunit has its own logic. What we have described in earlier chapters as 'modern' policing, for example, strictly differentiated between the work of the CID and that of crime prevention. This approach distinguished between different kinds of organisation by the differences in their functions. Under such a regime, functional specialisation implies that policing is the business of the police. The provision of local services is the business of local authorities. Banking is the business of bankers and education that of educators. According to Clegg (1990), however, this is changing. The phenomenon of 'de-differentiation' denotes a radical change to this structure. What an organisation previously regarded as its defining functions, it may have to share or even discard completely. New kinds of organisation are evident. Differences in function are now less important (see Clegg, 1990: 11–12, 180–1). Familiar examples of this are the arrangements that now exist for obtaining telephone services from British Gas, electricity from a water authority and so on.

Changes of this kind are certainly evident in policing. Other agencies have taken over many functions that were previously an integral part of policing practice, either wholly or in part. For example, police have already shed much of the responsibility for the enforcement of parking offences. Traffic wardens, the local authority or contractors have taken over these tasks. Investigation of drug offences now includes a very substantial role for HM Customs and Excise. Definition in terms of local, national and international levels no longer ensures strict demarcation between the agencies that are tackling drugs trafficking. As we saw in Chapter 4, some intelligence and enforcement functions are now carried out by the NCIS or NCS (or by private agencies) rather than by police forces. Consequently, improved communication between the agencies has become an imperative to avoid undue competition between them (Wright *et al.*, 1993).

For perhaps the most striking example of de-differentiation of functions in the field of policing, we must return to the Crime and Disorder Act 1998. This is an important example because it shows the extent to which de-differentiation is driven by policy. It is also important because it challenges the primacy of the modern police in responsibility for crime prevention that has existed since 1829. The Act gives local authorities increased responsibility for the reduction of crime. It also seeks to involve the private, commercial and voluntary sectors in community safety. Indeed, as discussed in Chapter 5, the current approach to crime prevention and community safety fostered by the government is entirely that of inter-agency partnership. The government has introduced similar models for national and local strategies to tackle drugs misuse. In the case of both community safety and drugs, these arrangements involve as wide a spectrum of players as possible. Each of these forms of de-differentiation has an impact on the status and character of the public police and on that of the other agencies involved.

Although much of the debate in Chapters 3–6 is about public policing, there are now strong reasons for accepting that the term 'policing' can no longer mean just the public police. The existence of a number of other means indicates a radical change to the nature of policing. This includes the work of local authorities, hybrid policing which has both public and private elements, commercial security and action by communities and individuals. The lack of effectiveness of the police in providing security and protection for the public has had a considerable influence on policy debates about policing. There is little doubt that policy has responded in recent years to what Johnston (1992) has aptly called the 'rebirth of private policing'. Johnston provides an extensive review of the development of private policing. This covers conditions before and during the development of the modern public police. Indeed, the fact that private policing is making incursions into policing more generally is no longer controversial. Johnston (2000) points to the comment made two decades ago by Shearing and Stenning (1981) that the Peelian vision of an 'unremitting watch' was in fact more likely to be provided by commercial means rather than by the public police (Johnston, 2000: 171).

In practice, the resurgence of private policing and the attenuation of public police activity in some areas is becoming unremarkable. However, we need to say a little more about the impact of the public–private dichotomy for governance. At first sight, the development of private policing appears to be an economic rather than a political issue. If the public police cannot provide protection and security for a variety of reasons, perhaps commercial or quasi-public bodies that are part of 'civil society' can do so? While it is certainly true that the rise of private policing has been concerned with questions of instrumental effectiveness, this is only part of the argument that surrounds it. If private enterprise provided all policing, it is highly possible that the negotiation of justice between free agents in the marketplace may finally undermine its very meaning. The key question relates to the way in which the legitimacy of such private institutions is established. According to Johnston (2000), such private agencies are legitimised if a democratic body with responsibility for policing in its widest sense employs them. He says:

> ... It does not follow that commercial security must, invariably, involve the exercise of illegitimate power. My decision to employ a security guard to prevent youths from gathering outside my house may be illegitimate. A decision made by a democratic body to operate, with the police and others, under the aegis of an optimal policing plan would be a different matter.
>
> (Johnston, 2000: 180)

Much of the contemporary debate on this issue, therefore, concedes that public institutions such as the police should be part of a 'mixed model' for meeting democratically agreed goals. A plurality of providers who are democratically accountable serve the public better (so the argument goes), than do state-controlled institutions. For Loader (1997), both policing and commercial security should work towards dissolution of demand rather than towards a maximal policing style. There is, according to Loader, '... no purely *policing* solution to problems of crime and the "fear of crime" ' (Loader, 1997: 155). Dissolution of demand in this sense requires pluralised activity, within which the police may play a part. For Loader, however, there is always a danger in proliferating security by making it into a commodity. This in itself, is likely to lead to a dangerous excess of policing. What is required is the provision of a democratic framework to make decisions. Only in this way can these decisions be associated with policing that contributes to the 'common good'.

The current answer to this problem is to retain an element of the public police but to complement their activities with other providers who do not generally have coercive powers. The problem is, despite legislation such as the Crime and Disorder Act 1998, there is no constitutional framework that makes these relationships explicit. It is difficult to bring people and institutions into a rational framework without specifying conditions (powers and accountabilities) that both enable and constrain their mandate. As Johnston (1992) suggests, it is not possible simply to bring agents of private policing into the role of public (state) functionaries by giving them constabulary powers. He says:

> The problem is, of course, that once private agents in the employ of commercial companies are granted constabulary powers, it is no longer possible to define the public (state) sphere in terms of its monopoly of legitimate force and the commercial (market) sector as something else. Instead one has a hybrid form of public commercial coercion, and the state–market distinction upon which so much political theory depends, is undermined.
>
> (Johnston, 1992: 218)

For Johnston, this example confirms the fragility of the state/market and public/private dichotomies. However, without some universal system of law and adjudication (and the possibility of coercion), no private or public agency can be made accountable for its actions. This takes the debate beyond the ambit of civil society into that of law. The Human Rights Act 1998 (HRA) has made publicly accountable many organisations that the law previously has regarded as 'private'. When they undertake roles that affect citizens' rights, such as in the management of prisons, court security duty or investigation, they become 'public authorities' in much the same sense as the public police or the prison service. In this way, the HRA extends the principles originally instituted to protect people from the misuse of power by state institutions. This recognises that it is public authorities rather than the associations of civil society that infringe fundamental rights. Although there has been a shifting of the balance of institutional responsibility, policing is not a role for civil society as a grouping of freely associated bodies and individuals. From wherever it draws its participants, these principles anchor policing firmly in the public domain. In this sense, it remains a 'public good'.

New public management: modernity's finest hour?

The ethos of the sovereign state has meant that governments have always sought to influence the broad strategies of public sector organisations. More recently, however, governments have also increasingly sought to control their more detailed objectives and the means by which they achieve them. The promotion of so-called 'new public management' has been a response to the perceived failure of performance of many public sector organisations. This began even before the coming to power of the Thatcher administration in 1979. The emphasis on goals and objectives that characterises new public management was central to much of the 'business' thinking in the public sector in the 1960s. Government initiatives in the Thatcher era increased the focus on this form of 'management by results'. These principles continue to dominate. Since the coming to power of New Labour in 1997, centralised control through legislation, regulation, audit and 'best value' policies have continued to affect all public sector institutions. New Labour has also continued the attack on professional autonomy that Thatcher initiated. Professionalism based on expertise, and trust has been under continual pressure. Managerialism has been in the ascendant, characterised by hierarchical authority, compliance with rules and the drive for effectiveness through planning and audit. The use of external audit for assessment of performance has replaced self-regulation in every part of the public sector.

New public management both reflects and encourages a wider trend towards rational management in the public sector. Policing has been understood by both Conservative and New Labour administrations as an activity that should be subject to rational management techniques. From 1979 onwards, the government's Financial Management Initiative (FMI) insisted that police forces should give value for money. Home Office Circular 114/83 made them pay more attention to the so-called three 'E's: effectiveness, efficiency and economy. It required, among other things, that forces should have a clear idea of their priorities. It required them to consult with local communities and to develop ways of assessing whether their objectives have been achieved (Home Office 1983). This put more emphasis than was previously the case on the development of rational, scientific systems of management. In particular, it emphasised the importance of planning and of the measurement of outputs.

The adoption of this approach by the police owed much to contemporary thinking at the Police College at Bramshill during the tenure of Sir Kenneth Newman as its head. Bramshill encouraged the use of a systems-based model of 'policing-by-objectives' (PbO), which had been used in some US police forces to encourage more scientific methods of police management (Lubans and Edgar, 1979). Although most British police forces did not explicitly adopt PbO, they used some form of management by objectives (MbO) in response to the Home Office Circular. Butler's work on police management, described by Weatheritt as a 'do-it-yourself guide for British police managers', draws heavily on the philosophy and practice of MbO (see Butler, 1984, 1992; Weatheritt, 1986: 124n.). After the issue of Home Office Circular 114/83, police forces prepared and published plans. HM Inspectorate of Constabulary reviewed these during inspections. The Audit Commission also reviewed the planning systems in place in a number of forces with a focus on objective-setting (Audit Commission, 1990).

The application of rational management to policing, however, has not been uncontroversial. For Bittner, the criterion of workmanship in policing 'calls for standards of excellence that cannot be formulated in advance of the occasion of use' (Bittner, 1983: 3). Similarly, Waddington (1986a,b) argues that police work, by its very nature, cannot be planned. The best the police can hope to do is cope with complex and un-predictable contingencies when they arise. Police officers need to exercise knowledge, skill and judgement. Each situation must be judged on its merits and the only possible evaluation is the one made after the event when all the facts are known (Waddington, 1986a, 1986b). This has negative implications for the evaluation of performance recommended by some advocates of the rational management approach.

A study of two forces that had adopted MbO showed they did not always implement the process effectively. These forces were at opposite ends of the spectrum as regards resources. However, the research found similarities in terms of police attitudes towards objective-setting. In most cases, the completion of a specific task was the main output. They usually achieved this objective. There was little evidence, however, that they were attaining real outputs and outcomes, especially in relation to crime reduction. For this reason, the researchers regarded objective-setting at that time as 'doomed to success'. In some cases it amounted to little more than a presentational strategy to comply with policy (Wright, 1992; Chatterton et al., 1994). Further studies of performance showed that the problem of 'loose coupling' between inputs and outputs often thwarted achievement. Intervening variables, such as lack of training, inadequate information technology and poor management systems were often the cause. Unpredictability in the events themselves also sometimes caused it (Chatterton et al., 1995).

The picture, however, is not entirely negative. Butler (1985a, 1985b), for example, did not accept Waddington's criticisms. He argued that Waddington overstates the difficulties and fails to consider large areas of police performance which are amenable to direction and evaluation. There is some support for this argument. Chatterton and Rogers (1989) found that positive rewards and a system for providing accurate, up-to-date information on crime and other incidents could effectively focus the work of the lower ranks. Weatheritt's study of a force that implemented policing by objectives suggested that it could be successful with the support of higher management (Weatheritt, 1986).

In developing a wide range of local problem-solving schemes in conjunction with other agencies and with communities, however, most police forces have now abandoned a formal reliance on MbO. Instead, they have tried to concentrate more flexibly on the management of performance. Here objectives are still set: in community safety strategies at local borough/basic command unit levels and in policing plans at force level. However, the process now tends to be more embedded in routine operations management or in specific projects. Nevertheless, it is still often far from clear how police managers can guarantee the linkage between inputs and outputs. There is also a danger that the audit of performance measures will fail to recognise the importance of some variables in making comparison between boroughs or between police command units. In the past, assessments of police performance have rarely taken into account such variables as relative social deprivation, levels of resources or the distribution of populations. There are signs, however, that this is now starting to happen in the crime audits required under the Crime and Disorder Act 1998.

Other more recent measures have also tended to confirm the predominance of rational management in government thinking. New Labour has introduced a statutory requirement under the Local Government Act 1999 for the adoption of the principles of *best value* for the management and control of public services. This provides the most compelling evidence yet available of the high level of government commitment to control of planning and expenditure in this field. According to Leishman *et al.* (2000):

> *Best value* stands as a monument to New Labour's firm commitment to place the public sector under continuing and intensifying scrutiny and the police have been no less exposed to this agenda than the rest of the public services.
>
> (Leishman *et al.*, 2000: 3)

Under *Best value*, the government expects year-on-year improvements in services in terms of increased efficiency, effectiveness and quality. The Home Secretary has power to deal with serious or persistent failures. The role of HMIC in ensuring value for money enforces the centralised influence on policing. The report, *What Price Policing?* (HMIC 1998), provided an overview of value for money initiatives, and emphasised the need for costing police activities as an important part of planning policing services. A number of police forces have adopted management models, such as the European Foundation for Quality Management model (EFQM) or the Business Excellence Model (BEM), to enable them to deal with these developments. There is no space here for a more detailed account of the development of quality, performance, value-for-money and 'best value' measures in the police service. For further analysis of these developments, readers should refer to Waters (2000).

As we have discussed, new public management includes an interesting range of technical measures. However, the actual processes are not central to the debate. The key issue is the extent to which new public management attempts to canonise modernity. In doing so, it replaces professional autonomy at every level with managerial control. If the model were effective, the result would be the enforcement of strict hierarchical compliance for the achievement of 'performance' at every stage down the chain of management. Only those at the top of the pyramid remain autonomous. As such, new public management is a highly authoritarian process. It represents a power structure and a degree of closure rarely matched by the professional and administrative models that it seeks to replace. According to Cooper and Burrell (1988), this preoccupation with functions and performance is defining of modernism. They say:

> The significance of the modern corporation lies precisely in its invention of the idea of performance, especially in its economizing mode, and then creating a reality out of the idea by *ordering social relations* according to the model of functional rationality.
>
> (Cooper and Burrell, 1988: 96)

We have already discussed this at length in Chapter 2. Modern though new rational management may be, there are many objections to this approach.

The deep ambiguity of many activities defines a number of objections to rational management as a way of solving social, ethical and political problems. These are at their height in relation to dilemmas in the field of health, education and other forms of risk management, including policing. Some theorists have pointed to the difficulty of objective-setting for the achievement of large-scale outcomes. For example, Lindblom (1959) and Braybrooke and Lindblom (1963) have argued that synoptic goals must be illegitimate because they rely on knowledge of end-states that are both logically and practically unknowable. If this is correct, health, learning and security are meta-concepts that are not accessible through objective-setting in the way that new public management seems to suppose. Instead, Braybrooke and Lindblom argue for an alternative policy perspective where a process of discrete steps describes change. This they refer to as 'disjointed incrementalism'. They maintain that, although individuals and organisations may have a general sense of direction, the limitation of the logic of action entails that we cannot specify large-scale synoptic goals with any validity. Similarly, according to Lane (1995):

> Policy studies have shown that comprehensive rational decision making no longer works. It is simply not possible to reach all the outcomes aimed at by means of large scale decision making.
>
> (Lane, 1995: 169)

The problem of macro-level planning to achieve targets in crime reduction is a good example of this difficulty. Change may become apparent as a vector of a number of micro-initiatives. However, all the variables are simply not controllable at the macro level by police or by any amalgam of police and other agencies. This presents problems assessing performance, for example in crime reduction. We must look for performance at the micro level. Then we will see the significance of the fact that outputs and outcomes are subject to loose coupling and local effects.

New public management also ignores the importance of the social organisation of workgroups and creativity to performance. Mintzberg (1995) has argued that, rather than adopting measures for strategic planning based on rational management, organisations should recognise the advantages of 'adhocracy' and role adaptability to develop creativity and effectiveness. 'Adhocracy' is a form of organisation suited to the performance of complex tasks through project teams and innovative groupings. Over-reliance on bureaucratic forms of rational management also tends to devalue the ethical dimension of action. This is especially important in policing where, all too often, systematic modernism has substituted instrumental rationality for moral values in its pursuit of measurable ends. In contrast to the interlocking expected by new public management, commentators such as Weick (1977) suggested that effective organisations are characterised by their diversity. He says:

> Specifically I would suggest that the effective organisation is (1) garralous, (2) clumsy, (3) superstitious, (4) monstrous, (5) octopoid, (6) wandering and (7) grouchy.
>
> (Weick, 1977: 193–4)

Claims of this kind provide a totally different perspective to that of new public management. They endorse the idea that we should not look to any single set of factors to ensure effectiveness. According to Pfeffer and Salancik (1978): '... the effectiveness of an organisation is a socio-political question' (Pfeffer and Salancik, 1978: 11, quoted in Scott, 1992: 361).

However, the adoption of new public management by all administrations since the beginning of the 1980s may reflect a deeper, more ideological belief, suggesting that social control is best generated by government, working through a subordinate structure of institutions. At its worst, this generates an authoritarian command-oriented strategy that gives little recognition to anything but compliance. New public management is a high point in late-modern thinking about political and organisational control. Although it continues to bear some similarities to the business principles upon which it was founded, it departs from them in significant ways, especially in its emphasis upon central control, rather than in the empowerment of subordinates to optimise performance. Perhaps (rather fortunately), it is also drinking in the 'last chance saloon' of modernity. We will have to wait to see whether the actual trajectory of public sector institutions will finally justify this far from positive evaluation.

Policing futures

Assuming that public policing will not wither away in any significant sense, in the first two decades of the twenty-first century it will need to respond to a considerable amount of external change. This simple assertion, however, hides a great deal of complexity. To get clear about how policing and the public police will develop, it is necessary to discuss the trajectory of political, economic, social and technological change and to produce credible scenarios of how it might affect policing. Recognition of contingency is the key to understanding change. Generally speaking, police have been highly skilled in responding to set-piece events, such as those relating to public order or major disasters. They are good at handling contingencies of this kind, often working in conjunction with other agencies and emergency services. They have consulted the public by means of surveys to set their policing priorities and to test public satisfaction. The broader contingencies brought about by political, economic, social and technological change, however, have not always been well handled.

Here the literature has been ahead of the practice. For Lawrence and Lorsch (1967), organisations must be adaptable to deal with the wide variety of contingencies in order to survive. They must also be able to influence the development of their working environment. They coined the term 'contingency theory' to express this symbiotic relationship. Police management, however, has largely ignored the more difficult long-term changes in social structure and attitudes. For this reason, police have often been unprepared to deal with political, economic, social and technological change. In short, they have not developed suitable adaptive mechanisms to enable them to survive in rapidly changing conditions. The failure to anticipate the challenge of changing social values is perhaps the best example of all of the failure of modernity in police management.

Police are now making attempts to identify the threats and opportunities to which they should respond. For many police organi-sations, this has not yet become a routine activity of management. How-ever, the environmental scanning that they have carried out has been worthwhile. For example, the review carried out in 1990 by a consortium of police staff associations included a systematic assessment of the future of policing (see Joint Consultative Committee 1990). ACPO have pro-duced an extensive analysis of influences on the police and their implications at the national level (ACPO 1996). Individual police forces and organisations such as National Police Training have also carried out scanning for their own purposes. Kennedy and Wright (1997) carried out a pilot project to provide a regional scanning database for West Mercia Constabulary. Lancashire Constabulary has carried out an analysis of trends in the working environment and has integrated them into its corporate planning. Reportedly, ACPO now intends to make such future studies a routine part of top-level planning. The methodologies for such programmes are well established. What is remarkable about this process, however, is the difficulty which police planners have experienced in making use of this material. Reports have often just remained 'on the shelf'. This is all the more surprising, given the need for adaptability.

What are the factors that are likely to affect policing over the next decade? In 1998, the Public Management Foundation carried out an extensive survey to identify factors affecting the future of public services until the year 2008 (Public Management Foundation 1998). This survey has generated two contrasting scenarios which are summarised below. The first scenario entitled 'A Third Way', was the more optimistic. This scenario suggested that the decentralisation of power and the stability of the economy have led to increased prosperity. The shedding of power by central government, the transfer of responsibility to citizens, clearer ideas of partnership and local and regional corporatism have achieved this. The public has retained confidence in the political process. Local government retains few core functions, as an enabler rather than a provider of services. There is widespread acceptance that Britain should exercise its influence through Europe. The government has introduced the euro. The use of information technology has created increased prosperity. There are modest increases in taxation and in public spending, although there is direct charging for some public services.

According to the analysis, the welfare state continues but this is only possible through compulsory insurance and pension contributions. There is a fall in reported crime and widespread use of 'virtual' incarceration. Society is more tolerant. There is rejection of racism and homophobia but a decrease in obsession with family structures. The public no longer sees the distinction between the genders as important. More networking is evident. This is especially the case among the elderly. There is a shortage of labour and increased self-employment and home-working. The national learning grid is thriving and there is a general increase in educational standards. The environment is at the centre of public policy. There is a reduction in road transport through disincentives with a corresponding increase in public transport. Citizens are more active and better informed. Rights arguments apply not just to governments but to corporations and all public service providers. The increased role for 'civil society' and a belief in emancipatory politics reflects the adoption of this so-called 'third way' in the politics of New Labour in Britain (see Giddens, 1994; Giddens and Pierson, 1998: *passim*).

The second (more pessimistic) scenario is entitled 'Pay as You Go'. Here, the government has not effectively transferred political power away from the centre. There is a great deal of disillusionment about politics. The loss of power and sovereignty has created a crisis of English national identity. The government has not introduced election by means of proportional representation in England. There is no regionalisation in England. The state has not 'delivered' on many promises. Local government has been forced to shed direct service provision. Britain has joined the euro but there is a weakening of national government. Expansion of the European Union by the inclusion of Eastern and Central European states has hit depressed UK areas. EU directives are having an increasing effect on citizens' lives. The economy is stable although Britain has fallen behind its competitors. Growth is modest but there is a widening gap between the rich and the poor. The use of information technology increases social exclusion rather than reducing it. In the post-industrial malaise there is more family breakdown and truancy. More people live alone. The public sees large public bodies as being out of touch. There is an increase in crime and drug abuse above the level of the 1990s. The government cannot sustain increases in public spending and personal taxation is a key issue. Long-term unemployment continues for some people. There is a continuing squeeze on public services that have to meet rising demands, with rationing and charges in key areas. There is obsession with standards and a barrage of critical measurement. Educational institutions are the equivalent of factories rather than places of learning. Citizens are more vocal and single-issue pressure groups rather than politicians are at the forefront of politics. Rights still take precedence over responsibilities. There is an increasing concern over pollution. The government introduces road charging but there is still a lack of an integrated transport system. The middle classes protect their homes with a siege mentality. Widespread alienation with the political process has led to protest. As a result of these pressures, Britain has become one of the least cohesive societies in Western Europe (Public Management Foundation, 1998; Wright, 2000: 296–7).

Clearly, both of these scenarios represent a world quite unlike that of the 1980s and early 1990s. What is striking about them, however, is that, despite their differences, they both describe a trajectory of globalisation of commerce and information. Both point to a world that will inevitably become more demanding for what remains of public sector management. In the second more pessimistic scenario, it is questionable whether the modern agenda of progress is realistic. In these circumstances, organisations may have to discard rational management systems in favour of other modes of operation that simply aim at survival (Wright, 2000: 297).

It is within this turbulent environment that we must consider the long-term future of policing practice. In both scenarios summarised above there are factors which seem likely to demand radical change to the foundations and rationale of public sector institutions, especially in their relationship to the public and private worlds. In reviewing the developments in policing through the lenses of new public management and futures studies we need to ask whether society has moved into a distinctively post-modern era, where meaning itself has begun to erode. Does a paradigm shift in meaning suggest a requirement for a totally new and radically different form of policing? Or are the claims of post-modernism simply a vacuous and confusing way of describing the difficulties that late modernity is experiencing? We discuss some of the implications of post-modernism in the following section of this chapter.

Reflexive modernisation

There are a number of conflicting trends and tensions that foreshadow further fragmentation of the institutional basis of public policing. These bring into doubt its organisational and political stability. New public management has produced more problems than it has solved in terms of improving modern policing. Futures studies have shown the potential for tension and conflict across the political, economic, social and techno-logical domains. The expansion of civil society presents a plurality of interests and cultural diversity. However, it is by no means clear how these are to be reconciled with the continued universal requirement of the rule of law. De-differentiation of functions has characterised the policing role in recent years. The tensions between the public and private worlds are endemic. Democracy itself is a contested concept. It is increasingly unable to deal with the many challenges to political legitimacy which confront it. As presently constituted, it provides little ground for con-fidence that ineffective public institutions can be repaired.

These objections present significant difficulties for modernity in policing, if we define it in terms of progress and evolution. However, some commentators have proposed a means of escape. Beck *et al.* (1994) argue that modernity cannot progress without reflection on its achievements and failures (including their unintended consequences). According to Beck (1998), it is reflexive modernisation that can sustain the promise of progress. He summarises the concept as follows:

1. The more modern a society becomes, the more knowledge it creates about its foundations, structures, dynamics and conflicts.

2. The more knowledge it has available about itself and the more it applies this, the more emphatically a traditionally defined constellation of actions within structures is broken up and replaced by a knowledge dependent, scientifically mediated global reconstruction and restructuring of social structures and institutions.

3. Knowledge forces decisions and opens up contexts for action. Individuals are released from structures, and they must redesign their context of action under conditions of constructed insecurity in forms and strategies of 'reflected' modernisation.

(Beck, 1998: 85)

For Beck, this identifies the basis on which we can reconstruct modernity. It also expresses the inevitability of change for individuals and institutions. Other theorists have found similar ways to express these possibilities. Reflexive modernisation is also the sense in which Habermas (1984) speaks of the 'communicative society' and Luhmann

(1995) of the 'self-referentiality of systems' (Beck, 1998: 85). If the thesis of reflexive modernisation were valid, its impact would be very relevant to the development of modern institutions, including policing. In this sense, policing would be able to redefine itself and its role in the new millennium, reflexively drawing on the best of the past but recasting it in the light of new conditions.

Risk and cultural diversity are factors that point towards communication as the key concept in the new millennium. In the sense in which the term is used here, however, this goes far beyond communication as simply the effective sending or receiving of messages or 'marketing'. According to Habermas (1984, 1987), the key to the reconstruction of modernity is to overcome the systematically distorted communication that is inherent in power relationships. Communication that is free from power provides the possibility of getting at the truth. This is because participants are concerned to come to a genuine understanding, rather than just confirm their power relations. He says:

> … communicative action has nothing to do with propositional truth, but it has everything to do with the truthfulness of intentional expressions and with the rightness of norms … Rationalisation here means extirpating those relations of force that are inconspicuously set in the very structures of communication and that prevent the conscious settlement of conflicts.
>
> (Habermas, 1979: 119)

For Habermas (1984: 21–42), therefore, true communication is not strategic communication. Force is always the basis of the latter, as, for example, when we use it to get across a particular point of view or strategic goal. We can only judge true communication, exemplified as communicative action, by tests that do not entail external validation. We test them by 'redemption in argument'. This means that there should be mutual reasons for accepting the validity of the argument. These reasons are the shared meanings that are arrived at through the interpretation of the specific cultural situations of ourselves and of others. For Habermas, a discourse ethics of this kind not only becomes possible in principle. It is also a sociological and political imperative.

Similarly, for Reed (1992), what is required is an understanding of how modern organisations can begin to live through dialogue and intellectual activity. This dialogue will be characteristic of new ways of organisational thinking. He says,

The 1990's seem set to witness a substantial move away from the polarised thinking that has shaped the agenda for and towards a search for intermediation between competing, but nevertheless communicating perspectives, programmes and narratives.

(Reed, 1992: 281)

This sense of communication also underpins the idea of reciprocity in policing practice that we discussed in Chapter 2. Through communication, policing becomes a search for truth: truth in the resolution of conflict; truth in the management of risk; truth in the achievement of justice for a victim or an offender. It is no longer simply the assertion of authority or the application of power. It also entails rejecting the idea of policing in terms of consent, primarily ensured by means of contract. There can be no contract, in this sense, because there is no longer a monopoly of knowledge and expertise. This requires recognition by policing agencies that the search for truth and conflict resolution is more important than the power relationship. It also requires recognition by them that they tend to conceal power in subtle ways.

Again, however, there are sceptical voices. For example, Ericson and Haggerty (1997) have complained that policing agencies have misappropriated the communication of risk. Police information systems are obsessed with registering minutiae for accountability purposes or on the grounds that it might be useful in future surveillance and intelligence. As a result, police have become 'knowledge workers' in a field flooded with information and configured by communication rules, formats and technologies. Such knowledge is 'commodified' and used in a variety of ways for risk management rather than, as before, for coercive or disciplinary reasons (see Ericson and Haggerty, 1997: 318 *et seq.*, 426–52). They say:

Risk communication systems require surveillance. Surveillance provides knowledge for the selection of thresholds that define acceptable risks and justify inclusion and exclusion. Surveillance agents such as the police front-load the system with relevant knowledge that is later sorted for distribution to interested institutional audiences. Coercive control gives way to contingent categorisation. Knowledge of risk is more important than moral culpability and punishment. Innocence declines as everyone is assumed to be 'guilty' until the risk communication system reveals otherwise and one is admitted to the institution for the purpose of a specific transaction.

(Ericson and Haggerty, 1997: 448–9)

In harnessing communication for wider programmes of risk management, therefore, policing has not even succeeded in satisfying its critics. Even if the information collected by the police is true, the problems remain.

This will not surprise those who have interpreted the boundary between modernity and post-modernity. Bauman (1991, 1993) and Smart (1999) both emphasise that the tensions evident in late modernity are a product of the search for order against the prevailing conditions of conflicting emotions, attitudes, uncertainties and ambiguities. In this sense, they are the very products of modernity, paradoxically reflecting an 'ambivalence of which we can be reasonably certain' (Smart, 1999: 6–7; Bauman, 1991: 95, 97). Concurring with Giddens (1990: 7), Smart maintains that in this sense 'modernity is double edged ... there is both security and danger, trust and risk' (Smart, 1999: 6). Postmodernity, on the other hand, is also itself full of danger and uncertainty. According to Bauman (1993):

> The postmodern mind does not expect any more to find the all-embracing, total and ultimate formula of life without ambiguity, risk danger and error, and is deeply suspicious of any voice that promises otherwise ... The postmodern mind is reconciled to the idea that the messiness of the human predicament is here to stay.
>
> (Bauman, 1993: 245)

If this is correct, there are considerable difficulties in assuming that the police can simply redefine itself for all to be well. Even in trying to change, policing must also take note of this 'dangerous boundary' between modernity and post-modernity.

Indeed, there is already some evidence that post-modern influences have started to affect policing. Reflexive modernisation sees fragmentation, ambivalance, tension and conflict as the very reason for change and improvement. Post-modern thinking see them as fragmenting, inevitable and ironic. In this sense, post-modernity does not even, as Lyotard (1984: 81) puts it, allow us the 'solace of the good forms'. According to Sim (1998):

> ... post-modernism is ... the end of the enlightenment dream of mastery and definitive improvement to human society, thought, knowledge and technology.
>
> (Sim, 1998: 239)

Of course, 'post-modernism' is a controversial term. It reflects the supposed death of reason and its replacement with a world which questions or ignores modern certainties about meaning, theory and the intellectual autonomy of the individual. It signifies a deep change in thought patterns and an epistemological scepticism about the extent to which the intellect can control the world. Whereas 'modern' constructions seem to suggest that no problem is insurmountable given the right appliance of science, post-modern thinking is sceptical about such claims.

Much of the evidence in the second scenario set out above seems to point to radical fragmentation in the political, economic, social and technological environments. Globalisation of commerce and information means that the nation state itself is under pressure (Rosenau, 1990). Ritzer (1995) has argued that there is an emerging transnational paradigm of consumption, a 'McDonaldisation' of society, which includes the standardisation of products and delivery in ways that ignore local culture and history. Debates about post-modernity, therefore, are debates about boundaries – debates about whether we can in any sense understand concepts beyond the context of modernity. For Baudrillard (1983), we have already moved into a time characterised by the destruction of meaning and the absence of a regulatory ideal. Consumers 'culturise' everything. This, in itself, is a form of 'extinction': a denial of communication as reciprocity. For Baudrillard, technology can only offer a series of 'simulations' that begin to constitute the reality. The world (political, economic, social and technological) becomes like a theme park. Spectacles such as Disneyland *become* the reality: they are no longer distinguished from it. Goals and actions are no longer to be represented by reality. There is no end game or purpose: only 'simulations', which are symbolism without sanction.

What are the implications for policing? If the post-modern thesis is correct, we can no longer understand the products of policing as differentiated from other products: they are just a product among products for consumption. The adoption of the language of consumerism in late modern policing is already clear, through the discourse of 'services' (notably not 'service' which has moral connotations). Police carry out surveys mainly to establish 'customer' satisfaction. If the post-modern thesis is correct, there is also a shift from the idea of policing as a 'real presence' to something akin to Baudrillard's 'simulations'. Indeed, there are many indications that this is the case. Reiner (1992) has shown that for the public, accounts of policing in the media determine the social reality more than does 'knowledge by acquaintance'. Inordinate public fascination with both documentary and fictional accounts of crime and policing in the media provides an enormous influence on public perceptions. Technology replaces the real image with a virtual image. The simulated 'tele-reality' becomes the hyper-reality. It replaces the real. Of course, the images are confusing and contradictory. The policeman-as-hero, from Dirty Harry to Judge Dredd, is contrasted with the police-person as intellectual or as paragon of social concern, from Inspector Morse to Juliet Bravo, and so on. Here, instead of knowledge about the real nature of police work, the public is confronted with a choice of 'favourites' – and cases generally lead to a conclusion. The position of the viewer is that of *voyeur*. It is of little wonder, therefore, that public expectations of policing bear little relationship to the actuality of experience. Perhaps more significantly, as Mawby (2000) has suggested, the police themselves have responded to the predominance of the media. They have become 'image workers' rather than 'knowledge workers' of the kind suggested by Ericson and Haggerty (1997). Here, *contra* Habermas, strategic rather than true communication confronts us. For reasons of presentational strategy, the projected image masks the reality of policing. The strategy maintains the appearance of transparency, but the projection of the image is more important than the reality of the events themselves. For the public, the 'unknown policeman', to whom *Control in the Police Organisation* (Punch, 1983) was dedicated, is still unknown. Only the simulation is real.

For those who think that policing is on the slippery slope of post-modernity, neither reflexive modernisation nor communication can stop the slide. The possibility that communication can underpin the notion of reciprocity in policing practice has become fragile. For those who are more optimistic, however, communication provides a provisional link between reciprocity and particular kinds of policing practice. It keeps the debate about the nature of policing open through argumentation and deliberation, agreement and disagreement. Communication is not a form of emancipatory politics in itself, but holds open the possibility of such a politics through dialogue.

Concluding remarks

The primary purpose of this book has been to answer (tentatively in many respects) the question 'what is policing?' The rise of the police institution and its rational function as a means of social control within the paradigm of modernity was an appropriate starting point. The development of the police institution was a major achievement and one appropriate to its time. However, no institution is perfect or immune to change. British policing since the 1960s has certainly produced a number of dis-appointments. It is all too easy to lay this 'fall from grace' at the door of individual police officers or police leaders. In Chapter 1, we saw that deeper difficulties are present. From the 1960s onwards, it has seemed increasingly difficult to produce an 'anchored' notion of policing or one that perpetuates its comfortable role in the 'golden age' of the 1950s. The public no longer views the police institution as the predominant champion of truth and justice. It no longer resonates with rhetoric about its role in support of the democratic ideal (Reith, 1943). A large amount of criminological evidence has confirmed the existence of a crisis. We can properly describe this evidence as an epidemiography of policing.

As we saw in Chapter 2, it has not been possible to reconstruct the earlier and more settled notion of modern policing by relying on the analysis of institutional functions. Despite several attempts to do so in the past two decades, some of which were concerned more with cost-saving than with creating new approaches, policing has not been amenable to functional analysis. On the contrary, it has increasingly been character-ised by a diversity of meanings. It has also exhibited a conceptual contestability that has begun to call into question previous certainties about its character. These ambiguities demand a different approach to analysis. For this reason, we have argued that it is preferable to understand the concept of policing from the viewpoint of the logic of its modes of practice rather than through its institutional structure and functions. The central claim of this book is that it is now necessary to understand the concept of policing from different perspectives: as modes of practice that make up the whole, rather than as the functions of a single institution. We also argued that these modes of practice are capable of representing a less controlling, more managerial and enabling approach to policing. This idea of a 'practice' is characterised by reciprocity between policing and the policed. The concept of performativity ties policing practice to the need to achieve goals of agreed relevance.

In Chapters 2–6, therefore, we argued that there are four logical answers to the question 'what is policing?' Four modalities represent the plurality of policing practice in contemporary conditions. These include policing as peacekeeping; policing as crime investigation; policing as the management of risk; and policing as the promotion of community justice (see Figure 2.1). These, we argued, are reciprocal modes of policing practice in late-modernity. They reflect contemporary policing practice as a whole from four different perspectives (see Figure 2.2). We emphasised that these modes are not functional descriptions. Policing as risk management, for example, is the whole of policing from that perspective, not a functional part of it. The identification of these modal categories of practice also marks a transition from the functional constructs that drove it at an earlier stage, namely those of keeping order, controlling and preventing crime and enforcing the law. Figure 2.1 shows this transition in outline, signifying the decline of the ethos of control based on power or authority and the rise of a more 'managerial' approach. In this sense, it is the management of conflict, the management of the investigation process, the management of risk and the management of offending in diverse communities that increasingly direct late-modern policing. Although not yet always evident in reality (for there is still plenty of conflict to manage), this potentially represents an 'enabling' framework for late-modern policing for the promotion of peace, justice, security and law-abidingness.

The modes of policing practice are important because of the reciprocity that they imply. However, this has not yet been recognised in the control-oriented methods that continue to characterise government policies under new public management. New Labour's second term in office has brought forward proposals for the 'modernisation' of the police by means of the Police Reform Bill in the autumn of 2001. And yet, in a world that continues to change very rapidly, there is certainly some credible evidence to suggest that policing is already challenging its 'modern' status. A new paradigm of fragmentation is replacing the old organisational certainties. As is the case with social change, changes in meaning and organisational fragmentation point in the direction of post-modern deconstruction. Initially, there will be a seemingly never-ending drive for reorganisation and 'modernisation' of the police and policing agencies. The point of this is to find workable rational structures within the political framework of late modernity. Ultimately, however, there will be deconstruction of the old forms of organisation and hierarchy. Policing is already becoming 'de-differentiated'. A number of agencies are delivering policing services and carrying out policing tasks beyond the professional public police. This will produce a pressing need for a degree of coordination and communication which will not be solved by means of new structures or by turning the screws of central control.

The role of communication is at best that of a 'fusion of horizons' through which a network of informational agencies and communities may interpret and negotiate new opportunities to ensure justice. However, communication will not directly solve problems. It only keeps open the political space through which participants may resolve them through argumentation, deliberation, agreement and disagreement. Communication does, however, exemplify the idea of reciprocity that has been a central theme in this book. This is in contrast to the more controlling ethos that still continues to characterise public policy and new public management during late modernity. Whereas the idea of modernity implies control, new understandings will need to include a more symbiotic and discourse-based relationship between government and the governed and between policing and the policed. This is the sense in which a new rationality of policing is required. As such, communication should be the primary concept that configures police management in the early decades of this millennium.

The more positive 'futures' scenario set out above provides a starting point for a new understanding of the enabling and negotiating role of policing. As argued in Wright (2000: 300), it implies a need to develop beyond the crass managerialism that masks power relationships to a more explicit and authentic adoption of the idea of working in and with a diversity of communities. It implies a diffusion of power and a balance between the concepts of social control and social care. At best, policing becomes part of society at every level, whether working on transnational organised crime or in highly localised surroundings. Inevitably, the immanent relationship between the concept of reciprocity and policing practice will mean that policing will need to look to these communities for support and legitimation.

Whatever the technical achievement, modernity in general and the apparatus of social control that it has adopted in modern policing in particular has not overcome the moral dilemmas which are part of community life. The promise of modernity for progress through social control towards some utopian 'end-game' of fairness and justice has not been realised. As Bauman rightly claims, all modernity managed to do was to:

> ... recast as inferior and doomed all those forms of life which did not harness their own pain to the chariot of Reason ... they also made the rule governed house which modernity built hospitable to cruelty which presented itself as a superior ethics.
>
> (Bauman, 1993: 226)

For this reason, if for no other, it is important to recognise that moral responsibility is more important than technique. However apparently complete and rational, modern policing will not be able to eradicate moral dilemmas. Nor will it be able to shed its ambivance of purpose and ambiguity of meaning. It should not be expected to do so in the future. Whatever the mode of practice, policing will have to continue to live with the consequences of moral responsibility.

References

ACPO (1986) *Final Report of the Working Party on Drugs Related Crime* (Chair: R.F. Broome). London: Association of Chief Police Officers.

ACPO (1990) *Strategic Policy Document: Setting the Standards for Policing: Meeting Community Expectation*. London: Association of Chief Police Officers.

ACPO (1993) *Quality of Service Committee*. London: Association of Chief Police Officers.

ACPO (1996) *Through the Millennium: The Policing Agenda*. London: Association of Chief Police Officers.

Alderson, J. (1979) *Policing Freedom*. Plymouth: Macdonald & Evans.

Alderson, J. (1985) 'Police and Social Order', in J. Roach and J. Thomaneck (eds), *Police and Public Order in Europe*. London: Croom Helm.

Alderson, J. (1998) *Principled Policing*. Winchester: Waterside Press.

Allen, R. and Wright, A. (1997) 'Learning the Right Lessons from New York: Direct Accountability and Zero-tolerance'. *Police Research and Management*, 1(1): 41–50.

Amey, P., Hale, C. and Uglow, S. (1996) *Development and Evaluation of a National Crime Management Model*. Police Research Series Paper No. 18. London: Home Office.

Anderson, D., Chenery, S. and Pease, K. (1995) *Biting Back: Tackling Repeat Burglary and Car Crime*, Crime Detection and Prevention Series Paper No. 58. London: Home Office.

Ascoli, D. (1979) *The Queen's Peace*. London: Hamish Hamilton.

Ashworth, A. (1998) *The Criminal Process: an Evaluative Study*. Oxford: Oxford University Press.

Audit Commission (1990) *Effective Policing: Performance Review in Police Forces*. London: Audit Commission.

Audit Commission (1993) *Helping with Enquiries: Tackling Crime Effectively*. London: Audit Commission.

Audit Commission (1996) *Streetwise: Effective Police Patrol*. London: Audit Commission.

Audit Commission (2001) *Best Foot Forward: Headquarters Support for Basic Command Units*. London: Audit Commission.

Austin, J.L. (1962) *How to Do Things with Words*. Oxford: Oxford University Press.

Babington, A. (1969) *A House in Bow Street: Crime and the Magistracy in London 1974–1881*. London: Macdonald.

Banton, M. (1964) *The Policeman in the Community*. London: Tavistock.

Banton, M. (1986) *Investigating Robbery*. Aldershot: Gower.

Baudrillaud, J. (1983) *Simulations*. New York: Semiotext(e).

Bauman, S. (1991) *Modernity and Ambivalence*. Cambridge: Polity.

Bauman, S. (1993) *Postmodern Ethics*. Oxford: Blackwell.

Bayley, D. (1985) *Patterns of Policing: a Comparative International Analysis*. New Brunswick, NJ: Rutgers University Press.

Bayley, D.H. (1994) *Police for the Future*. Oxford: Oxford University Press.

Bayley, D.H. (1996) 'What Do the Police Do?', in W. Saulsbury, J. Mott and T. Newburn (eds.), *Themes in Contemporary Policing*. London: Independent Enquiry into the Roles and Responsibilities of the Police.

Beavon, D. J. K., Brantingham, P.L. and Brantingham, P.J. (1994) 'The Influence of Street Networks on the Patterning of Property Offenses', *Crime Prevention Studies*, 3: 115–48.

Beck, U. (1992) *Risk Society: Towards a New Modernity*. London: Sage.

Beck, U. (1998) *Democracy without Enemies*. Cambridge: Polity Press.

Beck, U., Giddens, A. and Lash, S. (1994) *Reflexive Modernization: Politics, Tradition and Aesthetics in the Modern Social Order*. Cambridge: Polity Press.

Becker, L. (1986) *Reciprocity*. London: Routledge.

Beetham, D. (1991) *The Legitimation of Power*. London: Macmillan.

Beiner, R. (1992) *What's the Matter with Liberalism*. Berkeley, CA: University of California Press.

Bell, D. (1980) 'The Social Framework of the Information Society', in T. Forester (ed.), *The Microelectronics Revolution*. Oxford: Blackwell.

Bellamy, J. (1973) *Crime and Public Order in England in the Later Middle Ages*. London: Routledge & Kegan Paul.

Benke, M., Buzas, P., Finzster, G., Mawby, R.C., Szikinger, I. and Wright, A. (1997) *Developing Civilian Oversight of the Hungarian Police*. Brussels: European Commission.

Bennett, T. (1994) 'Recent Developments in Community Policing', in M. Stephens and S. Becker (eds), *Police Force, Police Service: Care and Control in Britain*. London: Macmillan.

Berlin, I. (1969) *Four Essays on Liberty*. Oxford: Oxford University Press.

Berry, G., Mawby, R.C. and Walley, L. (1995) *Serious Crime Investigation*. Stafford: Staffordshire University, Centre for Public Services Management and Research.

Bittner, E. (1967a) 'Police Discretion in Emergency Apprehension of Mentally Ill Persons', *Social Problems*, 14: 279–92.

Bittner, E. (1967b) 'The Police on Skid Row: A Study of Peacekeeping', *American Sociological Review*, 32: 699–715.

Bittner, E. (1970) *The Functions of the Police in Modern Society*. Chevy Chase: National Institute of Mental Health.

Bittner, E. (1974) 'Florence Nightingale in Pursuit of Willie Sutton', in H. Jacob (ed.), *The Potential for Reform of Criminal Justice*. Beverley Hills, CA: Sage.

Boland, V. (1997) *Financial Times*, 14 February.

Boon, A. and Levin, J. (1999) *The Ethics and Conduct of Lawyers*. Oxford and Portland, OR: Hart Publishing.

Bottomley, K. and Coleman, C. (1981) *Understanding Crime Rates*. Aldershot: Gower.

Bottomley, K. and Pease, K. (1993) *Crime and Punishment: Interpreting the Data*. Milton Keynes: Open University Press.

Bottoms, A.E. (1994) 'Environmental Criminology', in M. Maguire, R. Morgan and R. Reiner (eds.), *Oxford Handbook of Criminology*. Oxford: Oxford University Press.

Bradley, F.H. (1927) *Ethical Studies*, 2nd edn. Oxford: Oxford University Press.

Bradley, R. (1998) *Public Expectations and Perceptions of Policing*, Police Research Series Paper No. 96. London: Home Office

Braithwaite, J. (1989) *Crime, Shame and Reintegration*. Cambridge: Cambridge University Press.

Braithwaite, J. and Pettit, P. (1990) *Not Just Deserts: A Republican Theory of Criminal Justice*. Oxford: Clarendon Press.

Brake, M. and Hale, C. (1992) *Public Order and Private Lives*. London: Routledge.

Brantingham, P.J. and Brantingham, P.L. (1991) *Environmental Criminology*, 2nd edn. Prospect Heights, IL: Waveland Press.

Bratton, W. (1997) 'Crime is Down in New York City: Blame the Police', in N. Dennis (ed.), *Zero Tolerance: Policing a Free Society*. London: IEA Health and Welfare Unit.

Braybrooke, D. and Lindblom, C.E. (1963) *A Strategy of Decision*. New York: Free Press.

Broderick, J. (1973) *Police in a Time of Change*. Morristown, NJ: General Learning.

Brogden, M. (1982) *The Police: Autonomy and Consent*. London and New York: Academic Press.

Brooks, P.R., Devine, M.J., Green, T.J., Hart, B.L. and Moore, M.D. (1988) *Multi-Agency Investigation Team Manual*. Washington, DC: US Department of Justice.

Brown, J. and Waters. I. (1996) 'Force versus Service: a Paradox in the Policing of Public Order', in C.Critcher and D. Waddington (eds.), *Policing Public Order: Theoretical and Practical Issues*. Aldershot: Avebury.

Burrows, J. and Tarling, R. (1982) *Clearing up Crime*, Home Office Research Study No. 73. London: HMSO.

Butler, A.J.P. (1984) *Police Management*. London: Gower.

Butler, A.J.P. (1992) *Police Management*, 2nd edn. Aldershot: Dartmouth.

Butler, T. (1985) 'Objectives and Accountability', *Policing*, 1(4): 174–86.

Butler, T (1986) 'Objectives and Accountability', *Policing*, 2(2): 160–66.

Cain, M. (1973) *Society and the Policeman's Role*. London: Routledge & Kegan Paul.

Cain, M. (1979) 'Trends in the Sociology of Police Work', *International Journal of the Sociology of Law*, 7(2): 143–67.

Canter, D. and Alison, L. (2000) *Profiling Rape and Murder*. Aldershot: Ashgate.

Castells, M. (1989) *The Informational City*. Oxford: Blackwell.

Chapman, B. (1970) *Police State*. London: Macmillan.

Chapman, T. and Hough, M. (1998) *Evidence Based Practice: A Guide to Effective Practice*. London: Home Office (HM Inspectorate of Probation).

Chatterton, M.R. (1979) 'The Supervision of Patrol Work under the Fixed Points System', in S. Holdaway (ed.), *The British Police*. London: Edward Arnold.

Chatterton, M.R. (1983) 'Police Work and Assault Charges', in M. Punch (ed.), *Control in the Police Organisation*. Cambridge, MA: MIT Press.

Chatterton, M. and Rogers, M. (1989) 'Focused Policing', in R. Morgan and D. Smith (eds.), *Coming to Terms with Policing*. London: Routledge.

Chatterton, M.R., Weatheritt, M. and Wright, A. (1994) *Rational Management in Police Organisations: A Comparative Study in Two Forces*. Manchester University: Henry Fielding Centre.

Chatterton, M.R., Gibson, G., Gilman, M., Godfrey, C., Sutton, M. and Wright, A. (1995) *Performance Indicators for Local Anti-Drugs Strategies*, Crime Detection and Prevention Series Paper No. 62. London: Home Office.

Chenery, S., Holt, J. and Pease, K. (1997) *Biting Back II: Reducing Repeat Victimisation in Huddersfield*, Crime Prevention and Detection Series Paper No. 82. London: Home Office.

Choong, S. (1997) *Policing as Social Discipline*. Oxford: Clarendon Press.

Clarke, R. (1980) 'Situational Crime Prevention: Theory and Practice'. *British Journal of Criminology*, 20: 136–47.

Clarke, R. (1983) 'Situational Crime Prevention: Its Theoretical Basis and Practical Scope', in M. Tonry and N. Morris (eds.), *Crime and Justice* (Vol. 4). Chicago: University of Chicago Press.

Clarke, R. and Felson, M. (1993) *Routine Activity and Rational Choice*. New Brunswick, NJ: Transaction.

Clarke, R. and Hough, M. (1984) *Crime and Police Effectiveness*. London: Home Office.

Clegg, S.R. (1990) *Modern Organisations: Organisation Studies in the Post-modern World*. London: Sage.

Cohen, S. (1985) *Visions of Social Control*. Cambridge: Cambridge University Press.

Cohen, S. (1994) 'Social Control and the Politics of Reconstruction', in D. Nelken (ed.), *The Futures of Criminology*. London: Sage.

Cohen, L. and Felson, M. (1979) 'Social Change and Crime Rate Trends: A Routine Activities Approach'. *American Sociological Review*, 44: 588–608.

Coleman, C. and Moynihan, J. (1996) *Understanding Crime Data: Haunted by the Dark Figure*. Buckingham: Open University Press.

Coleman, C. and Norris, C. (2000) *Introducing Criminology*. Cullompton: Willan.

Colquhoun, P. (1796) *A Treatise on the Police of the Metropolis*. London: Dilly.

Conan Doyle, A. (1890) 'The Sign of Four', in *Lippincott's Magazine*. London.

Cooper, R. and Burrell, G. (1988) 'Modernism, Post-Modernism and Organisational Analysis: An Introduction', *Organisation Studies*, 9(1): 91–112.

Cox, B., Shirley, J. and Short, M. (1977) *The Fall of Scotland Yard*. Harmondsworth: Penguin.

Cressy, D.R. (1972) *Criminal Organisation*. London: Heinemann.

Critcher, C. and Waddington, D. (eds.) (1996) *Policing Public Order: Theoretical and Practical Issues*. Aldershot: Avebury.

Critchley, T.A. (1978) *A History of Police in England and Wales*, revised edn. London: Constable.

della Porter, D. and Reiter, H. (eds.) (1998) *Policing Protest: The Control of Mass Demonstrations in Western Democracies*. Minneapolis, MN: University of Minnesota Press.

Dennis, N. (ed.) (1997) *Zero Tolerance: Policing a Free Society*. London: IEA Health and Welfare Unit.

Dennis, N. and Mallon, R. (1997) 'Confident Policing in Hartlepool', in N. Dennis (ed.),) *Zero Tolerance: Policing a Free Society*. London: IEA Health and Welfare Unit.

Derrida, J. (1976) *Of Grammatology*, trans. G.S. Spivak. Baltimore, MD and London: John Hopkins University Press.

Dorn, N., Murji, K. and South, N. (1992) *Traffickers: Drugs Markets and Law Enforcement*. London: Routledge.

Douglas, M. (1970) *Natural Symbols*. London: Crescent Press.

Douglas, M. (1978) 'Cultural Bias', Royal Anthropological Institute, Occasional Paper No. 35, in M. Douglas (1982) *In the Active Voice*. London: Routledge & Kegan Paul.

Douglas, M. (1992) *Risk and Blame*. London: Routledge.

Douglas, M. and Wildavsky, A. (1982) *Risk and Culture: An Essay on the Selection of Technical and Environmental Dangers*. Berkeley, CA: University of California Press.

Dunnigham, C. and Norris, C. (1999) 'The Detective, the Snout and the Audit Commission: the Real Costs in Using Informants'. *Howard Journal*, 38: 67–86.

Eck, J. (1982) *Solving Crimes: The Investigation of Burglary and Robbery*. Washington, DC: Police Executive Research Forum.

Egger, S.A. (1998) *The Killers Amongst Us: An Examination of Serial Murder and its Investigation*. Upper Saddle River, NJ: Prentice Hall.

Ehrenberg, V. (1968) *From Solon to Socrates: Greek History and Civilization during the 6th and 5th Centuries BC*. London: Methuen.

Ekblom, P. and Heal, K. (1982) *The Police Response to Calls from the Public*, Home Office Research and Planning Unit Paper No. 9. London: Home Office.

Emsley, C. (1983) *Policing and its Context 1750–1870*. London: Macmillan.

Emsley, C. (1996a) *The English Police: A Political and Social History*, 2nd edn. London: Longman.

Emsley, C. (1996b) *Crime and Society in England: 1750–1900*, 2nd edn. London: Longman.

Ericson, R.V. (1982) *Reproducing Order: A Study of Police Patrol Work*. Toronto: University of Toronto Press.

Ericson, R.V. and Haggerty. K.D. (1997) *Policing the Risk Society*. Oxford: Clarendon.

Eriksen, T.H. (1997) 'Multiculturalism, Individualism and Human Rights: Romanticism, the Enlightenment and Lessons from Mauritius', in R.A. Wilson (ed.), *Human Rights, Culture and Context*. London: Pluto Press.

Etzioni, A. (1995) *The Spirit of Community*. London: HarperCollins.

European Union (1998) *Joint Action Making it a Criminal Offence to Participate in a Criminal Organisation*. Brussels: European Union, Council of Justice and Home Affairs Ministers.

Evans, E.J. (1996) *The Forging of the Modern State: Early Industrial Britain 1783–1870*, 2nd edn. London: Longmans.

Fagan, J. (1989) 'The Social Organisation of Drug Use and Drug Dealing among Urban Gangs'. *Criminology*, 29: 565–90.

Farrell, G. and Pease, K. (1993) *Once Bitten, Twice Bitten: Repeat Victimisation and its Implications for Crime Prevention*, Crime Prevention Unit Series Paper No. 46. London: Home Office.

Farrell, G., Chenery, S. and Pease, K. (1997) *Crackdown and Consolidation in Boggart Hill: Evaluation of the Anti-burglary Project*. Huddersfield: University of Huddersfield Applied Criminology Group.

Feeley, M.M. and Simon, J. (1992) 'The New Penology', in J. Muncie, E. McLaughlin and M. Langan (eds.) (1996) *Criminological Perspectives*. London: Sage.

Felson, M. (1994) *Crime and Everyday Life*. Thousand Oaks, CA: Pine Forge Press.

Fielding, H. (1757) *An Enquiry into the Causes of the Late Increase of Robbers*. London.

Fielding, N. (1984) 'Police Socialisation and Police Competence'. *British Journal of Sociology*, 35: 568–90.

Fielding, N. (1995) *Community Policing*. Oxford, Clarendon.

Fielding, N. (1996) 'Enforcement, Service and Community Models of Policing', in W. Saulsbury, J. Mott and T. Newburn (eds.) *Themes in Contemporary Policing*. London: Independent Enquiry into the Roles and Responsibilities of the Police.

Fijnaut, C., Bovenkerk, F. and van den Bunt, H. (1998) *Organized Crime in the Netherlands*. The Hague: Kluwer Law International.

Forrester, D., Chatterton, M., Pease, K. and Brown, R. (1988) *The Kirkholt Burglary Prevention Project, Rochdale*, Crime Prevention Unit Series Paper No. 13. London: Home Office.

Forrester, D., Frenz, S., O'Connell, M. and Pease, K. (1990) *The Kirkholt Burglary Prevention Project: Phase II*, Crime Prevention Unit Series Paper No. 23. London: Home Office.

Foucault, M. (1972) *Power/Knowledge: Selected Interviews and Other Writings 1972–1977*. New York and London: Harvester Wheatsheaf.

Frosdick, S. and Walley, L. (1997) *Sport and Safety Management*. Oxford: Butterworth-Heinemann.

Frost, G. (1948) *Flying Squad*. London: Rockliff Press.

Gallie, W.B. (1964) 'Essentially Contested Concepts', in *Philosophy and the Historical Understanding*. London: Chatto & Windus.

Garland, G. (1996) 'The Limits of the Sovereign State: Strategies of Crime Control in Contemporary Society'. *British Journal of Criminology*, 36(4): 445–71.

Gatrell, V.A.C. (1990) 'Crime, Authority and the Policeman-State', in J. Muncie, E. McLaughlin and M. Langan (eds.) (1996) *Criminological Perspectives*. London: Sage.

Gerth, H.H. and Wright Mills, C.W. (eds.) (1970) *From Max Weber*. London: Routledge & Kegan Paul.

Giddens, A. (1990) *Modernity and Self-identity*. Cambridge: Polity.

Giddens, A. (1991) *The Consequences of Modernity*. Cambridge: Polity.

Giddens, A. (1994) *Beyond Left and Right: the Future of Radical Politics*. Cambridge: Polity Press.

Giddens, A. and Pierson, C. (1998) *Conversations with Anthony Giddens*. Cambridge: Polity Press.

Gilling, D. (1997) *Crime Prevention: Theory, Policy and Politics*. London: UCL Press.

Gilling, D. (2000) 'Policing, Crime Prevention and Partnerships', in F. Leishman, B. Loveday and S.P. Savage (eds.), *Core Issues in Policing*, 2nd edn. London: Pearson Education.

Glidewell, Sir I. (1998) *Review of the Crown Prosecution Service*, Cm 3969. London: Stationery Office.

Goldblatt, P. and Lewis, C. (1998) *Reducing Offending: An Assessment of Research Evidence on Ways of Dealing with Offending Behaviour*, Home Office Research Study No. 187. London: Home Office.

Goldstein, H. (1990) *Problem-oriented Policing*. New York: McGraw-Hill.

Gorta, W. (1998) 'Zero Tolerance – The Real Story or the Hidden Lessons of New York'. *Police Research and Management*, 2(1): 15–22.

Graef, R. (1990) *Talking Blues*. London: Fontana (Collins-Harvill).

Gray, J. (1989) 'Limited Government', in D. McKevitt and A. Lawton (1994) *Public Sector Management: Theory Critique and Practice*. London: Sage.

Green, T.H. (1880) 'Liberal Legislation and Freedom of Contract', in R.L. Nettleship (ed.) (1885–8) *Collected Works of T.H. Green*. London: Longmans.

Greene, J.R. and Klockars, C.B. (1991) 'What Police Do', in C.B. Klockars and S.D. Mastrofski (eds.), *Thinking about Police*. New York: McGraw-Hill.

Greenwood, P.W., Petersilia, J. and Chaiken, J. (1977) *The Criminal Investigation Process*. Lexington, MA: D.C. Heath.

Habermas, J. (1979) *Communication and the Evolution of Society*, trans. T. McCarthy. London: Heinemann.

Habermas, J. (1984) *The Theory of Communicative Action, Vol. I – Reason and the Rationalization of Society*, trans. T. McCarthy. London: Heinemann.

Hall, S., Critcher, C., Jefferson, T., Clarke, J. and Roberts, B. (1978) *Policing the Crisis: Mugging, the State and Law and Order*. London: Macmillan.

Hamilton, E. and Cairns, H. (1961) *Plato: the Collected Dialogues*. Princeton NJ: Princeton University Press:

Hampsher-Monk, I. (1992) *A History of Modern Political Thought*. Oxford: Blackwell.

Hill, C. (1969) *Reformation to Industrial Revolution*, revised edn. Harmondsworth: Penguin.

Hirschi, T. (1969) *The Causes of Delinquency*. Berkeley: University of California Press.

HMIC (1998) *What Price Policing? A Study of Efficiency and Value for Money in the Police Service*. London: HM Inspectorate of Constabulary.

Hobbes, T. (1651) *Leviathan* (ed. C.B. Macpherson, 1986). Harmondsworth: Penguin.

Hobbs, D. (1988) *Doing the Business*. Oxford: Oxford University Press.

Hobbs, D. (1994) 'Professional and Organised Crime in Britain', in M. Maguire, R. Morgan and R. Reiner *Oxford Handbook of Criminology*. Oxford: Oxford University Press.

Holdaway, S. (ed.) (1979) *The British Police*. London: Edward Arnold.

Holdaway, S. (1983) *Inside the British Police: A Force at Work*. Oxford: Blackwell.

Home Office (1981) *The Brixton Disorders 10–12 April 1981: Report of an Enquiry by the Rt. Hon. the Lord Scarman OBE*, Cmnd 8427. London: HMSO.

Home Office (1983) *Circular 114/83: Manpower, Effectiveness and Efficiency in the Police Service*. London: Home Office.

Home Office (1984) *Circular 8/84: Crime Prevention*. London: Home Office.

Home Office (1991) *Report of Independent Working Group of Standing Conference on Crime Prevention* (Chair: James Morgan). London: Home Office.

Home Office (1993a) *Police Reform: A Police Service for the Twenty-First Century*, Cmnd 2281. London: HMSO.

Home Office (1993b) *Report of the Inquiry into Police Responsibilities and Rewards* (Chair: Sir Patrick Sheehy), Cm 2280, I, II. London: HMSO.

Home Office (1993c) *Fourth Safer Cities Progress Report*. London: Home Office.

Home Office (1995) *Review of Police Core and Ancillary Tasks*. London: HMSO.

Home Office (2000a) *Interception of Communications Act 1985: Report of the Commissioner for 1999*, Cmnd 4778. London: HMSO.

Home Office (2000b) *Police Personnel Statistics*. Home Office: Research and Statistics Directorate.

Hough, M. (1985) 'Organisation and Resource Management in the Uniformed Police', in K. Heal, R. Tarling and J. Burrows (eds.), *Policing Today*. London: HMSO.

Hough, M. (1996) 'The Police Patrol Function: What Research can Tell Us', in W. Saulsbury, J. Mott and T. Newburn (eds.), *Themes in Contemporary Policing*. London: Independent Enquiry into the Roles and Responsibilities of the Police.

Hough, M. and Tilley, N. (1998) *Auditing Crime and Disorder: Guidance for Local Partnerships*, Crime Detection and Prevention Series Paper No. 91. London: Home Office.

Hunter, V.J. (1994) *Policing Athens: Social Control in the Attic Lawsuits 420–320 B.C.* Princeton NJ: Princeton University Press.

Innes, M. (1999a) 'The Media as an Investigative Resource in Murder Enquiries'. *British Journal of Criminology*, 39(2): 269–86.

Innes, M. (1999b) 'An Iron Fist in an Iron Glove? The Zero Tolerance Policing Debate'. *The Howard Journal*, 38(4): 397–410.

Irving, B., Faulkner, D., Frosdick, S. and Topping, P. (1996) *Reacting to Crime: The Management of Police Resources*. London: Home Office.

James, A. and Raine, J. (1998) *The New Politics of Criminal Justice*. London: Longman.

Jefferson, T. (1987) 'Beyond Paramilitarism'. *British Journal of Criminology*, 27(1): 47–53.

Jefferson, T. (1990) *The Case Against Paramilitary Policing*. Milton Keynes: Open University Press.

Jefferson, T. (1993) 'Pondering Paramilitarism: a Question of Standpoints?', *British Journal of Criminlogy*. 33(3): 374–81.

Jefferson, T. and Grimshaw, R. (1984) *Controlling the Constable*. London: Frederick Muller.

Johnston, L. (1992) *The Rebirth of Private Policing*. London: Routledge.

Johnston, L. (2000) *Policing Britain: Risk, Security and Governance*. London: Longmans.

Joint Consultative Committee (1990) *Operational Policing Review*. Surbiton: Surrey.

Jordan, P. (1998) 'Effective Policing Strategies for Reducing Crime', in P. Goldblatt and C. Lewis, *Reducing Offending: an Assessment of Research Evidence on Ways of Dealing with Offending Behaviour*, Home Office Research Study No. 187. London: Home Office.

Kelling, G.L. (1998) 'The Evolution of Broken Windows', in M. Weatheritt, *Zero Tolerance: What Does It Mean and Is It Right for Policing in Britain?* London: Police Foundation.

Kelling, G.L. and Coles, C.M. (1997) *Fixing Broken Windows*. New York: Touchstone.

Kelling, G.L., Pate, T., Dieckman, D. and Brown, C. (1974) *The Kansas City Preventative Patrol Experiment: Summary Report*. Washington DC: Police Foundation.

Kennedy, J.A. and Wright, A. (1997) *Environmental Scanning for West Mercia Constabulary: Report on Methodology and Substantive Findings*. Stafford: Staffordshire University Business School.

Killingray, D. (1997) 'Securing the British Empire: Policing and Colonial Order, 1920–1960', in M. Mazower, *The Policing of Politics in the Twentieth Century*. Providence, RI and Oxford: Bergbahn Books.

Kinsey, R., Lea, J. and Young, J. (1986) *Losing the Fight Against Crime*. Oxford: Blackwell.

Klein, M. and Maxson, C. (1994) 'Gangs and Cocaine Trafficking', in D.L. Mackenzie and C.D. Uchida (eds.), *Drugs and Crime: Evaluating Public Policy Initiatives*. Thousand Oaks, CA: Sage.

Klein, M., Maxson, C. and Cunningham, L. (1991) 'Crack, Street Gangs and Violence', *Criminology*, 31: 623–50.

Klockars, C.B. (1980) 'The Dirty Harry Problem', in *The Annals*, 452: 33–47.

Klockars, C.B. (1985) *The Idea of Police*. Beverley Hills, CA: Sage.

Knapp, W. (1972) *Report of a Commission to Investigate Alleged Police Corruption*. New York: George Brazillier.

Knox, T.M. (1952) *Hegel's Philosphy of Right*. Oxford: Oxford University Press.

Kraska, P.B. and Paulsen, D.J. (1997) 'Grounded Research into US Paramilitary Policing: Forging the Iron Fist Inside the Velvet Glove'. *Policing and Society*, 7(4): 253–70.

Kukathas, C. and Pettit, P. (1990) *Rawls: A Theory of Justice and its Critics*. Cambridge: Polity.

Lane, J.-E. (1995) *The Public Sector: Concepts, Models and Approaches*, 2nd edn. London: Sage.

Lawrence, P.R. and Lorsch, J.W. (1967) *Organisation and Environment: Managing Differentiation and Integration*. Boston: School of Business Administration Harvard University.

Lea, J. and Young, J. (1984) *What is to be Done About Law and Order*. Harmondsworth: Penguin Books.

Lee, J.A. (1981) 'Some Structural Aspects of Police Deviance in Relations with Minority Groups', in C. Shearing (ed.), *Organisational Police Deviance*. Toronto: Butterworth.

Leigh, A., Read, T. and Tilley, N. (1996) *Problem-Oriented Policing: Britpop*, Crime Detection and Prevention Series Paper No. 75. London: Home Office.

Leigh, A., Read, T. and Tilley, N. (1998) *Britpop II: Problem-Oriented Policing in Practice*, Police Research Series Paper No. 93. London: Home Office.

Leigh-Kyle, D. (1998) *Lawyers on the Spot*. London: Vision.

Leishman, F., Cope, S. and Starie, P. (1996) 'Reinventing and Restructuring: Towards a New Policing Order', in F. Leishman, B. Loveday and S.P. Savage (eds.), *Core Issues in Policing*. London: Longmans.

Leishman, F., Loveday, B. and Savage, S.P. (eds.) (1996) *Core Issues in Policing*. London: Longmans.

Leishman, F., Loveday, B. and Savage, S.P. (eds.) (2000) *Core Issues in Policing*, 2nd edn. London: Pearson Education.

Liddle, M. and Gelsthorpe, L. (1994a) *Interagency Crime Prevention: Organising Local Delivery*, Crime Prevention Unit Series Paper No. 52. London: Home Office.

Liddle, M. and Gelsthorpe, L. (1994b) *Crime Prevention and Interagency Co-operation*, Crime Prevention Unit Series Paper No. 53. London: Home Office.

Liddle, M. and Gelsthorpe, L. (1994c) *Interagency Crime prevention: Further Issues*, Supplementary Paper to Crime Prevention Unit Papers Nos. 52 and 53. London: Home Office.

Lindblom, C.E. (1959) 'The Science of Muddling Through'. *Public Administration Review*, 19: 79–88.

Lloyd, S., Farrell, G. and Pease, K. (1994) *Preventing Repeat Domestic Violence: A Demonstration Project in Merseyside*, Crime Prevention Unit Series Paper No. 49. London: Home Office.

Loader, I. (1997) 'Private Security and the Demand for Protection in Contemporary Britain'. *Police and Society*, 7: 143–62.

Locke, J. (1690) *Two Treatises of Government* (ed. P. Laslett, 1967). Cambridge: Cambridge University Press.

Loveday, B. (1996) 'Crime at the Core', in F. Leishman, B. Loveday and S. Savage (eds), *Core Issues in Policing*. London: Longman.

Loveday, B. (2000) 'New Directions in Accountability', in F. Leishman, B. Loveday and S. Savage (eds.), *Core Issues in Policing*, 2nd edn. London: Pearson Education.

Lubans, V.A. and Edgar, J.M. (1979) *Policing by Objectives*. Hartford, CT: Social Development Corporation.

Luhmann, N. (1995) *Social Systems*, trans. J. Bednarz. Stanford, CA: Stanford University Press.

Lupsha, P.A. (1996) 'Transnational Organised Crime Versus the Nation State', in *Transnational Organised Crime*. Pittsburg, PA: Cass. 2(1): 21–48.

Lyotard, J.-F. (1984) *The Postmodern Condition*. Manchester: Manchester University Press.

McClure, J. (1980) *Spike Island*. London: Pan Books.

McConville, M., Sanders, A. and Leng, R. (1991) *The Case for the Prosecution*. London: Routledge.

MacIntyre, A. (1985) *After Virtue: A Study in Moral Theory*. London: Duckworth.

McKenzie, I. (2000) 'Policing Force: Rules, Hierarchies and Consequences' in F. Leishman, B. Loveday and S.P. Savage (eds.), *Core Issues in Policing*, 2nd edn. London: Pearson Education.

McLaughlin, E. and Murji, K. (1995) 'The End of Public Policing: Police Reform and the New Managerialism', in L. Noaks, M. Levi and M. Maguire (eds.), *Issues in Contemporary Criminology*. Cardiff: Cardiff University Press.

Macpherson, C.B. (1962) *The Political Theory of Possessive Individualism*. Oxford: Oxford University Press.

Macpherson of Cluny, Sir W. (1999) *The Stephen Lawrence Inquiry*, Cm 4262-1. London: HMSO.

Maguire, M. (1982) *Burglary in a Dwelling*. London: Heinemann.

Maguire, M. and John, T. (1995) *Intelligence, Surveillance and Informants: Integrated Approaches*, Crime Detection and Prevention Series Paper No. 64. London: Home Office.

Malinowski. B. (1944) *A Scientific Theory of Culture*. Chapel Hill, NC: University of North Carolina Press.

Manning, P.K. (1977) *Police Work: The Social Organisation of Policing*. Cambridge, MA: MIT Press.

Mark, R. (1979) *In the Office of Constable*. London: Fontana (paperback edition).

Mars, G. (1983) *Cheats at Work: An Anthropology of Workplace Crime*. London: Counterpoint (Unwin).

Marshall, G. (1965) *Police and Government*. London: Methuen.

Mawby, R.C. (2000) *The Police Image: A Study of Construction, Communication and Legitimacy*. PhD thesis, University of Keele.

Mawby, R.I. (1979) *Policing the City*. Aldershot: Gower.

Mawby, R.I. (1990) *Comparative Policing Issues*. London: Unwin Hyman.

Mawby, R.I. (2000) 'Core Policing: the Seductive Myth', in F. Leishman, B. Loveday and S.P. Savage (eds.), *Core Issues in Policing*, 2nd edn. London: Pearson Education.

Mayhew, P., Mirrlees-Black, C. and Aye Maung, N. (1994) *Trends in Crime: Findings from the 1992 British Crime Survey*, Research Findings No. 14. London: Home Office Research and Statistics Directorate.

Merton, R.K. (1957) *Social Theory and Social Structure*, 2nd edn. Glencoe, IL: Free Press.

Metropolitan Police (1851) *General Regulations, Instructions and Orders for the Government and Guidance of the Metropolitan Police Force*. London: W. Clowes & Sons for HM Stationery Office.

Mill, J.S. (1859) 'On Liberty', in G. Williams (ed.) (1993) *Utilitarianism and Other Essays*, revised edn. London: Everyman (Dent).

Mill, J.S. (1861) 'Utilitarianism', in G. Williams (ed.) (1993) *Utilitarianism and Other Essays*, revised edn. London: Everyman (Dent).

Milne, A.J.M. (1962) *The Social Philosophy of English Idealism*. London: George Allen & Unwin.

Milne, R. and Bull, R. (1999) *Investigative Interviewing: Psychology and Practice*. Chichester: Wiley.

Mintzberg, H. (1995) *The Rise and Fall of Strategic Planning*. London: Prentice Hall.

Mirrlees-Black, C. and Budd, T. (1997) *Policing and the Public: Findings from the 1996 British Crime Survey*. Research Findings No. 60. London: Home Office.

Mollen Commission (1994) *Report of the Commission to Investigate Allegations of Corruption and Anti-corruption Procedures of the Police Department*. New York: Mollen Commission.

Morgan, J.B. (1990) *The Police Function and the Investigation of Crime*. Aldershot: Avebury.

Morgan, R. and Newburn, T. (1997) *The Future of Policing*. Oxford: Clarendon Press.

Morton, J. (1993) *Bent Coppers*. London: Little, Brown.

Muir, W.K. (1977) *Police: Street Corner Politicians*. Chicago: University of Chicago Press.

Muncie, J., McLaughlin, E. and Langan, M. (1996) *Criminological Perspectives*. London: Sage.

Newman, O. (1973) *Defensible Space*. London: Architectural Press.

Nicholl, C. (2001) 'Managing Crime through Restorative Justice'. *Police Research and Management*, 5(1): 21.

Nippel, W. (1995) *Public Order in Ancient Rome*. Cambridge: Cambridge University Press.

Nolan, Lord (1998) *First Report of the Committee on Standards in Public Life*. London: Stationery Office.

Norris, C. (1989) 'Avoiding Trouble: the Patrol Officer's Perception of Encounters with the Public', in M. Weatheritt (ed.), *Police Research: Some Future Prospects*. Aldershot: Avebury.

Northam, G. (1988) *Shooting in the Dark*. London: Faber.

Nozick, R. (1974) *Anarchy, State and Utopia*. Oxford: Blackwell.

Oakeshott, M. (1933) *Experience and Its Modes*. Cambridge: Cambridge University Press.

Oakeshott, M. (1975) *On Human Conduct*. Oxford: Clarendon Press.

O'Malley, P. (1992) 'Risk, Power and Crime Prevention'. *Economy and Society*, 21(3): 252–75.

Orwell, G. (1949) *Nineteen Eighty-Four: A Novel*. London: Secker & Warburg.

Packer, H.L. (1964) 'Two Models of the Criminal Process'. *University of Pennsylvania Law Review*, 113: 1–68.

Packer, H.L. (1968) *The Limits of the Criminal Sanction*. Stanford, CA: Stanford University Press.

Paine, T. (1984) *The Rights of Man (1791)*. Penguin: Harmondsworth: Penguin.

Pavarini, M. (1994) 'Is Criminology Worth Saving?', in D. Nelken (ed.), *The Futures of Criminology*. London: Sage.

Pease, K. (1998a) 'What Shall we Count when Measuring Zero Tolerance?', in M. Weatheritt, *Zero Tolerance: What Does it Mean and Is It Right for Policing in Britain?* London: Police Foundation.

Pease, K. (1998b) *Repeat Victimisation: Taking Stock*, Crime Detection and Prevention Series Paper No. 90. London: Home Office.

Pfeffer, J. and Salancik, G.R. (1978) 'The External Control of Organisations', *Administrative Science Quarterly*, 19: 135–51.

Phillips, C. and Brown, D. (1998) *Entry into the Criminal Justice System: A Survey of Police Arrests and Their Outcomes*, Home Office Research Study No. 185. London: Home Office.

Pidgeon, N., Hood, C., Jones, D., Turner, B. and Gibson, R. (1992) 'Risk Perception', in *Risk: Analysis, Perception and Management*, Report of a Royal Society Study Group. London: Royal Society.

Police Foundation (1981) *The Newark Foot Patrol Experiment*. Washington, DC: Police Foundation.

Police Foundation/Policy Studies Institute (1994) *Independent Committee of Enquiry into the Role and Responsibilities of the Police: Discussion Document* (Chair: Sir John Cassels). London: Police Foundation/Policy Studies Institute.

Police Foundation/Policy Studies Institute (1996) *The Role and Responsibilities of the Police: Report* (Chair: Sir John Cassels). London: Police Foundation/Policy Studies Institute.

Pollard, C. (1997) 'Zero Tolerance: Short-Term Fix, Long-Term Liability?', in N. Dennis (ed.), *Zero Tolerance: Policing a Free Society*. London: IEA Health and Welfare Unit.

Public Management Foundation (1998) *The Future for the Public Services: 2008*. London: Public Management Foundation.

Punch, M. (1979a) 'The Secret Social Service', in S. Holdaway (1979) *The British Police*. London: Edward Arnold.

Punch, M. (1979b) *Policing the Inner City*. London: Macmillan.

Punch, M. (ed.) (1983) *Control in the Police Organisation*. Cambridge, MA: MIT Press.

Punch, M. (1985) *Conduct Unbecoming*. London: Tavistock Publications.

Punch, M. (1997) 'The Dutch Criminal Justice System: A Crisis of Identity'. *Security Journal*, 9: 177–84.

Punch, M. and Naylor, T. (1973) 'The Police: A Secret Social Service'. *New Society*, 24.

Raeff, M. (1983) *The Well-Ordered Police State*. New Haven, CT: Yale University Press.

Rawlings, P. (2002) *Policing: a Short History*. Cullompton: Willan Publishing.

Rawls, J. (1972) *A Theory of Justice*. Oxford: Oxford University Press.

Reed, M.I. (1992) *The Sociology of Organisations*. London: Harvester Wheatsheaf.

Reiner, R. (1984) 'Is Britain Turning Into a Police State?', *New Society*, 2 August: 51–6.

Reiner, R. (1985) *The Politics of the Police*. London: Harvester Wheatsheaf.

Reiner, R. (1992a) *The Politics of the Police*, 2nd edn. London: Harvester Wheatsheaf.

Reiner, R. (1992b) 'Policing a Postmodern Society'. *Modern Law Review*, 55(6): 761–81.

Reiner, R. (1994) 'Policing and the Police', in M. Maguire, R. Morgan, and R. Reiner (eds), *Oxford Handbook of Criminology*. Oxford: Oxford University Press.

Reiner, R. (1995) 'From Sacred to Profane: The Thirty Years War of the British Police'. *Police and Society*, 5(2): 121–8.

Reiner, R. (1998) 'Copping a Plea', in S. Holdaway and P. Rock (eds.), *Thinking about Criminology*. London: UCL Press.

Reiner, R. (2000a) *The Politics of the Police*, 3rd edn. London: Harvester Wheatsheaf.

Reiner, R. (2000b) 'Police Research', in R.D. King and E. Wincup (eds.), *Doing Research on Crime and Criminal Justice*. Oxford: Oxford University Press.

Reiss, A.J. (1971) *The Police and The Public*. New Haven CT: Yale University Press.

Reith, C. (1938) *The Police Idea: Its History and Evolution in England in the Eighteenth Century and After*. London: Oxford University Press.

Reith, C. (1943) *British Police and the Democratic Ideal*. Oxford: Oxford University Press.

Ritzer, G. (1995) *'The McDonaldization of Society'*. Thousand Oaks, CA: Pine Forge Press.

Rose, D. (1996) *In the Name of the Law*. London: Vintage.

Rosenau, J.N. (1990) *Turbulence in World Politics*. London: Harvester Wheatsheaf.

Royal Commission on Criminal Justice (1993) *Report*, Cm 2263 (Chair: Viscount Runciman). London: HMSO.

Royal Commission on Criminal Procedure (1981), *Report*, Cmnd 8092 (Chair: Sir Cyril Phillips). London: HMSO.

Royal Commission on the Police (1962) *Final Report* (Chair: Sir Henry Willink) Cmnd 1728. London: HMSO.

Royal Society (1983) *Study Group Report on Risk-Assessment*. London: Royal Society.

Royal Society (1992) *Risk: Analysis, Perception and Management – Report of a Royal Society Study Group*. London: Royal Society.

Rubenstein, J. (1973) *City Police*. New York: Farrar, Strauss & Giroux.

Ryle, G. (1951) 'Thinking and Language', in G. Ryle (1971) *Collected Papers*. London: Hutchinson.

Sampson, A. and Phillips, C. (1995) *Reducing Repeat Racial Victimisation on an East London Estate*, Crime Detection and Prevention Series Paper No. 67. London: Home Office.

Schwartzmantel, J. (1994) *The State in Contemporary Society*. Hemel Hempstead: Harvester Wheatsheaf.

Scott, H. (1957) *Scotland Yard*. Harmondsworth: Penguin Books.

Scott, R. (1992) *Organisations: Rational, Natural and Open Systems*. London: Prentice Hall.

Scraton, P. (1985) *The State of the Police*. London: Pluto.

Shapland, J. and Vagg, J. (1988) *Policing by the Public*. London: Routledge.

Sharpe, A.N. (1995) 'Police Performance Crime as Structurally Coerced Action', *Police and Society*, 5(4): 201–20.

Shearing, C. and Stenning, P. (1981) 'Modern Private Security: Its Growth and Implications', in M. Tonry and N. Norris (eds), *Crime and Justice: An Annual Review of the Research*. Chicago: University of Chicago Press.

Sheldon, B. and Macdonald, G. (1999) *Research and Practice in Social Care: Mind the Gap*. Exeter: University of Exeter Centre for Evidence-Based Social Work.

Sher, G. (1987) *Desert*. Princeton, NJ: Princeton University Press.

Sherman, L.W. (1974) *Police Corruption*. New York: Anchor Press.

Sherman, L.W. (ed.) (1997) *Preventing Crime: What Works, What Doesn't, What's Promising*. Office of Justice Programs Research Report. Washington, DC: US Department of Justice.

Sherman, L.W. (1990) 'Police Crackdowns: Initial and Residual Deterrence', in M. Tonry and N. Morris (eds.), *Crime and Justice: A Review of the Research*, 12. Chicago: University of Chicago Press.

Silberman, C. (1978) *Criminal Violence, Criminal Justice*. New York: Random House.

Sim, S. (1998) *The Icon Critical Dictionary of Postmodern Thought*. Duxford: Icon Books.

Sims, L. and Mynhill, A. (2001) *Policing and the Public: Findings from the 2000 British Crime Survey*, Research Findings No. 136. London: Home Office.

Skogan, W. (1990) *Police and the Public in England and Wales. A British Crime Survey Report*, Home Office Research Study No. 117. London: HMSO.

Skogan, W. (1994) *Contacts between Police and Public: Findings from the 1992 British Crime Survey*, Home Office Research Study No. 134. London: HMSO.

Skolnick, J. (1966) *Justice without Trial*. New York: John Wiley.

Skolnick, J. (1990) 'The Social Structure of Street Drug Dealing'. *American Journal of Police*, 9: 1–41.

Smart, B. (1999) *Facing Modernity: Ambivalence, Reflexivity, Morality*. London: Sage.

Smith, D.J., Gray, J. and Small, S. (1983) *Police and People in London*, (4 vols.) London: Policy Studies Institute.

Smith, N. and Flanaghan, C. (2000) *The Effective Detective: Identifying the Skills of an Effective SIO*, Police Research Series Paper No. 122. London: Home Office.

Stead, P.J. (1957) *The Police of Paris*. London: Staples Press.

Steer, D. (1980) *Uncovering Crime: The Police Role*, Royal Commission on Criminal Procedure Research Study No. 7. London: HMSO.

Stephens, M. and Becker, S. (eds.) (1994) *Police Force, Police Service: Care and Control in Britain*. London: Methuen.

Stockdale, J. and Gresham, P.J. (1995) *Combating Burglary: An Evaluation of Three Strategies*, Crime Detection and Prevention Series Paper No. 59. London: Home Office.

Stoffels, J.D. (1994) *Strategic Issues Management: A Comprehensive Guide to Environmental Scanning*. Oxford: Pergamon/Planning Forum.

Storch, R. (1975) 'The Plague of Blue Locusts: Police Reform and Popular Resistance in Northern England 1840–57', *International Review of Social History*, IX: 4.

Sykes, E.E. and Brent, R.E. (1983) *Policing: A Social Behaviourist Perspective*. New Brunswick, NJ: Rutgers University Press.

Taylor, A.E. (1945) *Plato: The Man and his Work*. London: Methuen.

Thompson, M., Ellis, R. and Wildavsky, A. (1990) *Cultural Theory*. Boulder, CO: Westview Press.

Tilley, N. (1992) *Safer Cities and Community Safety Strategies*, Crime Prevention Unit Series Paper No. 38. London: Home Office.

Tilley, N. (1993a) *After Kirkholt – Theory, Method and Results of Replication Evaluations*, Crime Prevention Unit Series Paper No. 47. London: Home Office.

Tilley, N. (1993b) *Understanding Car Parks, Crime and CCTV: Evaluation Lessons from Safer Cities*, Crime Prevention Unit Series Paper No. 42. London: Home Office.

Tilley, N. (1993c) *The Prevention of Crime Against Small Businesses: The Safer Cities Experience*, Crime Prevention Unit Series Paper No. 45. London: Home Office.

Tilley, N. and Webb, J. (1994) *Burglary Reduction: Findings from Safer Cities Schemes*, Crime Prevention Unit Series Paper No. 51. London: Home Office.

Toch, H. and Grant, J.D. (1991) *Police as Problem Solvers*. New York and London: Plenum Press.

Trasler, G. (1986) 'Situational Crime Control and Rational Choice: a Critique', in K. Heal and G. Laycock (eds.), *Situational Crime Prevention: from Theory into Practice*. London: HMSO.

Trasler, G. (1993) 'Conscience, Opportunity, Rational Choice and Crime', in R. Clarke and M. Felson (eds.), *Routine Activity and Rational Choice*. New Brunswick, NJ: Transaction.

Trinder, L. and Reynolds, S. (2000) *Evidence-Based Practice: A Critical Appraisal*. Oxford: Blackwell.

Trojanowicz, R. and Bucqueroux, B. (1990) *Community Policing: A Contemporary Perspective*. Cincinnati, OH: Anderson Publishing.

United Nations Drugs International Control Programme (1998) *World Drugs Report*. Oxford: Oxford University Press.

University of Kent (1995) *Development and Evaluation of a National Crime Management Model: Progress to Date February 1995*, Police Research Group Briefing Note 1/95. London: Home Office.

Van Maanen, J. (1978) 'On Watching the Watchers', in P.K. Manning and J. Van Maanen (eds.), *A View from the Streets*. Santo Monica, CA: Goodyear.

Vennard, J. and Hedderman, C. (1998) 'Effective Interventions with Offenders', in P. Goldblatt and C. Lewis, *Reducing Offending: An Assessment of Research Evidence on Ways of Dealing with Offending Behaviour*, Home Office Research Study No. 187. London: Home Office.

Vincent, A. and Plant, R. (1984) *Philosophy, Politics and Citizenship: The Life and Thought of the British Idealists*. Oxford: Blackwell.

von Hirsch, A. (1976) 'Giving Criminals their Just Deserts', *Civil Liberties Review*, 3: 23–35.

Waddington, D. (1989) *Flashpoints: Studies in Public Disorder*. London: Routledge.

Waddington, D. (1998) 'Waddington versus Waddington: Public Order Theory on Trial'. *Theoretical Criminology* 2(3): 373–94.

Waddington, P.A.J. (1986a) 'Defining Objectives'. *Policing*, 2(1): 17–26.

Waddington, P.A.J. (1986b) 'The Objectives Debate'. *Policing*, 2(3): 225–35.

Waddington, P.A.J. (1987) 'Towards Paramilitarism: Dilemmas in Policing Civil Disorder'. *British Journal of Criminology*, 27(1): 37–46.

Waddington, P.A.J. (1991) *The Strong Arm of the Law: Armed and Public Order Policing*. Oxford: Oxford University Press.

Waddington, P.A.J. (1993) 'The Case Against Paramilitarism Considered'. *British Journal of Criminology*, 33(3): 353–73.

Waddington, P.A.J. (1994) *Liberty and Order: Public Order Policing in a Capital City*. London: UCL Press.

Waddington, P.A.J. (1996) ' Stop and Search'. *Police Review*, 25 April: 16–17.

Waddington. P.A.J. (1999) *Policing Citizens*. London: UCL Press.

Waddington, P.A.J. (2000) 'Public Order Policing: Citizenship and Moral Ambiguity', in F. Leishman, B. Loveday and S.P. Savage (eds.), *Core Issues in Policing*, 2nd edn. London: Pearson Education.

Wadham, J. and Mountfield, H. (1999) *Human Rights Act 1998*. London: Blackstone Press.

Walker, C. and Starmer, K. (1999) (eds.), *Miscarriages of Justice*. London: Blackstone Press.

Walker, N. (1996) 'Defining Core Policing Tasks: The Neglect of the Symbolic Dimension'. *Policing and Society*, 6(1): 53–71.

Walta, M., Ramirez, D.A. and McDevitt, J. (1999) *Rethinking the Culture of Professional Policing: A Community Justice Model of law Enforcement*. Paper presented to the New York University Conference on Police Integrity and Democracy, 20–23 May.

Walzer, M. (1983) *Spheres of Justice*. Oxford: Blackwell.

Waters, I. (2000) 'Quality and Performance Monitoring', in F. Leishman, B. Loveday and S.P. Savage (eds.), *Core Issues in Policing*, 2nd edn. London: Pearson Education.

Weatheritt, M. (1986) *Innovations in Policing*. London: Croom Helm and Police Foundation.

Weatheritt, M. (1998) *Zero Tolerance: What Does it Mean and is it Right for Policing in Britain?* London: Police Foundation.

Weber, M. (1918) 'Politics as a Vocation', in H.H. Gerth and C. Wright Mills (eds.) (1970) *From Max Weber: Essays in Sociology*. London: Routledge & Kegan Paul.

Weick, K.E. (1977) 'Re-punctuating the Problem', in P.S Goodman and L.S. Sproul (eds.), *New Perspectives in Organisational Effectiveness*. San Francisco, CA: Jossey-Bass.

White, R. and Haines, F. (1996) *Crime and Criminology: An Introduction*. Melbourne: Oxford University Press.

Williams, P. (ed.) (1997) *Russian Organized Crime: The New Threat*. London and Portland, OR: Frank Cass.

Williams, P. and Savona, E. (1996) *The United Nations and Transnational Organized Crime*. London and Portland, OR: Frank Cass.

Williamson, T. (1996) 'Police Investigation: The Changing Criminal Justice Context', in F. Leishman, B. Loveday and S.P. Savage (eds.), *Core Issues in Policing*. London: Longmans.

Williamson, T. (2000) 'Policing: The Changing Criminal Justice Context – Twenty-five Years of Missed Opportunities', in F. Leishman, B. Loveday and S.P. Savage (eds.), *Core Issues in Policing*, 2nd edn. London: Pearson Education.

Wilson, J.Q. (1968) *Varieties of Police Behaviour*. Cambridge, MA: Harvard University Press.

Wilson, J.Q. (1975) *Thinking about Crime*. New York: Vintage.

Wilson, J.Q. and Kelling G.L. (1982) 'Broken Windows: The Police and Neighbourhood Safety'. *Atlantic Monthly*, March : 29–38.

Winch, P. (1958) 'Understanding a Primitive Society, in *Ethics and Action*. London: Routledge & Kegan Paul.

Wright, A. (1992) *The Objective-Setting Process: Doomed to Success?* Paper presented to Conference on Information Technology and Targeted Police Work, Manchester University, September 1992. Manchester: University of Manchester Henry Fielding Centre.

Wright, A. (1994) 'Short-Term Crackdowns and Long-Term Objectives', *Policing*, 10(4): 253–9.

Wright, A. (1996a) 'Organized Crime in Hungary: The Transition from State to Civil Society', *Transnational Organized Crime*. 3(1): 68–86.

Wright, A. (1996b) 'Police Research and the Role of the Policing Futures Forum', *Collected Papers from the 3rd National Police Research Conference*. London: Home Office (Police Research Group).

Wright, A (1998) 'Slippery Slopes: The Paramilitary Imperative in European Policing', *Police Research and Management*, 2(2): 31–41.

Wright, A. (2000) 'Managing the Future: An Academic's View', in F. Leishman, B. Loveday and S.P. Savage (eds.), *Core Issues in Policing*, 2nd edn. London: Pearson Education.

Wright, A. and Irving, B. (1996) 'Value Conflicts in Policing. Crisis into Opportunity: Making Critical Use of Experience'. *Policing and Society*, 6: 199–211.

Wright, A. and Mawby, R. (1999) 'Civilian Oversight of Policing in Transitional States: the Case of Hungary', *International Journal of the Sociology of Law*, 27: 335–50.

Wright, A. and Pease, K. (1997) 'Cracking Down on Crime'. *Policing Today*, 3(3): 34–6.

Wright A., Waymont, A. and Gregory, F. (1993) *Drugs Squads: Law Enforcement Strategies and Intelligence in England and Wales*. London: Police Foundation.

Yeo, H. and Budd, T. (1999) *Policing and the Public: Findings from the 1998 British Crime Survey*. Research Findings No.113. London: Home Office.

Young, J. (1988) 'Radical Criminology in Britain: The Emergence of a Competing Paradigm', *British Journal of Criminology*, 28(2): 289–313.

Young, J. (1997) 'Left Realist Criminology' in M. Maguire, R. Morgan and R. Reiner (eds.), *The Oxford Handbook of Criminology* (2nd edn.). Oxford: Oxford University Press.

Young, J. (1999) *The Exclusive Society*. London: Sage.

Young, M. (1991) *An Inside Job*. Oxford: Clarendon.

Zander, M. (1994) 'Ethics and Crime Investigation by the Police'. *Policing*, 10(1): 39–47.

Index